# School and Schooled

## A Flight Plan for Life and an All-American Story of Hard Work and Success

Airline Captain
**Frank J. Donohue**

Not-Y
Virginia Beach, VA

School and Schooled: A Flight Plan for Life and an All-American Story of Hard Work and Success
by Frank J. Donohue

© 2014 Frank J. Donohue

All rights reserved.

No part of this publication may be reproduced or transmitted in any form or by any means, mechanical or electronic, including photocopying and recording, or by any information storage and retrieval system, without permission in writing from author or publisher (except by a reviewer, who may quote brief passages and/or show brief video clips in a review).

Published by Not-Y, Virginia Beach, VA

ISBN 978-0-9894678-0-3  (Print)
ISBN 978-0-9894678-1-0  (E-Book)

Library of Congress Control Number: 2013955499

Cover and Book Design: Nick Zelinger, www.NZGraphics.com

Although the author and publisher have made every effort to ensure that the information in this book was correct at press time, the author and publisher do not assume and hereby disclaim any liability to any party for any loss, damage, or disruption caused by errors or omissions, whether such errors or omissions result from negligence, accident, or any other cause.

First Edition

Printed in the United States of America

I dedicate this book to Francis and Jared
and all pilots around the world.

# Contents

Foreword .................................................. 1

**Introduction:**
*How did I become a pilot?* ............................ 3

**Chapter 1: Low School 0–14**
*After now and before later* ........................... 5

**Chapter 2: High School 15–18**
*Always remember and you'll never forget* .............. 14

**Chapter 3: Military School (USAF) 18–22**
*Doing better than most but not as good as some* ....... 21

**Chapter 4: Undergraduate School (ERAU) 23–24**
*Fifty-four college credits in one year* ............... 51

**Chapter 5: Aviation School 25–26**
*Five pilot jobs in two years* ......................... 66

**Chapter 6: 1989: Hell of a Year**
*Why didn't you do the To Do list and the Re-Do list?* . 109

**Chapter 7: FedEx® Career**
*We make our money above planet earth
and it is serious business* ............................ 126

**Chapter 8: Flight 1340**
*One flight to Memphis proved challenging* ............. 159

**Chapter 9: Family Schooling**
*It is better to have no friends then to have bad friends.* . . . . 181

**Chapter 10: Money Schooling**
*Anything and everything else is extra.* . . . . . . . . . . . . . . . . . . 201

**Chapter 11: Religion Schooling**
*Jesus and I love you* . . . . . . . . . . . . . . . . . . . . . . . . . . . . . . . . 220

**Chapter 12: Body and Soul**
*Any stresses I can help you with?.* . . . . . . . . . . . . . . . . . . . . . 236

**Chapter 13: Retirement Thinking**
*I made a deal with God* . . . . . . . . . . . . . . . . . . . . . . . . . . . . . 260

**Appendix** . . . . . . . . . . . . . . . . . . . . . . . . . . . . . . . . . . . . . . . . . . 269

**Bibliography** . . . . . . . . . . . . . . . . . . . . . . . . . . . . . . . . . . . . . . 277

**Acknowledgments** . . . . . . . . . . . . . . . . . . . . . . . . . . . . . . . . . 283

**About the Author** . . . . . . . . . . . . . . . . . . . . . . . . . . . . . . . . . . 285

# Foreword

## *"How did you become a pilot?"*

The question is a favorite that I pose to my colleagues. Although I didn't know I wanted a career in aviation until I was twenty years old, I achieved that momentous goal in only six years—a fact that I hope you find motivating.

I've held many titles—sergeant, instructor, sir, coach, boss, captain, brother, son, husband. The one that gives me the most pride is "Dad." Being a father to my sons has been my greatest challenge and my greatest reward in life. I began writing this book for my sons as a way of providing them insight into some of the things I have done and who I am. I think of it as a resource, because it also contains survival tools that I hope will help them and others manage their lives. I have witnessed death. On ten occasions, I have come close to death myself. I know that I will not always be there for my sons, but maybe this book will be the second best thing for them.

This book begins as the memoir of a pilot and the process of becoming a pilot. But it is also a self-help book on family, money, religion, and the human body and soul. It is based on wisdom that I have learned during the first half of my life. There are sections of this book that are funny, poetic, historical, motivational, inspirational, and educational with some suspense and love included in the mix. Occasionally, at random, I recall specific events and mini-stories. In this book I have tried to recreate events, locales and conversations from my memories. To protect privacy, some names and identifying details have been changed; I may have also changed some identifying characteristics and details such as physical properties, occupations and places of residence.

In addition to writing for my sons, I am also writing for parents, high school grads, college grads, military personnel, and everyday people who want to improve their financial situation, personal health, and spiritual life. Hence the title *School and Schooled*, because I write about the schooling I have obtained and then provide schooling for the reader.

It is my goal to inspire and motivate you to pursue your dream career, become a better parent, improve your financial situation, and improve the health of your body. You will get the *Ten Healthy Rules*. And you will be guided to explore and improve your spiritual life. In fact, a custom prayer just for you is included in this book, so go ahead: read and be entertained and learn.

# Introduction

School and Schooled is authored by me—Francis by birth, also known as Francois Jon, Franco, Francisco, Fran, Frankie, Frankolino, Frankenstein, and most commonly Frank John Donohue, Jr.

In the USA there are around a million lawyers and around 900,000 doctors, but there are only about 100,000 airline pilots. Each profession serves its own purpose but consider this: airline pilots transport almost 2 million passengers and almost 5 million packages per day. And here's a question to ponder—what kind of mental and physical ability does it take to be one of the 100,000? In his book about the early days of space flight, *The Right Stuff*, Tom Wolfe talked about the special characteristics and detailed psychological and physical tests that were required to be given that very special title of "astronaut." Being a pilot is not quite at the same level, of course, but there is a certain frame of mind required to guide an extremely large man-made machine, with hundreds of passengers or 100,000 pounds of cargo on board, across country or around the world. When equipment malfunctions or when the visibility is near zero, it takes a certain toughness and point of view to keep things together and maintain control. Remember, flying remains the safest form of transportation.

Scheduled airlines have a death rate of 0.003 fatalities per 100 million passenger miles, according to widely-available statistics. That's in part because of the training of the pilots—and the lessons we were taught about preparation, execution, trouble-shooting and paying attention to details. These are all valuable lessons for everyone—even if you never desire to pilot a plane of any size.

That's what "School and Schooled" is about—the opportunity for an experienced pilot to share some lessons and suggest how they might apply to the lives of others.

## School and Schooled

How did I become an airline pilot at such a young age? You are about to find out. I left Long Island at age 18 with only a high school diploma and an automobile driver's license. I returned at age 26 with college degrees and pilot's licenses. I left John F. Kennedy International Airport and flew around the world. I almost died ten times. But I lived. I lived to write poetry and to write songs. I lived to write this history and, I hope, to make you laugh and motivate you, inspire you, and perhaps help you become a better parent or coach, help you improve your financial situation, inspire you with healthy rules for your body and a prayer for your soul.

So please enjoy these stories and ideas and learn to become a better parent and a better money manager, increase the health of your body and soul, and come fly with me through the interesting life of an airline pilot.

# CHAPTER 1
# Low School (Age 0-14)

**Almost Died: Age 2**
**Falling out of a car on the Long Island Expressway**

My father and I were in his faded yellow Plymouth cruising at probably 60 miles per hour on the Long Island Expressway. At least, that's what they tell me. I was two. I wasn't taking notes at the time, imagining I would be writing this book a few decades later, so my parents helped me with these details.

If it was like most trips, I probably asked, "when are we going to get there daddy?" and he probably responded with the unhelpful reply, "after now and before later."

Anyway, I was curious about the shiny handle on the door. With one hand holding the bottle I enjoyed for nourishment, I used my other hand to investigate. I was in the front seat. My mother was in the back seat with my two-month-old baby brother. Dad was driving. It was Christmas night and were on the way from my grandmother's house in Floral Park to my aunt's house in Central Islip.

I couldn't stop looking at that shiny handle. It begged to be yanked.

So I did.

And the handle did what it was supposed to do. The door opened. My precious bottle fell out of the car and bounced down the LIE.

"Hey, that's my bottle," I said. Or thought. I attempted to leap out the door to retrieve it unaware, of course, of the danger. Remember, no seat belts or baby-bucket car seats back then. The 60 mph wind alerted my dad and he grabbed my rear snowsuit when I was about half-way out the door. He yanked me back—and saved my life.

*Thank you, Dad.*

One benefit: after watching my bottle bounce down the freeway, I was officially done with sucking my milk from a plastic nipple. I don't recommend it for others, but the incident weaned me off the bottle.

## First Things First

I think knowing where you've come from is as important as where you are. How else do you know who you are and what you're made of?

First things first: I love my father and mother. And the following is what I know about my genealogy—my roots. My father is of Irish blood heritage and my mother is of Yugoslavian blood heritage. Great-grandfather John Donohue, born in New York in 1865, husband of great-grandmother Lorrette Sweeney, begot grandfather Francis Damien Donohue. John and Lorrette's parents were born in Ireland. Grandfather Francis Damien Donohue, born in New York in 1907, husband to grandmother Margaret Veronica O'Donnell, begot father Francis John Donohue. Father Francis John Donohue, born in New York in 1936, husband to mother Antoinette Grgas, begot Francis John Donohue Jr. (me) in New York in 1961. Mother Antoinette Grgas, born in New York in 1940, is daughter to grandfather Benjamin Siska Grgas, who was born in 1909 in Sibenik, Yugoslavia. Benjamin's parents, great-grandfather Paul Siska Grgas and great-grandmother Geraldine Jerka, were born in Yugoslavia. Antoinette Grgas's mother, grandmother Catherine Dobrilla Antich, was born in New York in 1916. Catherine Dobrilla Antich's parents, great-grandfather Antich and great-grandmother Antoinette Rossini, were born in Yugoslavia. Francis John Donohue Jr.'s father's heritage was pure Irish, and his mother's heritage was pure Yugoslavian, resulting in Francis J. Donohue Jr. born the first half-breed in the family.

I was born on the cusp of Capricorn (Dec. 22–Jan. 20) and Aquarius (Jan. 21–Feb. 19) during the worst snowstorm of the year. Capricorns have the traits of being practical, prudent, ambitious, disciplined, humorous, and reserved. Aquarius has traits of being friendly, humanitarian, honest, loyal, original, inventive, independent, and intellectual. Because I was born on the cusp I could read the Capricorn daily horoscope, and I if didn't like what I read, then I would read the Aquarius horoscope and pick the best reading. How's that for both practical (Capricorn) and original (Aquarius)? Guess I am a bit of both.

## Primary School: Age 0–7

During this stage of life you learn, learn, and learn. You start putting your own thoughts into your own words and speak to other humans. You go to school and learn to socialize, sing, play, read, and write. You learn to put your right hand over your heart and pledge:

*I pledge allegiance to the flag of the United States of America, and to the Republic for which it stands, one nation under God, indivisible, with liberty and justice for all.*

This is the version revised by President Eisenhower and the Congress of the United States of America in 1954. It's very important to me—much more than just words. We live in the greatest country on Planet Earth. I've believed that since I was young. I did not know, of course, that I would later devote my life to service to my country in the military.

I started primary school at John H. West School in Bethgate, New York (on Long Island). It's public grammar school, and there I learned to sing songs like "Jimmy Crack Corn," "One, Two Buckle My Shoe," "Wheels On The Bus," "Mary Had a Little Lamb," "Ring Around the Rosie," and "Twinkle, Twinkle Little Star." In first grade, I learned to read the "Dick and Jane" books (by William Grey and Zema Sharp). You know, "See Spot Run." At home I read the Dr. Seuss books like *Hop on Pop, Green Eggs and Ham, The Cat in the Hat,* and *One Fish, Two fish, Red Fish, Blue Fish.* Who didn't like Dr. Seuss?

And who didn't need to learn how to share?

Sharing can be a tough concept when you're young. One Christmas, I received a red wagon with black wheels and white rims. This was a very special gift and I had no interest in sharing it with my brother.

My father was blunt: "If you don't want to share then you will not be allowed to live in this house."

It was dark and late, but I held my new red wagon, left our home and started walking down the sidewalk. To where? To somewhere. I didn't have much of a plan. At the time, of course, I did not know that later on in life my career would involve knowing every destination—filing flight plans and knowing your starting point and your destination. Anyway, it was crispy cold outside and I could hear strange frightful noises. I had done little to prepare for my departure. After bravely walking about the distance of two houses, I turned around and quickly returned to my warm, safe home.

And shared.

## Middle School: Age 8–14

I attended Saint James, a parochial Catholic school, from second through eighth grade. I graduated in June 1975. Every morning before class started, we said the Pledge of Allegiance and the "Our Father" prayer or the "Hail Mary" prayer. In sixth grade, I had Sister Constolatta. She was four foot eight inches tall, but she didn't lack authority. If you stepped out of line, she would point and poke her finger in your chest, yell at you in front of the whole class, and always finish by saying, "believe me you." We called her Hitler. In eighth grade, I had Sister Sauka. She made us memorize and recite the "Flanders Field" poem in front of the whole class. The "Flanders Field" poem was written on May 2, 1915 by John McCrae, a doctor and military officer. The Flanders Poppy was promoted as the miracle flower and the symbol of remembrance.

In Flanders fields the poppies blow
Between the crosses, row on row,
That mark our place; and in the sky
The larks, still bravely singing, fly
Scarce heard amid the guns below.

We are the Dead. Short days ago
We lived, felt dawn, saw sunset glow,
Loved and were loved, and now we lie
In Flanders fields.

Take up our quarrel with the foe:
To you from failing hands we throw
The torch; be yours to hold it high.
If ye break faith with us who die
We shall not sleep, though poppies grow
In Flanders fields.

Sister Sauka also recited the "Wreck of the Hesperus," written by Henry Wadsworth Longfellow in 1839. However, when Sister recited the poem, you never knew who she was looking at because she was cross-eyed. One day she was disciplining James and instructed him to stand up in front of the class of fifty students. All five of the boys named James stood up. We called her Crazy Eyes.

During the early middle school years I learned to play the guitar and played baseball, basketball, ran track, and swam. I was awarded my first gold medal in the backstroke finals at eight years old. I enjoyed playing sports and watching sports—and I was glad, later on, when physical fitness became a key part of my job. New York City was a fabulous hub for professional sports. The N.Y. Jets defied the odds and won the Super Bowl in 1969 behind Joe Namath, the N.Y. Mets won the World Series in 1969 and the N.Y. Knicks won the NBA Championship in 1970. I was also a member of the 4-H club. My father, brother, and I went on fun 4-H camping trips together. During the latter middle school years I started acquiring an interest in women after noticing that their appearance, body and personality were different than men. Natural attraction.

I also acquired the love for fishing. My father took my grandfather Benjamin Grgas, my brother Kevin and me fishing on our family boat. My grandfather took Kevin and me fishing at Wantaugh State Park. Kevin and I would go to great lengths to fish; we would even ride our bikes five miles to fish at Florence Avenue Beach. We fished for flounder, fluke, weakfish, blowfish (the Long Island variety is completely safe to eat). We cleaned the fish and mother cooked them up.

I was so keen on the fun of fishing that I wrote a poem.

### Wish a Fish

I miss my boat on the water
steering starboard or port,
Trolling lines for a big striper
or wreck fishing for any fish typer,
To hear the real clicker
I'll jump on the rod in a Flicker,
or to feel that tap tap of fish bites
I'll yank and crank the fish into my sights,
hoping for a beauty of a monster and a fighter
I will give her drag until she's fighting lighter,
I'll always set my hook
so she can be took,
and then take a picture for my book,
so the other mates can take a look,
And then cut, clean, smell, and feel.
For the ultimate satisfaction of a fish meal.

## Almost Died: Age 13
## Trick-or-Treat with a Real Gun

Halloween has always been one of my favorite holidays but one night stays with me more than others.

One dark, gloomy Halloween night, our group of six teenagers was in the wrong neighborhood at the wrong time.

Okay, I'll be clear about one thing. Some of us were out Trick-or-Treating for candy but some of us were out looking for tricks and trouble. We weren't necessarily angels. We were on foot and probably walking around like we owned the town.

Not for long.

A car filled with older kids stopped right next to us. I remember a Frankenstein mask and Count Dracula.

One of the monster costume masks rolled down the window, pointed a gun at us, and said "trick-or-treat." It was too dark and I was too scared to even imagine that the gun might not be real.

Shell-shocked and frozen in our tracks for what seemed like eternity, no one spoke. Then the armed monster laughed in a crazy way and the car sped off.

Lessons learned?

1. When looking for trouble, you may find more than expected. (I was genuinely scared, down to my bones.)

2. Beware of strangers in a car, especially at night on Halloween and do not approach strangers. If you get a bad feeling about a situation then back away.
   And get out.

As I started getting interested in girls we played a game called "Spin the Bottle." To play the game you need at least two boys and two girls and a bottle. In the 1970's, Coca-Cola twelve-ounce soda was sold in bottles and they worked perfectly. To play, boys and girls sit down in a circle in an alternating boy-girl pattern and a bottle is placed in the middle of the circle. To start the game, one person spins the bottle, and when the bottle stops, pointing to a person of the opposite sex, that person has to kiss the other person of the opposite sex. The person chosen by the bottle is now the new spinner of the bottle, hence "Spin the Bottle." Do you know how hard it is to get the bottle to stop on a particular person like Doreen De Marco?

I was 13 years old—and started to get an idea about the opposite sex. My attention was focused on Miss Doreen. Not much more detail to relay here. It was a young, early crush.

My neighbor and friend, Tommy Whatso, and I started our first business—landscaping/cutting grass. We only had two customers. Tommy would edge the grass along the sidewalk and I would cut the grass with a lawn mower. After we had collected our first payment, we went to the "Pizza Cove" to reward ourselves. Back then if I had a quarter, I could buy a slice of pizza for fifteen cents and a cup of Coca-Cola soda for ten cents.

My favorite TV comedy shows were *The Honeymooners* with Jackie Gleason, *The Odd Couple,* the *Three Stooges* (over time there was actually a total of six stooges*), Bugs Bunny,* and the *Little Rascals* (my third grade teacher Mrs. Knup's husband was Spanky's doctor). Sometimes, I would stay up late and watch the scary Alfred Hitchcock show. I also watched *Charlie's Angels, The Brady Bunch,* and *The Partridge Family*—but only for the good-looking women on those shows. I watched all the law and order shows for action and suspense: *Beretta, Kojak, Colombo,* and *Perry Mason.*

I watched all the movies of Clint Eastwood and John Wayne. I watched *Star Wars*, and of course, the original *Jaws* film. Supposedly, the movie *Jaws* took place on fictitious Amity Island. In the 1974 novel *Jaws* by Peter Benchley, Amity is located on Long Island. There is an Amity village on Long Island located only a few miles from where I swam, water skied, boated, and fished. The "Jaws" film fulfilled the lesson that your mind can describe some mysterious shark even better than a movie can display it. Try this: watch the original "Jaws" film and then go swimming in the ocean. No problem. Now go swimming at night.

There was a choice among several high schools that I could attend. There was the local Plain Edge Public and there were also about five private high schools. I could have attended the local public Plain Edge Public, but I wanted to attend the parochial private Holy Trinity. My father, mother, and I sat down to discuss the options.

My father said, "Everyone gets to vote, but I will decide." Therefore, my father decided that I would attend Saint Dominic High School in Oyster Bay, New York. Oyster Bay was called the Gold Coast of the United States of America because, at the time, it had the most expensive real estate with the highest concentration of the wealthiest people in the country. My family were not wealthy; we considered ourselves upper middle class.

# CHAPTER 2
# High School (Age 15-18)

In the summer of 1975, I went to football camp at St. Dominic's. So, as I entered my freshman year, I was lucky to know the five kids who had gone to St. James with me, and I knew most of the junior varsity and varsity football team before starting school. While in high school, I played one year of football, ran track for a couple years, and still swam competitively for the Catholic Youth Organization. I was definitely growing up; the girls on the swim team looked much better during the high school years.

When I was fifteen, my maternal grandpa, Benjamin Grgas, gave my brother, Kevin, and me a sixteen-foot Sears's aluminum boat with a ten-horse-power engine. In the summertime, Kevin and I fished all the time and occasionally camped on Zach's Bay Island near Jones Beach. The view from the top of the sand dunes was beautiful. We would watch the sunset and sunrise with 360 degrees of water surrounding us. We would dig for muscles and steamer clams and put the clams inside of a cut-open soda can. Then we would put the can onto a lit bonfire to steam the clams. In the evening, we would take the boat over to the Jones Beach Theatre, where the Guy Lombardo speed showboat would enter prior to the start of a concert. Afterward, we would watch music concerts like "Blue Oyster Cult."

With my bicycle, I had a job delivering the *Long Island Press*. Shortly after, I obtained a job working as a locker-room man (I mainly shined shoes) at the exclusive Meadow Brook Golf Club. Meadow Brook treated me very well. They served me two meals a day—a gourmet hot lunch and great thick sandwiches in late afternoon. The golfers gave me generous tips and I bought by first car from the club manager. Some of the most influential people in the country were members of Meadow Brook: the Whitneys, the Vanderbilts, the Rockefellers, the Mosbys, the Hunts, the Halls, the Hutttons, the Graces, the Bradys, and others.

In the clubhouse, they had a room called "The Shoe Room." Men only. In September and October, after the busy summer golf season slowed down, some of these influential men would eat lunch and talk business in the Shoe Room. Many times, I heard business arrangements made here and read about these arrangements months later in the Wall Street Journal. For instance, I heard them discuss holding their oil tankers off shore until the price of oil rose higher. This was during the supply-and-demand gasoline crisis of the early 1980s.

The Meadow Brook club was started in Westbury Long Island in 1881 as a hunting club and built a nine-hole golf course three years later. The existing 18-hole golf course was designed by Dick Wilson and built in Jericho, Long Island in 1955 with championship tees stretching 7,100 yards. The greens averaged more than 6,500 square feet. There were thirteen dog-leg holes, and many of those fairways were surrounded by woods. Hole number seven could be played at 635 yards. This par 72 golf course was a very tough golf course to play. In 1978, Judy Rankin won the ladies' Professional Golf Association (PGA) golf tournament at two over par, playing from the men's front tees. During that golf tournament weekend I met all the lady golfers. Many golf tournaments have been played at Meadow Brook. My boss, Chester Dobbie, taught me to play golf there. A few of my friends and I also played most of the five golf courses at the Beth Page State Park.

For additional funds, I also sold barbecue gas grills and worked at a warehouse as an inventory stock man. A few times, I even helped my dad deliver cases of beer to restaurants and delis or I worked the register at his store: White's Beer and Soda Distributor. While working at the Wine and Cheese Back Barn restaurant, I did various jobs:

dishwashing, cook's helper, valet parking, bus boy, hostess, waiter, front doorman. In the summer I would work Friday, Saturday, and sometimes Sunday nights at the Back Barn (they had live music on these nights), and on Saturday and Sunday I worked at Meadow Brook golf club. This schedule allowed me to make more money than my friends, who were working forty hours a week from 8 a.m. to 5 p.m. Monday through Friday (and I had Monday through Friday off).

At age sixteen, I obtained my New York state driver's license. At seventeen years and three months, I purchased my first car—a 1972 mezzanine blue Chevelle Malibu with a black hardtop. The first thing I did to my first car was upgrade the stereo system by installing new speakers and a power booster equalizer. So at age seventeen I had a car and a boat and was sitting atop of the world. I drove that car everywhere—to school, to work, to concerts at Madison Square Garden in New York City, to the great Long Island beaches, and so forth. I even drove that car during a snowstorm to a Grateful Dead concert in Rochester, New York and through the Bethpage State Park horse trails. Young teenage boys should not be driving cars. I paid the price with a handful of minor car accidents and a handful of tickets; no one ever got hurt. I thought this car would be my ticket to picking up girls, but that is a challenge in itself when you really don't know what to do to meet girls at age seventeen.

## Almost Died: Age 17
## Auto Skid during a snow storm

Everyone plays hooky from school at least once. Don't they?

My friend Glenn's girlfriend, Linda, called St. Dominic High School and, posing as my mother, explained that I was sick and would miss school for a week.

Tony, Glenn, Linda, and I had a plan to drive from Long Island, New York to Rochester, New York to attend a concert by a band that was already a legend—The Grateful Dead. I was no "Dead Head," the

## High School (Age 15-18)

term used to describe true fanatics. But I liked the Grateful Dead and had seen them perform. In fact, going to Nassau Coliseum or Madison Square Garden was a regular thing. I saw bands like Yes, The Steve Miller Band, Lynyrd Skinner, Charlie Daniels, The Marshall Tucker Band, Neil Young, Crosby-Stills and Nash, America, Heart, Jim Croce, Edgar Winter and many more.

A trip to Rochester? Playing hooky from school? Seeing The Grateful Dead again? Sure. Sign me up.

This 350-mile drive would be the longest drive I had ever made, but my calculations suggested that it would only take about six hours to drive.

*Right.*

Looking for every chance to keep our driving costs down, we decided to take a short cut and drive Route 17 instead of driving on the New York Thruway. The New York Thruway was a highway with much better roads, but also required frequent tolls. To us, every dollar mattered so we opted to skip the toll road.

As we drove north, snow flurries turned to heavy snow. In fact, it was a severe snow storm. As the snow density increased on the two-lane route, big trucks reduced their driving speed and stayed in the right lane. The truck tracks provided better traction and cleared a path for my car, but the trucks were only driving about 30 to 40 miles per hour when the speed limit was 65.

"Could I pass a truck using the left lane?" The question nagged at me. At the rate we were driving, we would never make it.

There were no tire tracks in the left lane and the snow was building up. I was drafting behind a trailer truck that was blocking the wind so even though we were going slow we were saving money on gasoline.

But we were on the drive to get to the concert. I had to pass a truck. At least, I had to try to pass one.

As I cautiously changed over to the left lane, I immediately felt the full force of Mother Nature's wind on the car. Slowly, I increased my speed to pass that first truck and learned to not get too close to the truck because his wind draft could suck me in. After slowly passing the truck, I switched back over to the better, right-hand lane.

We passed at least six or seven trucks, and I became an expert truck passer to the point where passing trucks was routine.

In short, I became slightly complacent in the truck-passing operation. After passing truck number seven or eight, reality caught up with me. The right lane was now just as bad as the left lane. The snowfall and wind had increased and my rear wheels started skidding to the left. I had no rear tire traction! I tried to compensate the skid and turned the steering wheel left.

The situation became worse.

My rear wheels started fishtailing to the right, and I made an aggressive right turn to compensate. Then, all hell broke loose and my 1976 Chevelle Malibu entered into a few 360-degree turns. My rear tail bumper hit something and whatever it was stopped the 360-degree spins. I stopped the car—with all the trucks blowing by us—and we all got out into the cold snowstorm and assessed the situation. The car had hit a guard rail. We had stopped at a spot on the road on the edge of a steep cliff that led to a gorge. The only thing that prevented us from going over that cliff was that guard rail. The four of us collected our thoughts, spoke a few kind words to each other, and agreed that we didn't have to pass any more trucks on Route 17. The car was drivable.

The big lesson I learned was that when you get into a skid:

1. Take your foot off the gas pedal and do not press hard on the brakes.

2. Steer in the direction of the skid slowly.

3. Do not overcompensate with steering.

4. Stay calm until the car's path straightens out.

After the Grateful Dead concert in Rochester, we drove safely back on the New York Thruway, the better roadway home.

## Brief Texas Detour

After graduating high school I wanted to travel so I took a train to New York City, called my mother and told her I was going to Texas. Actually, I had secretly signed to join the United States Air Force after I turned 18 while still in High School. I was supposed to enter service after high school graduation with a job in computers. There was only one problem. I had accumulated too many tickets in one year of driving. As a result, my entry date was changed to December and my job slot was changed to accounting.

I joined the USAF on Long Island because the air forced provided meals, lodging, world-wide travel and education in computers; I had a taste of computers in a class in high school and liked the field. And pay. USAF seemed like the best service.

My parents were on my case that summer about what I was going to do with my life. I told them I was going into the USAF but they did not take me seriously. After my entry date was changed due to the traffic ticket problem, I had a long block of free time on my hands.

I knew two things. First, I wanted to travel. (I guess that traveling bug has been inside me for a long time.) Second, I wanted to make money.

At the time, Texas was a booming state and the word was out that there was a shortage of skilled workers.

"Wait 'til your father hears about this," said my mother when she heard about the plan to head to Texas. (It wasn't the first time she had said that.)

I'm sure my parents didn't believe I would join the USAF until it happened. Looking back, I can't blame them for thinking otherwise.

I took a Greyhound bus to Dallas. There were many job opportunities available in Texas, and I obtained employment as a professional painter with the J.S. Trogdon Company. At first I had a job painting inside a public school where the temperatures were pleasantly cool. The next job was outside—the old wooden roller coaster at the Texas State Fair. The sizzling 110° F temperatures were unpleasant. After completing these two jobs, J.S. Trogdon assigned me to travel to Lawton, Oklahoma, Wichita, Texas, and St. Louis, Missouri to paint Kmart stores at night when the stores were closed. I was with a crew including five other painters. We returned to Dallas and a few days later I flew to Los Angeles, arriving on the day before Thanksgiving Day—Turkey day.

After spending Thanksgiving Day and a week with my aunt, uncle, and six female cousins in Los Angles, California, I left to visit a high school friend, Harold Everwhat, in San Jose. Next, I traveled up to San Francisco to meet with my parents, who were on a mini vacation. We went out to eat at Scoma's restaurant on the Fisherman's Wharf pier and sat at a table next to Marie Osmond—she was gorgeous in 1979. From San Francisco, I flew on a Pan Am Boeing B-747 aircraft to John F. Kennedy International Airport on Long Island. Little did I know at the time that such long-distance flights might one day become routine—and that my view out of the airplane would be from a completely different perspective (the pilot's seat). After spending a week at home, I entered the United States Air Force on December 26, 1979. I will always remember and never forget that at age eighteen I left home with a high school diploma, an automobile driver's license, and some traveling experience.

And my parents finally believed that I did what I said I was going to do.

# CHAPTER 3
# Military School (USAF) Age 18–22

With 49 other guys I entered the United States Air Force (USAF) and started basic training at Lackland Air Force Base in San Antonio, Texas.

Yes, back to Texas.

It seemed as if almost half of the squadron was from New York and the other half was from California, with a few guys from the middle of the country. During basic training, there was a major clash of personalities, slang, and opinions—like which football team was the best in the National Football League. On January 20, 1980, the Pittsburgh Steelers beat the Los Angeles Rams 31 to 19 in Pasadena, California to win Super Bowl XIV. Within the squadron, this was East versus West. But we were all Americans so the males bonded and we found a way to get along. As a fifty-member group, we were given a day off to see the Harlem Globetrotters play basketball, and that was fun.

**Almost Died: Age 19**
**Gang mugging at the New Orleans Mardi Gras**

While in technical accounting training at Shepherd Air Force Base in Wichita Falls, Texas the grand Mardi Gras carnival parades were about to begin in Rio de Janerio, Venice and New Orleans. Of those, New Orleans was closest—just 650 miles away. It is good to belong to a religion, especially Christianity. Bill Notwhy, an Air Force friend, and

I were religious Christians and we hitch-hiked to New Orleans for Mardi Gras of 1980. While we were hanging out in the French Quarter in New Orleans, five guys surrounded us and tried to mug us. These thugs wanted to rob us of what little money we were carrying. Maybe they had even more violent intentions. We were outnumbered. We stood no chance in a fight.

With my strong New York accent and our short military-style haircuts, however, they didn't know were in the military—or anything about us. But I knew the short hair and overall look could also serve another purpose. I quickly claimed we were two ex-convicts just released from Rahway prison in New Jersey. There had been a *60 Minutes* television documentary on Rahway prison (today East Jersey State Prison) and its rough reputation and brutal conditions. The documentary helped me concoct the spiel.

They believed me and backed off. A close shave.

We met a lot of people and had such a good time in New Orleans, but we drank too much, and as a result, we had to buy a plane ticket to get back to base in time to avoid being considered AWOL, a serious crime in the military.

## To Lakenheath

While at Sheppard AFB, I took several CLEAP (College Level Exam Aptitude Program) tests and passed a few, obtaining my first college credit hours. On April 20, 1980 I purchased land in Port LaBelle, Florida and would later trade the lot for one closer to the ocean in Port St. Lucie (in 1989). After finishing Accounting Technical School and receiving a General Accounting Specialist certificate, I went home to Long Island. After one week, on May 29, my parents drove me to McGuire Air Force Base in New Jersey and the USAF flew me to the Royal Air Force base in Lakenheath, England for my first assignment.

Years later, my mother revealed to me that this moment at McGuire Air Force Base was the first time she saw my father with tears in his eyes. My mom was crying, too. My father probably thought that I would meet an English girl, settle down overseas and never return home. First-borns have an effect on parents like that.

Royal Air Force Lakenheath, the 48th fighter wing, is located in East Anglia in Suffolk County, about 70 miles northeast of London and 25 miles east of Cambridge. New Market, the horse racing center of England, is only thirteen miles away.

The name Lakenheath was derived from the Saxon word "kokenhyte," which meant the "landing place of Loka's people." This area, known as Lakenheath Warren, was initially built in the 1930's as a decoy airfield with false runway lights and aircraft made of plywood to lure attacking German pilot bombers away from nearby RAF Mildenhall and RAF Feltwell airfields.

When I arrived in 1980, the base had a few squadrons of F-111 aircraft. The F-111 jet aircraft were installed with the Pave Tact System, which allowed the F-111 to deliver weapons around the clock from high or low altitudes. The F-111 was a multi-purpose tactical fighter bomber aircraft with variable-sweep wings, which allowed the pilot (it was a two-pilot jet) to fly from slow speeds to fast speeds up to Mach 1.2 at a sea level and Mach 2.5 at 60,000 feet.

The wings could sweep from 16 degrees full forward to 72 degrees full aft. The jet included afterburner turbofan engines that were each capable of producing 25,000 pounds of thrust. The aircraft could carry a variety of conventional and nuclear weapons. RAF Lakenheath participated in a number of USAFE (United States Air Force Europe) and NATO (North Atlantic Treaty Organization) simulated warlike exercises. [2]

After only a few months, I was fortunate to relocate from the base to a civilian flat in the town of Bury Saint Edmund. My Air Force friend Don Realget and I leased a flat located on the third floor of an old building on Guildhall Street, smack in the middle of the town.

Bury St. Edmund is located in the middle of East Anglia, about 17 miles east of RAF Lakenheath. The town was named after King

Edmund, who was crowned King of East Anglia in 850 A.D. Edmund was a Christian and a peaceful man, but in the year 869 he was martyred by Danish invaders. His remains were brought to Bury St. Edmund and a shrine was built there. The St. Benedictine monks incorporated the shrine in the Abbey in 1020 A.D. The Abbey was founded in 945 A.D. and completed in the 12th century. Parts of the Magna Carta were signed there in 1214.[3] The town included many other historical buildings like the Abbey Gate, the Cathedral Church of St. James, St. Mary's Church, Athenaeum Angle Hill, the Corn Exchange, a good market square and plenty of great pubs.

However, the pubs kept strange hours. They were open from about 11:00 a.m. to 3 p.m. and then the pubs would close and reopen from 7 p.m. to 11 p.m. Occasionally, they would even close at 10:30 p.m. This took some getting used to; I was definitely not at home in Long Island.

If you heard "last call," then you could buy one, two, or three more rounds of beer and stay inside the pub after the doors were closed at closing time. Sometimes, Bobbies (policeman) would come in after closing time and join in the drinking. You did not want to hear, "drink up, mate, pub's closed."

My favorite pub was the One Bull Inn. This was the pub where I was drinking when I received the sad news that John Lennon had been shot to death in New York City. Here I was an American drinking beer in an English pub mourning the death of an amazingly talented Englishman who died very close to where I grew up.

The One Bull Inn was where I would go to meet girls—also known as "birds" or "lassies" by the Brits.

## A Quick Lesson in Slang

Okay, a quick course in English slang. These are some of the terms I encountered, but never fully incorporated into the way I spoke. I was still an American, after all.

**Blimey:** an exclamation of surprise.
**Bloody or bloody hell:** one of the most used swears words; used as an exclamation of surprise.
**Blokes/Lads:** guys, men, boys.
**Bobbies:** cops or police. (They carry sticks, not guns.)
**Cheeky/Cheeky Bugger:** a bit of a smart ass with an answer for everything.
**Cheers/Cheers, mate:** a colloquial term meaning thank you.
**Cheerio:** Goodbye.
**Fag:** Cigarette. (Usually hand rolled.)
**Fancy Dress Party:** a costume party kind of like our Halloween. I went to one in London dressed as a U.S. football player.
**Football:** soccer.
**Knackered:** worn out or tired out (like the day after a night of drinking).
**Pissed:** really drunk.
**Nicked:** stolen.
**Oy, mate:** Hi, what's up?
**Randy:** Horny. I would usually introduce myself by saying, "It's my birthday. I'm Randy."
**Ta:** Thanks.
**Taking the mick:** making fun of.
**Up the wooden hill:** up the stairs to bed.

The language took some getting used to and so did the food, though I grew to enjoy some of the dishes such as Cottage Pie or Shepherd's Pie, Bangers and Mash, Black Pudding (made from dry pig's blood and fat), Yorkshire Pudding, Fish and Chips and tea. When asked by an English woman, "would you like tea?" I would always say, "Yes." As a growing young man, I was usually hungry and I did not know whether I was getting a cup of tea to drink or some small sandwiches to eat. The English, since the 1840's, have a custom called "afternoon tea" or "to take tea." It's usually between 2 p.m. and 5 p.m. and either a "small meal" or "large meal" is served. The "tea" I received usually included sandwiches made with a combination of cucumber, egg, onion, ham, tomato and sometimes scones, cakes or pastries. The English also had "high tea" or "meat tea," a real hot meal between 5 p.m. and 7 p.m., or what we called dinner or supper. And then, of course, the English had drinking tea, which they drank often—like five to six times a day, with or without food.

I like some of these drinks:

"Two pints of lager and packets of chips please." A pint is 16 ounces, and chips are what we call French fries, usually flavored with salt and vinegar.

Lager (beer): a cool fermented yeast beer cooled and stored at low temperatures. Pilsner pale lager is the most popular lager in the world.

Stout (beer) and Porter (dark beers): made by roasting malt or barley and brewing with slowly fermenting yeast.

Black and Tan (beer), sometimes called half and half, a mix of pale ale and dark stout, or porter. Usually, the town had local ale and they mixed it with a dark stout. This black and tan mixing of beer probably started in the early 18th century in England.

Cider: made from apples, has a medium to deep gold-like color and has an alcohol content ranging from 2 to 8.5 percent.

## First Flight Lesson

In England, people seemed much friendlier than Americans. In New York and the rest of the U.S.A., it was easy to meet someone, but it took a long time before you really got to know that individual. In England, it was hard to meet someone, but once you met that person, it was easy to get to know that person really well.

On April 10, 1981, friend Jeff Guysyou took me to the Lakenheath AFB Aero club where I met Simon Drey, a flight instructor. There, I experienced my first flight lesson as a student in a Cessna C-150 aircraft. The Cessna C-150 (and the C-152) was a two-seater. It was designed in the 1950's and it was capable of acrobatics. (See photo number one page 153.)

The C-150 had a four-piston, 100 horsepower continental engine driving a two-blade fixed prop. The wingspan was about thirty-three feet and the aircraft was about twenty-two feet long. The airplane weighed about 1,000 pounds and the max takeoff gross weight was around 1,500 pounds. The airplane had the basic instruments of VHF radio, transponder, altitude indicator, altimeter, airspeed indicator and a compass. The C-150 could fly to an altitude of about 12,500 feet, a distance of around 500 miles and a speed of just over 100 knots or around 120 miles per hour (mph). Over 23,800 C-150 aircraft were built, making it the seventh most-produced civilian aircraft.[4]

The next day, I return for another flight lesson, and on April 12, 1981, I completed my third flight lesson. Why do I remember the date? That's easy.

On the morning of April 12, 1981, astronauts Robert Crichton and John Young strapped themselves into their seats on the Columbia space shuttle (Space Transportation System STS-1).

The Columbia space shuttle was the world's first manned, reusable rocket launcher—100 tons of U.S. space technology. This was the first time NASA had put man on an untested launcher. For hours, engineers had been pumping hundreds of thousands of gallons of liquid hydrogen and oxygen into Columbia's fuel tanks. When combined, the two elements would generate more than 1 million pounds of thrust. Two huge solid fuel boosters containing a highly explosive mixture of aluminum powder and perchlorate oxidizer, if all went well, would provide supplemental thrust.

Seconds before liftoff, the shuttle's turbo pumps (each powerful enough to empty a swimming pool in twenty seconds) started to force hydrogen and oxygen into the spacecraft's three main engines, where the two elements combined with unbridled ferocity. (I know this now because I would later write a college term paper about the shuttle.) In seconds, the temperatures in the engines soared to 6000° C. Superheated steam generated by the explosive combination of hydrogen and oxygen caused an eruption at the base of the spaceship, and within ninety seconds, the spaceship's computer signaled the two solid rocket boosters to launch the space shuttle into space. America had successfully launched the first reusable spaceship.[5]

I was fixated on the sight.

I decided right on the spot that I wanted to be a pilot. (Did you know that eighty percent of pilots are the first-born children in their families?)

I joined the RAF Lakenheath Aero Club, and on the back of my membership card was this poem:

**Safety First, and Live**

In days gone by, I proved my worth
By zooming low across the earth,
I buzzed the farms, the mountain ridges,
I flew beneath the river bridges,
I looped and spun, I snapped and rolled,
I took all dares for years untold,
I pressed my luck quite near the line,
But not for need—just thrills; that's fine
I tried most stunts, though it's bean said
I never tried to use my head,
So here's a toast—to you and me!
But you drink both, I'm dead, you see.
—Anon

In July of 1981, in a Cessna 150 aircraft (tail number N961L), I commanded my first solo cross-country flight. I flew from Lakenheath Air Force Base to Nottingham, England.

*Gulp*—solo. Just me, myself and I.

Was I nervous? Not really. I felt prepared. The instruction had been excellent. As the lone pilot, I do everything. I'm the flight planner, dispatcher, weatherman, mechanic, lawyer, and pilot. I compute the flight plan, evaluate the aircraft performance based on weather, check the atmospheric conditions, the weight and balance data and the flight plan route. Nottingham Castle is in the woods—supposedly the castle in the Robin Hood movies—and that that will be a good landmark on the way to Nottingham.

I file the flight plan with estimated time of departure and estimated time of arrival. In case I crash, my filed route will save rescuers time because they will have an idea of where to start looking. From the lawyer stand point of view, my flight instructor signs my flight log to verify I am competent to fly solo. I need all paperwork on hand at all times—my signed log book, student pilots' license, airworthiness certificate and lots of other paperwork including the weight-balance certificate. As a mechanic, I do a pre-flight on the aircraft to make sure it is safe to fly, looking for anything out of line. Then it's time to start the engine, contact ground control, get a taxi clearance, and taxi out. Before takeoff, I do an engine run up (to make sure the engine is operating correctly) and then call the tower for takeoff clearance. I'm on my way, with a keen eye out always looking for a place to land. With one engine, you are always looking for a place to land.

In Nottingham, I feel a bit of relief. But it's not over yet. I repeat all the steps—flight plan, aircraft check, everything. I get fresh fuel, check the weather, and update the flight plan for the return flight.

Back at Lakenheath, it's difficult to get out of the cockpit. I am feeling so confident and proud my head as swelled up with a feeling of pride and accomplishment. Even though I had flown only a few thousand feet above the ground, I felt like I had the whole world in my hand.

I was completely hooked on flying.

The total flight time was 1.2 hours each way. Flight Instructor Simon Drey certified my flight logbook. In less than five months—

on Sept. 4—I passed my private pilot's license exam in aircraft number N961L with FAA Examiner John J. Benton, Designated Pilot Examiner on a flight with an emergency divert to Thorpe Abbott's airport.

I was 20 years old, I had a total flight time of 64.3 hours and with this private pilot license the United States Federal Aviation Administration authorized me to command any aircraft for non-commercial purposes under visual flight rules (VFR)—and I could carry passengers. In other words, the passengers could share the expenses of a flight I was piloting, but they could not hire me in the commercial sense. In order to keep my license current, I had to make at least three takeoffs and three landings within the preceding ninety days. I also had to pass an FAA Second Class medical once a year, pass a flight review flight check once every 24 months, operate my aircraft in a safe and legal manner and comply with a litany of Federal Aviation rules and regulations.

Acquiring the pilot's license was a major accomplishment. But all was not well. Around October 1981, even though I had my private pilot's license and no one could take that away from me, I was about to get my Aero club membership revoked because my Aero club flight bill was growing larger than my ability to pay.

I was in debt. To make it worse, I had major car problems, too. I devised a plan to go AWOL. While hitchhiking to my flat in Bury St. Edmunds, an English man picked me up to give me a ride.

"Oy, mate, how is it going?" he said.

"Not good," I replied.

"I know what you mean," he said, and he told me his gloomy, sad story. After listening to his story, I had a change of heart and decided to tough it out.

Since then, whenever someone asks me how I'm doing, I reply:

"Better than most but not as good as some."

"What do you mean?" they might ask.

When someone asks me, I will say:

Whatso has no job so
Everwhat has no hut.
Notwhy is hungry and dry.
Realget is unhealthy and upset.
Realget lost his breath and is facing death.
Say-don't-you lost his I love you.
Guysyou is all-alone with no you
Guysu is all-alone with no "I have you" or "I love you"
Ycraz darken his soul and entered a no religion phase
Youhey cannot endure the pain anymore or any way.
Comehow hurt me real bad somehow.
Thatswhy

In life there is always someone in worse shape than you, and there is always someone doing better then you. On this earth, everyone lives in their own world and sometimes that world can feel like a prison, in a way. Each person's prison is defined differently. You may be in a marriage or relationship and the other partner is constantly arguing, complaining, and is never pleased. Maybe he or she always wants more money to spend. You may have a disability. You may have physical health issues or mental health issues. You may be poor, hungry, weeping, hated, lonely, insulted, or all of the above. My suggestion? Focus on the good things around you, on what is going well. Don't worry so much and try to be happy.

Jesus said: "Therefore I tell you, do not worry about your life, what you will eat or drink; or about your body, what you will wear. Is not life more important than food, and the body more important than clothes? Look at the birds of the air; they do not sow or reap or store away in barns, and yet your heavenly Father feeds them. Are you not much more valuable than they? Who of you by worrying can add a single hour to his life?" (*Matthew 6:25–27, New American Bible*)

There are no mistakes in life; everything is meant to happen for a reason. It's okay to make a mistake. Learn from that mistake and don't make the same mistake twice. If all hell breaks loose, don't worry, be happy; remember, you can always laugh and sing. In fact, here's a song I wrote:

**Sing a Song**

Tell me a lot about singing a song
Singing a song helps getting along

Doesn't matter what kind of song
Rhyming or not, short or long, right or wrong.

As long as you're singing your song
Life seems better, and less and less seems wrong.

When you are feeling unhappy and down
Start moving your mouth around and sing your song.

Now that you know you need your own song,
Time to produce and write your best personal song.

During the three years I spent in England I had several ways to get around. First, I had a Japanese-made Suzuki 250TS Motorcycle (I had to rebuild the engine before I could ride it). Next, I had a green English-made Austin Mini car, followed by a red German-made Audi 500 car, then a grey English-made Austin Cambridge car, and finally, a blue American-made Chevy LUV pickup truck with a camper shell. The USAF transported the Chevy LUV truck back to the USA for me. My air transportation consisted of a Cessna C-152 and a Cessna C-172 aircraft. Of course, I did not own the planes. I just rented them on an as-needed basis.

During my free time, I took college courses to pursue a degree in aviation and resource management. I also travelled throughout Europe, including:

- Amsterdam, Netherlands (visited Heineken Brewery and a diamond factory)
- Paris and Fontainebleau, France
- Athens and Mykonos, Greece
- Madrid, Spain
- Venice and Rome, Italy (met Pope John Paul II)
- Lucerne and Bern, Switzerland (with youth hostel friends went to a monastery for a fun night)
- Salzburg, Austria (did the Sound of Music tour)
- Frankfurt and Munich, Germany

## Around Europe

Embry-Riddle Aeronautical University (ERAU) had an affiliation branch in England through the USAF, and this is where I enrolled in college. One aviation class included a visit for the students to the Shuttleworth collection, located at the old Warden aerodrome near Biggleswade in Bedfordshire, England. The collection included flying machines from before the First World War, airplanes used in the 1914–1918 war, private and sporting airplanes used between First World War and the Second World War, and aircraft used by the flying services since 1918.

On another field trip we journeyed to visit Wing Commander Ken Wallis at his residence in Reymerston, where he built and flew a variety of auto gyrocopters. Commander Wallis piloted a demonstration flight for us in an "auto gyrocopter" called "Little Nellie." He logged 85 flight hours in the Little Nellie to film the auto gyro sequence in the James Bond film *You Only Live Twice* (1967).

World War I pilot William Fryer visited and spoke to our class one evening. Fryer was one of the three pilots claiming to have shot down the Red Baron (German Captain Manfred Albrecht Freiherr von Richthofen was the Red Baron) on April 21, 1918. The Red Baron had previously shot down 80 allied (mainly British) pilots through aerial aircraft dogfights. Mr. Fryer admitted there was so much smoke and confusion during that dogfight that he or one of the other two pilots may have shot the Red Baron down. Mr. Fryer was nearly deaf in his left ear from flying, so we had to speak loudly into his right ear, and I posed this question to him.

"Were you afraid of crashing when you landed in those days?"

He took out his log book and showed us many pictures of various airplanes he had flown and said: "To land was to crash because usually the landing gear failed."

He explained that it was not uncommon to fly two or three different types of airplanes in one week because in the day, you may have crashed your last airplane on your last landing. This was because the history of flying and building planes was very short; it had been only about fifteen years since Wilbur and Orville Wright flew the first sustained airborne aircraft flight in Kill Devil Hills, North Carolina on December 17, 1903. This was by far my favorite, most enjoyable and aeronautically-inspiring college course I have ever taken—at least up to this point in my life.

Amongst many of my peers, I was selected "Airman of the Quarter." The selecting board members question me:

"What are the branches of our government and which one is the most important?" Apparently, I was the only candidate who correctly answered, "The legislative, the executive and the judicial branch and they all shared equal power." This "Airman of the Quarter" award earned me an observation air refueling flight on a KC-135 Stratotanker aircraft. This was a flight that entailed a KC-135 aircraft refueling an F-15 Eagle fighter jet while in flight at an altitude of 30,000 feet. (This precision flying and the whole refueling operation was a spellbinding experience to watch.)

The Cessna C-172 airplane, called the Skyhawk, was bigger and faster than the C-150 and could seat four persons. The Skyhawk weighed about 1,500 pounds with a maximum takeoff gross weight of 2,500 pounds. It had a wingspan of 35 feet wide and it was 27 feet long. The Skyhawk had a 160 horsepower engine that could fly as fast as 125 KTS (about 145 MPH) to a distance of around 600 nautical miles. It could fly up to 17,000 feet in altitude. About 42,500 of these aircraft were built.[6] The C-150 had basic instruments in order to fly heading, altitude and airspeed during visual meteorology conditions (or in other words direction, height and speed during good weather).

The C-172 had more sophisticated aviation electronics, like Navigation Receiver (NAV REC) and a Horizontal Situation Indicator (HSI) to guide the pilot to fly an Instrument Landing System (ILS) approach and land safely on a runway during instrument meteorology conditions (such as clouds or fog). If a pilot faced limited visibility because of bad weather, he could execute an ILS Approach that could guide the pilot safely, via instruments, down to an altitude of two hundred feet. This point was called the decision height (DH), and at this altitude, the pilot had to decide whether or not he could see the runway and land visually. If he did not see the runway, the pilot would go around and try the approach again or he would go to land at another airport.

An electronic signal from a ground-based facility at the airport would be sent to the NAV REC, and the NAV REC would send a signal to the HSI. The HSI instrument would display to the pilot if he was high or low vertically, left or right horizontally from the correct course to the runway. The pilot would make the appropriate adjustments. If the visibility was good, the flight instructor would put a hood over the pilot's head so that the student pilot could only see the interior cockpit instruments, simulating flying in bad weather. On Sept. 27, 1981, I experienced my first flight in a C-172 (aircraft tail number N14496), my first ILS instrument approach instruction, and my first flight into a big airport (London Stanstead Airport EGSS). The ILS approach technology has increased the safety of air travel, reduced air disasters and improved the efficiency and flow at airports throughout the world.

On March 5, 1982, my friend and pilot partner Jeff Guysyou and I piloted a C-172 airplane to Nottingham, England to spend the night and to return the next day. When we went out that night, we acted like cool, big-time American pilots with big-headed egos. In reality, we were poor and barely had enough money for a few pints and a place to stay for the night.

While living in England my lovely sister Kathleen traveled from Long Island to visit for a week. This trip took the place of a high school graduation party—very nice of her. We toured all over southeast England and London. We even went to an English wedding. Kathleen had a great English time.

I would do anything to accumulate free flight time. On Jan. 16, 1983, I hitchhiked to Shoreham-at-Sea airport (EGKA), which is located about 100 miles south of London on the English Channel. That night, I slept in the back of the airplane (number N60626), and the next day I flew the airplane with no navigation aids and no radios back to RAF Lakenheath. The flight lasted 2.9 hours, and I had to circumnavigate around Heathrow International Airport in London with just a map and a compass susceptible to gyroscopic precession. Everything you see on an aeronautical map, you should be able to see on the ground, but not everything you see on the ground is on the map. Topography and geography change quicker than maps change. After navigating the airplane around London, I became disoriented and landed at another airfield for fuel and directions, then proceeded to RAF Lakenheath.

One Friday afternoon, Jeff and I received Permissive TDY (Temporary Duty Assignment) orders to take a military HOP (a free aircraft ride) to Ramstein Air Base in Frankfurt, Germany to pick up a plane from the Ramstein and fly it back. This was a great opportunity. We could get at least four or five hours of free flight time, spend Friday night in Germany, pilot the airplane back to England on Saturday or Sunday and be back to work on Monday.

No problem, right?

In fact, we didn't need to get our supervisor's permission. As previously mentioned, we were big time, cool pilots with big-headed egos. The HOP to Germany went fine. We met Mike, an Aero club member who took us out for our first German meal. At the restaurant, Jeff made the mistake of asking for pepper, salt, and ketchup. The cook came out from the kitchen and wanted to know what was wrong with the meal he had just prepared.

The next day, we went to the Ramstein Aero club to pick up the airplane and fly it to England. Bad news. The Aero club manager informed us that the aircraft was down for maintenance due to a hard landing made the previous day. The manager explained that he was able to obtain authorization for a special onetime "Ferry Flight" waiver and we could fly the aircraft back to England. We called our aero club manager Jack Benton and told him about the situation. Jack did not want the aircraft in that state, needing repair.

In that case, no problem. We could stay in Germany another night and go home Sunday.

Bad news. Guess what? There were no military HOPs to England on Sunday. Plus, because we had permissive TDY orders that would expire on Monday, we would be put on the bottom status of any list of others who wanted to HOP back to England on the limited available seats.

On Monday at 8:00 AM I called my supervisor and said, "Sergeant Rodney Bramilton, I am going to be a little late for work today."

"That's obvious," said Rodney, thinking I was calling from BSE, seventeen miles away.

"Well, I'm going to be a *lot* late for work today," I said. "I'm in Germany."

Bad news!

Yes, I was now officially AWOL (a serious crime in the military). Through hectic maneuvering to another German base, we did get back to England on Monday night. An AWOL punishment could lead to a conviction with reduction in rank, reduction in pay, expulsion from the military, hard labor, or any and all of the above.

Good news. My punishment was two weekends of hard labor, which turned into a blessing in disguise. For the two weekends, I was ordered to paint some of the rooms in our accounting office building. However, I was able to take the leftover paint back to my flat where I put it to good use. I guess I was a good guy with an interesting AWOL excuse and no prior trouble, so they went easy on me. Still, I vowed to never go AWOL again.

The next time I took a military flight HOP it was to Torrejón Air Base in Madrid, Spain, but that time I was absent from duty with permissive vacation leave.

## Almost Died: Age 21
## Auto accident en route from Madrid to Benador, Spain

On this trip, I was with three female friends. We were heading from Madrid to Benidorm (a Mediterranean beach resort in Spain). We were on the highway during a heavy rainstorm and the driver slid off the main road, hit a huge rock, and the car flipped over.

Flipped over, in fact, three times.

During the first flip, I leaped out of the right rear passenger seat (no one wore seat belts in those days) and through the window. The force cracked my head. After getting up onto my feet, I approached the car. Birdie, who was sitting next to me in the car, got out of the vehicle with minor injuries. Together, we pulled Jennifer, the driver, out of the wreck. She sustained minor shoulder and neck injuries and a broken leg. Orei, who sat in front of me, was trapped under the car. At this point, many Spaniards had stopped to help us. I directed some of the men to help lift the car off of Orei, who had broken her hip in several places.

An ambulance took the women away and the Guards (Spanish military police that carried small machine guns) approached me. The Guards looked at me with a serious, unhappy expression. I was thinking that with my looks (I was often being told I looked like Tony Curtis or Robert De Niro or Jerry Lewis or Tony Danza) they probably mistakenly thought I was wanted for some crime. While I was standing there soaking wet in the mud, my adrenaline started to wear off, and I soon realized my right leg was in great deal of pain and my head ached. In fact, my head was bleeding.

The Guards took me to a small, rudimentary police and First Aid facility in a small village. There, a person with some medical training (I don't think he was a certified, proper doctor) stitched the hole in my head without anesthesia (I did black out for a minute or two). He also placed an icepack on my leg.

Even though I had spent two years of Spanish classes in high school, I was only able to communicate with the Spanish police and the medical types on a basic level. However, I was able to communicate to two of the Guards to get a basic necessity. The two Guards escorted me across the street to a small bar and restaurant. There I purchased a glass of what we would call whiskey and a sandwich. I drank the glass of whiskey straight down in one mouthful immediately after receiving it. That move earned the respect, friendship, and mutual laughter of those two Spanish police officers. A few hours later, a couple of Air Force sergeants arrived, retrieved me, and transported me back to Torrejón Air Base in Madrid. Jennifer and Orei were in the hospital, Birdie wanted to mellow out and recuperate, and I wasn't going to let my injured leg spoil my vacation. Birdie's real name was Alberta. She was from Minnesota and she liked to be called Birdie.

Yes, *always tell the truth*—the Madrid leg story. I took my limping, aching, eye-catching leg, and joined a tour bus to Madrid. Well, you know how international foreign tourists are —they will use any line or any excuse to start up a conversation with you. Some spoke good

English; some did not. Some transmitted good body language; some did not. Some I wanted to speak to; some I did not. So, within that one day, the leg question and answer started getting old.

"What happened to your leg?"

Sometimes the whole story was worth telling. At other times, the short version sufficed. Well, I was never going to see these people again, so I started telling different versions of the leg story. I told short versions to the tourists I wasn't that interested in. And I told long versions to, well, the grandmother of the pretty blue-eyed brunette.

At the end of the tour, a Spanish meal with sangria was included. The tour bus group was subdivided into six 12-person tables. I positioned myself next to miss Pretty Brunette and quickly consumed two glasses of sangria. I needed it for medicinal purposes—my leg. Whew! She spoke first.

"I'm sorry to hear that XYZ happened to your leg." She spoke sweetly and was so pretty, so I waited for her to continue—mistake. Another person at the table who spoke better English cut in.

"I thought you said ABC happened to your leg."

"I thought you said NOP happened to your leg," said someone else.

My quick-wits were not functioning. What was I going to do? Tell the truth. I explained the original truthful leg story and how I started telling different versions of the story because the leg story response was getting old and boring. Everyone laughed. No, I didn't get the girl—but I eventually told the truth and felt better.

Shortly after, I flew back to England to rehabilitate my leg and to go back to work. Many different and some funny versions of the stories of what happened to me in Spain had already been circulating before I had arrived. Let people talk. They need something to talk about. Besides, some of their versions were very entertaining, and if they had the balls to ask me— I would *tell them the truth*.

# Almost Died: Age 21
# Auto skid on black ice in the Midland Mountains

At the end of December of 1982, three friends of male gender (Air Force Airmen) and I decided to go to Glasgow, Scotland to celebrate Hogmanay Night (the Scottish New Year's Eve).

How would we get there?

"I'll drive. It's less than 400 miles and less than a seven-hour drive, and I think my 1960 Austin Cambridge will make it," I said.

We pooled our money and off we went. As we were driving through the midland mountains at some of the highest elevations in the United Kingdom, I encountered Black Ice.

In aviation class, I had learned about Freezing Drizzle (FZDZ), Freezing Rain (FZRA), Hoarfrost (not whores), Rime Ice, and Clear Ice—but what was Black Ice?

Black Ice is a thin sheet of clear ice or glaze that is formed when freezing rain descends onto roads that are already sub-zero temperatures. Black Ice is dark and is very dangerous because the road appears wet rather than icy.[7] You cannot see Black Ice. Under Black ice conditions, drivers encounter little or no traction, little to no braking, extremely poor directional control.

And skidding.

Technically speaking, the factors affecting the friction between surfaces are as follows:

The static friction coefficient (μ) between two solid surfaces is defined as the ratio of the tangential force (F) required to produce sliding, divided by the normal force between the surfaces (N):

$$\mu = F/N$$

For a horizontal surface, the horizontal force (F) to move a solid resting on a flat surface:

$$F = \mu \times \text{mass of solid} \times g.[8]$$

If there are known black ice conditions, then black ice warnings are issued, therefore preventing Lorries (trucks) from jack-knifing and passenger cars from skidding off the road. We were in the midland mountains and I was happily driving. I knew of no warnings.

Suddenly, my rear wheels lost traction with the road

I lost control of the car.

Déjà vu.

Well, sort of. Remember the Rochester snowstorm trip—mountains on one side, cliffs on the other side? That was a four-lane roadway. This was two lanes. I slowly and delicately steered into the direction of the skid. I did not try to brake. I released the gas pedal and manually downshifted from fourth gear to third. The old Austin Cambridge car entered a few fish tails, but I avoided the 360-degree turn. Slowly and eventually, I obtained full steering control and brought the vehicle to a stop.

However, the left rear wheel was positioned off the road about twelve inches lower than the other three wheels. The English drive on the wrong side—the left side of the road. Déjà vu, take two. There, the mountains were on one side of the road (the right side this time) and a steep cliff leading into a valley on the other side of the road (the left side this time). There was no guard rail to prevent the car from going down the cliff. The vehicle was just a few feet from tumbling off and no guard rail to prevent the car from sliding into the mountain side, either.

After a brief discussion and a few "Thank Gods," we decided it would be safer to lift the rear wheel and push the car back onto the road. If we attempted to try to drive the car back onto the road, then maybe the car would skid down the cliff. We didn't want to lose the car.

We made it up to Glasgow in time to celebrate. On Hogmanay Eve, you could visit any house as long as you were carrying wine, beer, or liquor. The friendly Scottish would invite you into their house and offer you a drink and sometimes tasty snacks and you would offer them a drink of the poison you were carrying. Strictly to improve international socialization, I had already participated in the Hogmanay tradition in Edinburgh on Dec. 31, 1980. The poison we were carrying then was the U.S-made Jack Daniels. This beverage was very well received and helped promote great results. So I wasn't that interested in indulging again, tradition or not.

During New Year's, Edinburgh was populated mainly with tourists. Glasgow would be populated mainly with locals. I was interested in finding a Scott who had the Glaswegian Smile, or sometimes called the Glasgow Grin. The ancient rumor was that a Glaswegian Smile was obtained when another person slashed that person's face from the edges of the mouth to the ears with a knife or broken glass. We were warned to avoid certain rough areas of Glasgow and to avoid rough crowds in pubs where someone proclaims "drink up." While lifting your beer mug to drink up, someone may jam the beer mug into your mouth by ramming the bottom of the beer mug upwards into your teeth—the glass mug would break and cut your mouth edges, giving you the Glaswegian Smile. We did not believe the rumor and we were determined to prove or disprove the legend.

Glasgow was economically depressed at that time, having lost many jobs in the ship building and train building industries. As a result, we found establishments in the food and beverage industry that were selling products at a very reasonable price.

But being the rich USAF Airmen that we were, we just had to venture to the part of the city where we could purchase these products at the lowest cost. That is where we observed Scotts with Glaswegian Smiles and believed that the folklore was not some made up rumor, but a true story.

The people of Glasgow are some of the most friendly people I have met anywhere in the world, but be careful. There are some rough places in Glasgow where nobody would want to go—if he wanted to keep his beautiful smile. Nobody needs a Glaswegian Smile. We left Glasgow and drove back.

## Free Beer

In June of 1983, I flew as a passenger on a C141 Star-Lifter from RAF Mildenhall, England to Dover AFB Delaware and made my way to Bayonne, New Jersey to pick up my Chevy Luv pickup. I drove through New York City to my parent's home on Long Island. After hanging out for a week, I was "Going to California" (Led Zeppelin). My Long Island friend Ralf Saydontyou and I drove to Denver, Colorado in 48 hours. Arriving at daybreak we observed the sun rising through the side view mirror and saw the snow-covered tops of the Rocky Mountains light up in the distance. We hung out in Colorado and visited the Coors brewery. We did not participate in the brewery tour. You see, I observed some tourists exiting the brewery in a less-than-sober physical condition and my sober brain inspired me with this idea to enter the brewery through the exit door. Maybe I got the idea from the two bars located on the water on Long Island. The bars were called The In and The Out and they were located side by side.

After going through the exit door, there was a Coors Company complementary guest barroom with complementary (yes, *free*) beer. So we avoided the 90-minute boring tour and got right down to the business we intended to accomplish—drinking free beer.

If a person lives at sea level and goes to an altitude of around 10,000 feet, the oxygen density volume of air that human being's intake is half the density of air that humans are accustomed to inhaling at sea level altitude. Denver was the "Mile High City" at an elevation of 5,280 feet above sea level (there is a marker on the steps of the State Capitol). Therefore, consuming alcohol affects the inebriation of the human body at a faster rate. Here is Swedish physicist E.M.P. Widmark's basic formula for calculating Blood Alcohol Content (BAC).

$$\%BAC = (A \times 5.14 / W \times R) - (0.015 \times H)$$

- A = is the total number of ounces of alcohol consumed starting at the first drink. On average one twelve-ounce beer or one five-ounce glass of wine or one one point five-ounce shot of liquor is .60 liquid ounces of alcohol.
- W = is the weight of your body in pounds.
- R = is the distribution ratio for alcohol through the human body; on average 0.73 for men and 0.66 for women.
- H = is the number of hours since your first drink.

I drank my first beer at age \_\_\_, and I will drink my last beer at age \_\_\_. In fact I am drinking a beer right now. (☼ = Beer spot.)

I enjoy beer everywhere I travel. At the time, in Denver, I definitely noticed the elevation's impact on my ability to absorb the alcohol—and I enjoyed the taste of Coors, which was wasn't as well known around the country as it is today. Besides, free beer! What's not to like?

I like beer so much I've looked into the history of the beverage, so I know not everyone calls this great-tasting alcohol "beer." The Latins called it beer, the English ale, the Romans cerevisia, the Spanish cerveza, and the Slavics called it Pivo. About 10—15,000 years ago, some humans settled down to farm and grow grains. Most substances that contain sugars like grains can undergo a spontaneous fermentation due to wild yeast in the air. Various cultures from ancient Africa, Egypt, and Samaria may have independently invented a beer-like beverage by accident. There is evidence from ancient pottery that beer was produced 7,000 years ago in a place we today call Iran.

The oldest proven record of brewing beer was by the Samarians, about 6,000 years ago. The Babylonians brewed about 20 different types of beer. The Egyptians and Romans brewed beer, and even monks in the Christian abbeys brewed beer. The Germans, in 1516, instituted the first purity law (the Reinheitsgebot) regulating that German beers would be made using only the four ingredients of water, malted barley, malted wheat, and hops. In the sixteenth century, lager beer was discovered by accident after storing beer in cool taverns for long periods of time. During the Industrial Revolution, the thermometer and hydrometer enabled the increased quality production of various amber, brown, and pale malt beers.[9,10] Today, with advances in refrigeration and international shipping in the U.S.A., we have a choice to drink hundreds of different types of beers from various styles of local, regional, national, and foreign beers.

After spending a week in the Denver area, we drove to Salt Lake City, Utah. We only stopped to jump into Great Salt Lake for a swim. The lake has such a high concentration of salt that I could lay on my back in the water, exhale all the air out of my lungs, and still stay afloat. Plus, that high concentration of salt changed the color of the underwear that I was using as swim trunks! It dyed my red underwear into a pinkish orange. I left that underwear there, and we continued our drive to California.

## Almost Died: Age 22
## Highway break-down during the worst brush fire in Nevada

We almost didn't make it to California.

Ever since Denver, we were having car problems. We were driving west on Highway Route 80 near Carlin or Battle Mountain or some other small, hick town in Nevada and we exited to purchase gasoline.

We didn't talk to the locals and we weren't listening to the local radio station, so we were unaware that Route 80 was in the process of being closed because of an uncontrolled, 6,000-acre brush fire.

We quickly filled up and got back on Highway 80, probably the only highway entrance that had not been closed yet. After about fifteen minutes of driving, Ralf and I noticed that we were the only vehicle on the highway.

Very strange. The sunny skies disappeared behind smoky clouds.

We started seeing sporadic fires in the distance. The fires appeared widespread and close. Then my Chevy LUV pick-up stopped. The engine quit. When driving at a high altitude with a high temperature, the density altitude of air is very low, and that air did not provide the proper fuel-to-air mixture needed for the four-cylinder engine to run properly. Plus, the engine's fuel pump did not always work as it should.

Anxiously, I leaped out of the truck, opened the hood and removed the carburetor cover. As I had Ralf turn the ignition to start the engine, I manually adjusted the carburetor choke and the engine would start. At least, that was the theory. It had worked several times before.

This time, it was not working.

The wind shifted, and now the scorching brush fires were burning right up to the road. There I was on the westbound lane, gazing at ten-foot high flames, smelling fiery smoke and feeling heat on my face. Only the highway and the unburned median separated us from fire.

If the winds shifted again and jumped the road, we would die. Then I remembered I was carrying a spare 20-gallon plastic container filled with gasoline and a 22-foot hang glider kite –this could easily contribute to a vehicle explosion if the flames were to come closer.

It was a tense moment. "Why won't the engine start?" I asked myself. "What can I do?" "Should we abandon the pickup?"

I heard an airplane and shifted my smoky eyes up. A military-type aircraft was spreading chemicals over the fire.

Still trying to get the truck going, I poured a little gas from the spare gas tank into an empty soda can. This time, while Ralf was turning the ignition with the key, I poured gasoline into the carburetor and some fell on my hand. Now, I could smell smoke and gasoline—very dangerous!

"I hope the wind doesn't shift and the flames don't torch us!"

"I hope the engine starts."

A couple of emergency rescue firefighters showed up, perhaps alerted by the pilot, and just then, the engine started.

The firefighters followed us to the next highway exit and we escaped possible death from that windy, blazing brush fire. We made it to California, where I would spend the last six months of my USAF career at McClellan AFB in Sacramento, California.

## My Own Place

Sacramento is the capitol of California and I had arrived in July, the driest month with temperatures averaging 90º Fahrenheit and plenty of sunshine. California is the third largest US state and probably the most diverse state in nature, culture and demographics. There are beaches, mountains, farms, forest, deserts and cities to see; so I traveled to Lake Tahoe, San Francisco, Los Angeles, San Diego, and flew around in the C-172.

It was the first time in my entire life that I had my own place. That apartment in California was mine and only mine. However, I soon learned there are rights and responsibilities of having your own place.

On the plus side, you have the right to decide when to eat and sleep, when to come and go, and what guest can visit.

At the same time, you have the responsibility to pay the bills, maintain the residence and do certain chores, like cleaning. Cleaning is not my favorite activity.

Women, please read the following at your own risk. This is not for you. When the apartment got out of hand and really messy this is what I did:

1. I opened all the windows and doors.
2. I filled the bathroom tub with hot water and detergent and loaded all my dishes, glasses, and silverware into the tub.
3. I picked up all my clothes ran down to the laundry room and put the clothes into the washing machine.
4. I ran back to the apartment threw out all old food, wiped down the kitchen counter and table, picked up all trash

and vacuumed the floor. No mop for me; I mopped while in basic training and hated the task.
5. Went back to the bathroom, drained the tub and put the shower on. After rinsing all the dishes, glasses and silverware under the shower, I then spread them all over the kitchen counter and table to air dry.
6. Ran back to the laundry room, put the clothes in the dryer and ran back to the apartment.
7. Made the bed and with a wet washcloth or old T-shirt, cleaned the dresser, nightstand and bathroom sink.
8. Ran back to the laundry room, collected all my clothes and ran back to the apartment.
9. I put all shirts and pants on hangers and packed (maybe stuffed) the rest of the clothes into the dresser.
10. Collected all the dried dishes, glasses and silverware and stored them in the kitchen cabinets.
11. Closed all the windows and doors, lit a few candles, put on loud music, drank a cold beer, redressed and then went out.

After this, the apartment was good to go for at least two to three more weeks. I never went to cleaning school, but I figured that process was the most efficient way to clean a bachelor's pad in a few hours. Do you know that it is really important to most women that your place is clean?

So in December of 1983, my short Air Force career was coming to an end. What had I accomplished in four years? I had lived six months in Texas, three years in England, and six months in California. My travels had taken me all over the United Kingdom. They had taken me to Germany, Italy, Greece, Spain, Switzerland, Austria, France and The Netherlands. They had allowed me to drive from New York to California and then to Florida—and I had acquired lots of friends and memories during those four years.

The USAF awarded me:

- The Commendation Medal
- Good Conduct Medal
- Outstanding Unit Award
- Longevity Service Award
- Small Arm Expert Marksmanship
- Airman of the Quarter (twice)
- An Associate College Degree in Applied Science—Resource Management Technology

The Federal Aviation Administration issued me a private pilot license. After logging 114 hours of total pilot flight time in England. I logged another eight hours in California, acquiring a total pilot flight time of 122 hours while in the USAF.

Without any notice, ex-English girlfriend Linda travelled from London to Sacramento to pursue me. We spent time together and then we drove from Sacramento to Daytona Beach, Florida. After the realization that I was not ready to settle down, Linda went back to London.

After spending a few days rearranging a few of the college classes that I intended to take in 1984, my brother Kevin and I drove to Long Island. After spending the holiday week on Long Island, Kevin and I drove to Daytona Beach and I started undergraduate classes at Embry-Riddle Aeronautical University (ERAU).

CHAPTER 4

# Undergrad School (ERAU) Age 23–24

I n '84 I took 54.

In the year 1984 I completed 54 college credit hours at the main campus of Embry- Riddle Aeronautical University (ERAU).

ERAU's main campus today is located in Daytona Beach, Florida. Historically, the campus was founded at Lunken Airport in Cincinnati, Ohio on Dec. 17, 1925, exactly 22 years after the historic flight of the Wright Brothers. Barnstormer John Paul Riddle and entrepreneur T. Higbee Embry founded the Embry-Riddle company. The following spring, the company opened the Embry-Riddle school of aviation. Embry-Riddle began with a simple plan to train airplane pilots in a thorough, efficient manner and to cash in on the booming interest in flying after the end of World War I.

In 1965, with Jack R. Hunt as president, Embry-Riddle consolidated its flight training, ground school and technical training programs in one location and moved to Daytona Beach. In 1968, the ERAU institution was accredited by the commission of colleges of the Southern Association of Colleges and Schools and two years later Embry-Riddle attained university status."[11]

Today ERAU is known as the "Harvard of Aviation." In January of 1984 I started my attendance at the home campus of ERAU, taking courses in Aeronautics, Aviation History, Aviation Government, Aviation Law, Navigation, Meteorology, Flight Physiology, Flight Safety, Aerodynamics, Aircraft Engines, Aircraft Systems, Aircraft

Components, Aircraft Performance, Federal Rules and Regulations—and more.

In 1984 the campus was still small with a very high male-to-female ratio, but we did have Spring break. In fact Daytona Beach, famous as the "World Center of Racing" and home of NASCAR, was also known as the second-best place for Spring break on the East Coast of the United States. So every Saturday, on a weekly basis, busloads of college kids would come to Daytona Beach from all over America and Canada and stay for a week. These waves of students came for two months straight. So my Spring break consisted of driving five miles to the 23-mile stretch of white sandy beach and my Spring break lasted for two months.

Daytona is one of the few places in the world where you can drive your car on a sandy beach just a few feet from the Atlantic Ocean. Daytona has great subtropical weather with summer temperatures ranging from 70º to 90º Fahrenheit. The dry and mild winter temperatures range from the mid-40's to low 70's—a major improvement compared to the climate in England.

There was always something going on in Daytona Beach—like the Hawaiian Tropic Suntan Lotion Competition, the Daytona Speed Week, the Daytona 500 Auto Race, the Motorcycle Bike Week—and yes, we had to manage our time to fly, take college exams, and study as well.

So to capitalize on this situation I devised a plan that worked out well for us. We would stay home Friday and Saturday nights and go out Sunday through Thursday nights. This system increased the girl-to-boy ratio because most college kids stayed home during the week to study and went out on weekends. At age 23, I was more mature than the average student going to college, and I had three years of life experience in Europe.

While in school we had to make tough choices at times—like when to play and when to work. Several teachers selected me as the introducing speaker at the Communications College Night at ERAU and the next day there was a vets' party with free oysters and free beer, but I decided to stay home and write my Flight Physiology paper. The topic I chose was pilot stress.

John W. Young had given a speech at the university and I had asked him this question: "Do you think pilots endure more stress due to increased technology installed in aircraft that pilots fly today?"

He basically answered "yes" and talked about his experience commanding small airplanes, propeller airplanes, jet airplanes, rockets and space shuttles. I incorporated his response into my paper. That was a good choice and I earned an "A."

By the way, John W. Young was an astronaut, test pilot, naval officer and aeronautical engineer. He was the ninth person to walk on the moon. Young enjoyed the longest career of any U.S. astronaut and made six space flights, including as commander of two on the space shuttle.

The other term paper I wrote was about the spray-on foam insulation used in the thermal protection system of the external tank of the space shuttle. Trying to make good choices verses bad choices while attending college can be challenging at times.

My hard working father once stated to me, "No one is ever going to call you up and offer you a job; you have to go out and look for one."

Not always; there was an exception to this for me. At the time, I was renting a room in a shared house with other college students. One day, Loraine Comehow (a self-made millionaire) called. She was looking for a former roommate but the guy she was looking for had left and she offered me the work. You could say I was her Guy Friday because I did a wide variety of jobs including lawn maintenance, cutting bushes, weeding, fixing up rental properties, home renovation, painting, accounting and so on. . Another time when I didn't have enough money for food and gas to finish the week, a young professionally-dressed lady sustained a flat tire in her Monte Carlo right in front of the house that I was renting with college friends Douglas Olando and Donald Nilson. Being a good neighbor, I replaced the flat tire with the good spare tire, and she offered me a monetary reward. Initially I refused to accept, but after her persistence I did accept it and this money allowed me to survive that week, at least in the financial sense. For additional much-needed funds I listed in the United States Air Force Reserves for 20 months while attending undergraduate school. Money was not always available when I wanted it, but mysteriously money became available when I needed it.

Remember that 1972 Chevy Luv pick-up truck I bought in England, shipped to New Jersey and drove across the country to California and then to Florida? Well, after leaving Miami one weekend in 1985 en route to Daytona Beach, I blew an engine head gasket somewhere around West Palm Beach on I-95. My brother Kevin drove up, towed me back to Miami, and gave me a beat-up 1966 Chrysler Newport in exchange for my pick-up. I drove that car back to Daytona Beach. Even though the fuel efficiency was around eight miles per gallon, I would pull into a gas station and say, "Check the gas and fill her up with oil."

That boat (another word for a big, American car) had a 440 TNT four barrel V-8 engine that burned lots of oil. The vehicle was 18 feet long, six feet wide and weighed 4,300 pounds. However, on a good day the car would go over 120 mph and you could watch the gas gauge drop. At first, the car ran on only five of the eight cylinders. There were two holes in the rear floorboards. The passenger seat had a large hole that exposed the springs. The rear chrome bumpers were bent out like the Batmobile (the Batmobile from the Batman television shows and movies). The exterior exposed the original blue paint, rust, water spots and bird shit stains. So, being the rich college kid that I was, here is what I did.

1. I took the car to an auto repair shop. The mechanic, who was also a school auto mechanic instructor, took pity on

me. He changed a few wires and a few spark plugs, and only charged me for the cost of the parts.

2. Lorene Comehow owned and leased-out commercial buildings and one of those buildings was an auto-body repair shop. The owner kindly gave me fiberglass that I used to patch up the two floorboard holes.

3. I removed the five-foot-wide front passenger seat and took it to an upholster to repair the hole at a bare-minimum cost. So, for a week, I drove the boat with a beach chair as a driver's seat. The trick was to go easy on the brakes and try to ignore the many laughing onlookers while stopped at a red traffic light.

4. I couldn't straighten the bent-out, Batman-style chrome rear bumpers, but I had an idea for the paint job. I went to K-mart and purchased—at full retail price—one paint brush and one gallon of black gloss exterior Rustoleum paint. Yes, I hand-paint-brushed that 1966 Chrysler Newport boat—I mean automobile. Believe it or not from over ten feet away, you couldn't see any paint lines—just a few corroded holes here and there.

My pilot peers named the car "the Batmobile," I called her Black Beauty. Either way, I could seat seven college students (including me) as we ventured in comfort to the strip at Daytona Beach. All the passengers were shocked to see me parallel park that eighteen-foot Black Beauty Batmobile into a twenty-foot parking space on the first attempt. In New York, you have to successfully demonstrate parallel parking in order to earn a driver's license and to survive. When most of my friends' cars eventually died, my car was still alive and running, at least until the day I drove it to the junkyard in Dallas in 1987. However, one day I was asked, "Is the Bat mobile still running?" I had to reply, "It runs, but it won't stop." While in a parking lot, my brakes failed one day—a scary feeling when you press the brake pedal and a 4,300 pound vehicle will not stop. No injuries, no damage. I survived.

After taking twenty-two years to acquire my first degree (Associate in Applied Science in Resource Management Technology, Nov. 16, 1983) I started accumulating other certificates at a faster rate.

- July 13, 1985: Aircraft Dispatches License
- May 20, 1985: Commercial and Instrument Pilot License
- Aug. 13, 1985: Certified Flight Instructor License: Airplane Single-Engine Rating. (This single-engine option was a new option under a new program at ERAU; I was the first student to complete this program).
- Aug. 17, 1985: Bachelor in Aeronautical Science from Embry-Riddle Aeronautical University with 298 hours of total pilot flight time.
- Sept. 20, 1985: Multi-Engine Rated License
- Oct. 1, 1985: Ground Instructor License: Advanced and Instrument Rating.

In September of 1985, I was in pursuit of my first pilot flight position. I put on a professional suit and tie and I paced into the office of the flight department manager, Paul McDuffee. I requested an interview for a job as a certified flight instructor.

It didn't take long. Immediately after the interview, Mr. McDuffee offered me the position, teaching college students how to fly Cessna C-172 airplanes at ERAU. In the first nine months I instructed and signed off 54 students for solo flying. I loved my job so much that I was instructing eight flight hours a day and ground instructing four classroom hours a day. This scheduled was for six days a week—a total of 72 work hours per week.

This first flight job came with huge responsibility, which affected my ego and also produced a few sweaty, unwanted nightmares. Those nightmares always involved my students crashing into the ocean. They were triggered by my concern that I had signed-off too early, that they weren't ready to operate the C-172 aircraft solo.

The course I taught included:

- how to inspect and preflight the airplane
- how to start the engine
- when and how to communicate over the radio
- how to taxi to the runway
- how to take off
- how to depart the traffic pattern
- basic navigation
- basic airplane control of heading, altitude and airspeed about the three basic axes (longitude, latitude, and vertical)
- how to reenter the traffic pattern and land
- emergency procedures

As I have mentioned before, with an aircraft that has only one engine you are always looking for a field to land in case that engine fails. Once the student has mastered these skills, maneuvers, and procedures, the certified flight instructor (moi) would certify and endorse the student's logbook, permitting the student to fly solo—all by him or herself. The endorsement read:

> ***I have given Mr. John Ace Pilot Doe the flight training required by CFR 61.87 (n). He has met the requirements of CFR 61.87 (n) and is competent to operate a Cessna C-172 aircraft in solo flight during daytime at Daytona Beach Airport (DAB). This endorsement is valid for ninety days effective (date).***

What a deal. I was a college professor at the "Harvard of Aviation" and I was teaching college students how to fly airplanes. This helped me to meet girls as well. (See photo number two page 153.)

The first *aviation catastrophe* I observed was when I was instructing two students and our flight position was 4,000 feet above the Ormond VOR (OMN). Ormond VOR is located on the Ormond Beach Municipal Airport and it's less than 80 miles from the Kennedy Space Center at Cape Canaveral.

While in flight, we observed the Space shuttle Challenger (STS-51 L) blow up—a devastating sight.

The catastrophe occurred on Jan. 28, 1986—a scant seventy-three seconds into flight and above the Atlantic. The accident remains NASA's most visible failure. It was the world's first high-tech catastrophe to unfold on live TV.

Adding to the anguish was the young audience; school children everywhere tuned in that morning to watch the launch of the first schoolteacher and ordinary citizen bound for space, Christa McAuliffe. McAuliffe and six others on board perished because of the failure of an O-ring seal and feeble bureaucratic decisions. It was, as one grief and trauma expert recalls, the beginning of the age when the whole world knew what happened as it happened."[12]

The crew compartment shot out of the fireball, intact, and continued upward another three miles before starting to plummet. The free fall lasted more than two minutes. There was no parachute to slow the descent. There was no escape system whatsoever. NASA had skipped all that in shuttle development. In the public view, space travel was becoming ordinary and routine.

In a horrific flash, the most diverse space crew ever—including one black, one Japanese-American, and two women, one of them a Jew—was gone. NASA had safely launched shuttles 24 times before. The launches were being taken for granted, despite the enormous risk. The name of NASA's second oldest shuttle was forever locked in a where-were-you moment."[13] My students and I were 4,000 thousand feet above the ground and less than 80 miles away from the disaster. It was easy to see from our vantage point that something had gone wrong with the launch. It wasn't until I had landed and was changing students and aircraft that I was informed that I had watched seven people die. Hearing the news was very difficult to absorb, but you never know when your number is up. Later that night, I spent some time studying the emergency procedures for the Cessna C-172 aircraft.

In pursuit of additional flight time, I started moonlighting with a company that towed advertisement banners over Daytona Beach. The planes flew out of New Smyrna Airport (KEVB).

Here's how the tow operation worked. The pilot would first take off with the banner hook in the airplane's cockpit—no banner yet. The hook was tied to a rope and the rope was tied to the aircraft. Once in the air, the pilot would throw the hook out the window and make a dive-bomb attack toward the banner poles. The banner was built onto a long strap that had a huge loop at one end and the banner attached at the other. The banner could be as large as 35 feet high by 100 feet in length. The huge loop would be set atop two 10-foot poles, and the poles would be set upright, about 20 feet apart, and the rest of the banner would lay flat on the ground. The operation entailed flying directly over the huge loop that was set on top of the two 10-foot poles. Flying at top speed, as the aircraft passed over the loop, and just as the hook was about to snag the loop, the pilot would pull the airplane's yoke back so that the aircraft would pitch high toward the sky above the airplane's stall attitude. While transferring all your kinetic energy to potential energy, the airplane's airspeed would slowly decrease as the banner was lifted off the ground.

To prevent the aircraft from stalling (a stall is when the aircraft loses all its lift and will no longer fly) and to tow the banner at a slow speed, the aviator would slowly reduce just a little attitude as the banner was being lifted off the ground. Lifting the banner into the air would greatly increase the aircraft's drag force and weight force, thereby reducing the aircraft's thrust force and lift force. Then, the pilot would depart the aerodrome's traffic pattern and navigate to the

Daytona Beach shoreline, flying at only 200 feet above the Atlantic Ocean, and about 200 feet from the shoreline at the slowest possible speed (usually only five to ten knots above the stall speed—even though it's really the aircraft's angle of attack or attitude that determines the actual stall). Flying at a low attitude at a slow speed was the optimum way to present the banner to all those sun bathing customers on Daytona Beach. The key was to keep a safe distance from the other aircraft and the beach, while maintaining a safe air speed.

After making six or seven passes over the strip, it was time to return to the New Smyrna Beach airfield to get another advertisement banner and fuel. Approaching the field, the goal was to fly as low as possible to safely drop the banner by releasing the hook using the hook release latch located in the airplane's cockpit. After releasing the hook, enabling the banner to detach from the airplane, the aircraft's thrust force and lift force would drastically increase due to the loss of the drag force and loss of the weight force. The pilot could then climb and enter the downward leg of the traffic pattern, then the base leg and then the final leg in order to land on the runway.

One day I became the hero with a big-head ego among my banner pilot peers. That day, after dropping the banner, instead of continuing on an easterly heading to follow the normal route to land on the 5,000-foot runway twenty-four (RWY 24), I made a snap aerobatic decision. At around fifty feet above ground level (AGL), I viewed the remaining 2,000 feet of the 4,000-foot runway twenty (RWY 20) out of the corner of my eye and decided—"I could land on that!?!"

I banked the C-150 airplane 45 degrees, turned 90 degrees right, pulled the power to idle, extended all my flaps and attempted to land on the remaining portion of RWY 20. A few of the other banner pilots observed most of this aerobatic flight display and were immensely impressed. They bragged about me for weeks, and a few attempted to replicate my maneuver.

My id psychic function probably made the decision to land on RWY 20, my ego psychic function probably executed the landing maneuver, but my super ego psychic function (Sigmund Freud's three parts of the psychic apparatus—id, ego, super ego), certainly influenced me to tell the whole story of what happened that day. You see, I actually unintentionally taxied off the end of RWY 20, and almost ran into the trees ahead. However, as I approached the hard, grassy ground at the end of the runway, I released the brakes, grabbed the yoke full aft so that the nose wheel would stay off the ground, and made an immediate left turn onto the taxiway. This was a technique I had learned from flight training in England on actual soft-field, grassy runways. Yes—confess! *Tell the truth!* When I told the whole story, some of the banner pilots were even more impressed with the soft-field landing and taxiing technique.

My first a*viation emergency* was an emergency landing at Ormond Beach Municipal Airport (ORM) due to avionics smoke in a Cessna C-172 aircraft while towing banners. One beautiful, sunny day while flying a banner, I started smelling electrical smoke. Smoke and fire are the worst phenomenon that could occur on any airplane, especially with aviation fuel on board and no fire trucks on board. No problem. I would just turn off the avionics master switch, I thought, and that would turn off all the avionics. Something was probably overheating. Big problem! The burning smell and puffy white smoke, only a few feet from my face, did not extinguish. Big problem! I could not drop my banner on the sunbathers and I did not want to land in the water. I decided to divert to Ormond Beach Airport (OMN).

I turned every switch off in the aircraft and only turned on the radio on an as-needed base to conserve battery power and to contain a potential fire.

But—another problem.

There were ERAU flight instructors with student pilots flying in the same traffic pattern. Why was this a problem?

Simple: I was not supposed to be moonlighting while being employed by ERAU as a flight instructor. So I did my best to disguise my distinctive New York accent, declared an emergency, dropped the banner on the OMN airfield and landed safely. Afterward, I called my boss for a car ride and requested that they fix the airplane and arrange for someone else to fly that airplane back to New Smyrna Beach airport.

Apparently some of the avionics were hot-wired to the battery and not through the avionics master switch, which is the correct way to wire the avionics. So with the Cessna avionics dropout relay, if you start the aircraft's engine when the battery voltage is low, then the relay will fail to energize, which will let voltage spikes reach your avionics and cause them to overheat.

There is always risk in aviation. *It is better to tell a bad, embarrassing story then to die and not be able to tell a story at all.* I lived and landed the plane safely, but others weren't so fortunate. Hedrick Nickelson lost his C-150 G aircraft on April 14, 1985. The aircraft lost power while towing a banner off Daytona Beach. The pilot applied carburetor heat and checked the fuel controls. But the engine quit completely. Since the beach was crowded, the pilot elected to ditch the airplane into the rough sea water. The aircraft sank. The pilot survived but the wreckage was never recovered.[14]

---

In 1986 the major airlines were American, Delta, Eastern, Northwest, Pan Am, TWA, United and USAir. There were many regional airlines as well as the turbo jet airline companies. My first choice for a job was Pan Am, for one reason: they flew all over the world. My second choice was Eastern because they flew the most varied routes and varied types of aircraft. Then there was TWA, which was a first-class operation and also flew to Europe. USAir had the highest-paid pilots for the equipment type they flew. American Airlines, based in Dallas, was still a small airline, but growing. Northwest was in the process of merging with Republic Airlines and was not hiring. United Air was not hiring white males at the time, and Delta Air had a nepotism policy. Because my sister was employed with Delta, I would not be eligible to work for Delta unless my sister resigned her position. I had many good choices for possible employment and there were other national and regional airline companies such as:

>  Air Atlanta
>  Air Kentucky
>  Air Midwest
>  Air Tran Airways
>  Atlantic Southeast Airlines
>  ATA Airlines
>  Braniff Airlines
>  Colgan Airways
>  Frontier
>  Jet American Airlines
>  New York Air
>  Ozark Airlines
>  People's Express
>  Piedmont Airlines
>  Presidential Airways
>  Southwest Airlines
>  Sun World International Airways
>  Texas International
>  West Air Commuter Airlines
>  Western Airlines

There were lots of options but one big problem. Nearly all of these airlines required that pilots have minimum jet flight time and/or multi-engine flight time experiences. This was the hole in my resume and I needed to fill it.

In pursuit of acquiring multi-engine or jet flight time and after receiving a substantial pay raise of four dollars an hour, I resigned from my first flight job at ERAU.

On April 21, 1986 I wrote:

> Dear Mr. McDuffee:
>
> After serious consideration, I have reached a definite decision to resign from the Embry-Riddle Aeronautical University employment, effective May 5, 1986. You will readily understand my decision in view of my personal goals.
>
> My time with Embry-Riddle Aeronautical University has provided stimulation and challenge. I enjoyed working with you, and I regret very much the necessity of leaving because of the economic trend. I must seek a higher salary and a position with the opportunity for advancement in the line of work that best suits me.
>
> I am sure you will find that my work was satisfactory with the Embry-Riddle Aeronautical University, and I hope that I have proved worthy of the confidence you placed in me.
>
> If at any future time a problem should arise, I shall be happy to assist in any way I can.
>
> Sincerely,
>
> Frank J. Donohue, Jr.

With 996 hours of total pilot flight time and 23 hours of simulator time, I resigned from my first pilot job without having another lined up. At ERAU, the only flight time I logged was single-engine.

I drove to airports in Jacksonville (JAX), Orlando (ORL), Ft Lauderdale (FLL), and Miami (MIA) looking for a multi-engine or a jet engine pilot job.

## Undergrad School (ERAU) Age 23–24

College pilot friend Bill went to People's Express Airlines in New York, accepting a position as a Second Officer on a B 727 aircraft. College pilot friend John went to American Eagle Airlines in San Juan, accepting a position as a First Officer on a multi-engine turbo prop aircraft.

It didn't look good for me.

I thought I was failing and would end up on some corner in New York City, selling pretzels. With my resume and letters of recommendations in hand, I drove Black Beauty to Atlanta, Georgia.

# CHAPTER 5
# Aviation School (Age 25-26)

Going from airport to airport like a door-to-door salesman, a door opened.

On May 9, 1986 I accepted a position with Trans-American Airways as a Certified Flight Instructor to instruct all phases of single-engine and multi-engine flight students under Federal Aviation Regulations, Part 91.

In the process of checking my references, Benjamin Butler, the president and owner of Trans-American Airways, called Chester Dobbie. Chester was my previous boss at Meadow Brook Golf Club. No matter how minuscule the job you may have (remember that in 1979 I was shining shoes), do your best. You never know how far back someone may go to check on your character and performance. Ben later told me that Chester spoke highly of my work. "Frank is the greatest thing since sliced bread," said Chester to Ben. Thank you, Chester!

The Multi-Engine Rating License I had obtained in 1985 authorized me to fly multi-engine aircraft but it did not authorize me to teach students in multi-engine aircraft.

One of the best ways to accumulate pilot-in-command, multi-engine flight time is to enroll flight students to pay you to teach them how to fly those planes. Therefore, I worked out a deal with owner, Benjamin Butler, to rent a Piper Seminal aircraft (PA-44-180) at cost so that I could get the required hours to take my Multi-Engine Flight Instructor Rating exam. After obtaining the Multi-Engine Certified Flight Instructor (CFI-MEI) Rating License, I started teaching all types of multi-engine student pilots. I instructed many military pilots in their pursuit of earning an Airline Transport License (ATP).

On June 8, 1986 Benjamin and I flew a Cessna C-T210 aircraft from Atlanta, Georgia (ATL) to Kerrville, Texas (ERV) to pick up new student pilot, Eric Ranson. The 6.8 flight hour trip covered 750 miles and was the longest flight I have ever piloted. Eric's mother had been the second largest landowner in the state of Montana when she had lived there. Mrs. Ranson now lived in Kerrville and while we were there she arranged for us to get a private tour of the Mooney aircraft factory. I flew 16-year-old Eric back to Atlanta and spent the summer teaching him, along with my other students.

On July 2, 1986 I passed the Multi-Engine Instrument Instructor (MEI) flight check ride in a Seminole PA 44-180 airplane, tail number N810K. This was the most challenging flight check ride I had accomplished. This new MEI license authorized me to instruct basic and instrument students in multi-engine airplanes. Instructing enables you to build up flight time while getting paid and multi-engine pilot flight time was extremely valuable in strengthening my resume in order to get hired by a major airline company.

The day I heard Midnite Express Airline was conducting pilot job interviews, I arrived professionally dressed without an invitation.

Mentioning college pilot friend Robert as a personal reference, I politely requested an interview. Robert and I attended ERAU together and he was currently employed at Midnite Express. Robert's position at Midnite Express had helped him land a better job at United Airlines.

That day, Midnite Express interviewed and gave airplane simulator check rides to eight candidates. I was one of two pilots hired on Oct. 9, 1986 by Midnite Express to fly Cessna 402 aircraft under Federal Aviation Regulations Part 135. My job as the pilot in command (the captain) was to command the C 402 multi-engine aircraft as a solo pilot, during all weather conditions, five nights a week from Mobile, Alabama (MOB) to Atlanta carrying cargo freight.

## School and Schooled

So I resigned from Trans-American Airways with 1,300 hours of total pilot flight time, 103 hours of multi-engine flight time and 1,160 hours of Pilot-In-Command time (PIC).

The Cessna C 402 airplane was the largest airplane I had ever flown. Its wingspan was 44 feet and the plane was 36 feet long. It had a max takeoff gross weight of 6,850 pounds. The Cessna C 402 had two 325 horsepower, turbo-charged and fuel-injected engines. It could fly at 230 knots as far as 1,200 nautical miles and as high as 26,900 feet.[15]

The 402C had a seating capacity of ten passenger seats, but the plane I would fly was configured with only two seats so it could carry as much freight as possible.

My main route left Atlanta Hartsfield International Airport (ATL) around 6:00 a.m. and headed to Pensacola, Florida (PNB) and then to Mobile (MOB). At night around 9:00 p.m. I would fly the return route from Mobile to Atlanta. This was a Monday-through-Friday operation so Mobile became my new residence.

My first missed approach occurred while flying an Instrument ILS Approach into Atlanta on the Cessna C 402 as a single-pilot captain for Midnite Express. The air traffic controller instructed me to fly 170 knots (almost 200 miles per hour) to the outer marker final approach fix. The 170 knots airspeed is about 40 to 50 knots faster than the normal approach airspeed in this aircraft. We would generally fly this faster speed to the final approach fix (FAF) in order to maintain constant flow control with other jets, which were also flying at faster speeds into this very busy major international airport.

Most final approach fixes are about five miles from the end of the runway. Usually, the pilot has sufficient time to slow the aircraft to the normal final approach speed before landing. My final approach speed was about 125 knots, and I had slowed down to that speed before reaching the Decision Height (DH) on the ILS Instrument Approach to runway 26R. Remember, the DH is that point where the pilot decides whether he can see the runway or the runway's environment. The DH is the point when the pilot decides whether he is in a position to make a safe landing. The DH is usually around 200 feet above the ground and around a half a slant mile from the runway.

On this particular landing, the weather was bad with very poor visibility. It was so foggy that night that at the DH, I could not see the runway. All I could see was the red "Fly Delta" light sign on top of Delta's maintenance building, which was located in the middle of the airport. I made the decision to execute a missed approach and go around. It is not a good feeling when you are all by yourself, at night, in bad weather, and you cannot see the runway in order to land.

Could I attempt another ILS Instrument Approach again, see the runway and land? Or would I have to fly to another airport with good weather and land there? How much fuel did I have?

The missed approach procedure (MAP) tells the pilot in detail what heading and altitude to fly. As I was executing the MAP, the air traffic controller inquired whether I would like to attempt to fly a second ILS Instrument Approach to runway 26R. The fuel gauges indicated that I had enough fuel for another attempt. I accepted.

On the second time coming in, the controller authorized me to fly at any speed of my discretion. I slowed to my normal final approach airspeed a few miles before the FAF. I configured the aircraft for landing early and glued my eyes to see the approach lights and runway. This time, I decided to land. It's always a good feeling to touch down on planet earth.

My second major emergency occurred on Dec. 13, 1986 at the Mobile airport (MOB) when the nose gear of my aircraft failed to extend. Upon approaching MOB, the controller cleared me for a visual approach to RWY 36. I extended the landing gear after executing the pre-landing checklist, but the landing nose gear light did not illuminate. In order to test that the light bulb was working properly, I pressed the landing light indicator button. The light bulb illuminated, telling me the light bulb was working properly. I turned the plane onto the final approach and recycled the landing gear and again the same result—only the two main green lights illuminated, indicating the nose gear had not extended properly. (See photo number three page 154.)

I requested to the tower for permission to abandon the landing and to depart the traffic pattern for few minutes. The controller gave me clearance and asked to identify the problem. I told him that I had an indication that the front gear wasn't down. He asked me to fly a low approach to see if he could visually ascertain whether the nose gear was down.

While I was on the downwind leg in the traffic pattern, I attempted to manually extend the landing gear. Still no light.

I checked the circuit breaker, which was in its proper position. I verified the malfunction by retarding the throttles below 13 inches manifold pressure and I extended the flaps past the 30-degree position. I opened the emergency checklist manual to the "nose-gear not down and locked" section.

I executed the low approach. The controller reported that the nose gear did not appear to be fully extended. He said it appeared as if the landing gear was cocked to one side.

I asked the controller for time to troubleshoot the problem. He gave me clearance to fly right-hand turns west of runway 32.

Poring through the Cessna Emergency Checklist, I spent approximately twenty minutes troubleshooting the situation. I went through every detail three times. With the foot rudder, I yawed the aircraft left and right. With the hand yoke, I initiated erratic aircraft nose-up and nose-down pitch changes to try and get the nose gear to lock in place.

I asked the controller for another low approach and flew another low approach. The controller reported the same status. He asked my intentions. I told the controller that I would need a little more time and then I would make an emergency landing. My heart sinking and my worry level rising, I told the controller that I would need

## Aviation School (Age 25–26)

emergency ground crew assistance.

After completing the "landing with malfunction nose gear" checklist one more time, I requested landing clearance. I received clearance to land on the runway of my choice. With the wind direction of 40 degrees and 12-knot strength, I requested runway 36 and advised the controller that all electrical switches would be turned off after my final radio transmission. After receiving landing clearance for runway 36, I lined the aircraft up for final approach.

At 75 feet above the ground, I completed the checklist to perform the final shutdown. When the rear wheels touched down at the slowest speed possible, I held the nose off the ground for as long as possible. Finally, I had to let the nose down and it hit the runway and skidded about 100 yards. In my peripheral vision, I could see sparks igniting from the metal propellers scraping against the grey asphalt.

Upon full stop, I evacuated immediately. But there was no subsequent fire so I re-entered the aircraft and removed my belongings.

The airport manager approached me and asked me if I was all right. After giving him my name, aircraft number and my company's name, I requested a ride to the Aero One flight station.

At Aero One, I called Midnite Express part-owner Mario Rosario and reported the incident. Mario directed me to call maintenance chief Skip Wallace which, of course, I did.

Officers from the Mobile Police Department also requested my name, address, phone number, aircraft tail number and the name of the aircraft owner. I provided all the information the police requested. Then I phoned the airport manager to obtain permission to move the aircraft and remove its cargo. After receiving permission, I removed the cargo from the aircraft and transferred the cargo to the customer. Aero One moved the aircraft to their premises. Mario released me and I went home.

The next week, Midnite Express asked me for copies of my logbook. This was a tense time. For over a week, no one said "good job" or "bad job." I thought my aviation career was over. Again, the image loomed of a New York City street corner and yours truly as a vendor of pretzels.

About 10 days later, while I was at Midnite Express headquarters in Atlanta, the head mechanic approached me and congratulated me on the great job I had done saving the aircraft from total loss. Shortly afterward I received the following letter.

*Dear Frank:*

*I wish to personally express to you the gratitude of all of us at Midnite for the excellent and truly professional manner in which you handled a very challenging situation this past Saturday, December 13, 1986. Although the professional pilot is clearly expected to handle difficult occurrences, I have received feedback from several individuals, both from within and outside our company, indicating that the skill demonstrated in your landing of our Cessna 32, N320AR, after a nose-gear extension failure, was nothing short of remarkable.*

*It has also come to my attention that the reason for the gear failure was probably caused when a torque tube in the gear extension mechanism was bent during a towing. Clearly, this is most regrettable and we must strive to ensure that an unnecessary incident such as this never again occurs at our company.*

*We can ask no more of any employee, than the thorough attention to detail which you took prior, during and after your emergency landing. Please keep up the good work and please accept the small gift enclosed as a token of our genuine appreciation.*

*Sincerely,*
*Robert A. Milton*
*Chief Executive Officer*

That "small" gift of $100 was quite valuable to me, but not as much as keeping my aviation career. Besides, who wants to sell pretzels on a corner in New York in December?

## Second Missed Approach

My second missed approach occurred at Craig Field in Jacksonville, Florida. I was flying a VOR Non Precision Instrument approach in a Cessna C 402 aircraft to runway 32.

With a precision approach, the ILS system guides the pilot laterally and vertically to a point usually around 200 feet above ground level and around a half a slant mile to the end of the runway. At that point, the idea is that the pilot will be able to see the runway and land.

With a VOR Non Precision approach, the VOR only guides the pilot laterally to a position at which the pilot may be able to see the runway. A VOR is the acronym for "VHF omnidirectional radio range." A VOR is a type of a short-range radio navigation system, transmitting and receiving radio signals in the very high frequency band (VHF) from ground radio beacons to the aircraft's receiver unit to help a pilot navigate his aircraft position and stay on course. The VOR system was developed by the United States in 1937 and is used worldwide.

An ILS approach provides more precision guidance; therefore it is called a precision approach. A VOR approach is called a non-precision approach.

While executing a VOR approach, the pilot directs the airplane's vertical flight path based on reading of a pre-approved Federal Aviation Administration (FAA) authorized procedure. The procedure dictates when to descend and to what altitude to descend to. The instructions will vary based on the aircraft's air speed, time, and distance flown during the VOR approach.

The pilot uses a diagram that depicts the plan view and profile view of the procedure. The VOR receiver instrument in the cockpit displays the lateral guidance to fly, but the pilot must aviate the airplane vertically, based on interpreting the paper approach on the diagram.

The pilot flies this procedure to a Missed Approach Point. Note that a Missed Approach Point is different from Decision Height point. The Missed Approach Point could be anywhere from the end of the runway to up to a mile away from the end of the runway. The Missed Approach Point can also be much higher than the Decision Height— at a higher altitude of 400, 500 or 700 feet above ground level. [16]

I was executing a runway 32 VOR approach to Craig Field Airport on a bad weather day. Fog again.

I descended to 400 feet, flew to the missed approach point at which I had to make a decision: could I see the runway and *was I in a position to make a safe landing?*

I could see the runway, but I was 400 feet high and I was on top of the end of the runway, therefore I was *not in a position to make a safe landing* on the 4,000-foot runway.

I executed the missed approach procedure, did a go-around, and attempted a second approach.

On the second attempt, I saw the runway and I was in a good position and continued to land.

But there was one problem.

Around 20 feet above the ground, out of the right corner of my eye, I spotted a flock of seagulls standing in a V formation on the ground.

All of a sudden, the head seagull, followed by the rest of the flock, lifted up in unison and turned toward me, right smack in front of my flight path.

About 10 feet above the runway, while initiating the landing flair, about 12 of the birds slammed like torpedoes into my innocent airplane. If those birds had decided to ram me at 20 feet or higher, it's possible that the airplane would have stalled and I would have crashed.

After I had taxied in to a full stop, the aircraft mechanic spent hours cleaning seagull remnants off the airplane. The control tower closed the runway for over an hour to remove bird parts from the asphalt, too.

Because of the incident, other Midnite Express pilots issued me the aviator call sign name "Seagull." There are better ways to get yourself an aviator call sign. Soon after, the FAA issued and published this warning for Craig Municipal Airport (KCRG):

> *"Birds periodically on or near airport, increasing activity during inclement weather,"* and *"Wildlife on and in vicinity of airport."*

These pilot advisories still exist today for Craig Municipal Airport.

## ATP License

At age 25, with just over 1,500 hours of total pilot flight time, I passed the rigorous written exam for the Federal Aviation Administration (FAR) Air Line Transport Pilot (ATP) license. Then, I arranged a deal with the Midnite Express owners to rent the C-402 company aircraft at cost so that I could take the Airline Transport Pilot flight exam.

The Airline Transport Pilot (ATP) license is the highest level of aviation pilot license one can obtain. The ATP authorizes you to act as pilot-in-command of a scheduled air carrier's aircraft, having a max gross weight over 12,500 pounds or having over nine passenger seats. All airline captains have an ATP license.

The ATP license applicant is tested on Air Law, Aircraft General Knowledge, Flight Planning and Monitoring, Human Performance and Limitations, Meteorology, Operational Procedures, Principles of Flight, Communications (IFR and VFR), Performance, General Navigation, Radio Communications, Radio Navigation, Instrumentation and Weight and Balance.

On Feb. 2, 1987 in Jacksonville, with a total pilot flight time of 1,652 hours, I passed the Airline Transport Pilot flight check ride exam, which requires the highest level of pilot ability.

In January of 1987 I purchased a pilot-hiring service from Future Aviation Professionals of America (FAPA). Louis Smith was the president, and the phone number was 1-800-JET-JOBS. FAPA published pay listings for major, national, jet, and regional airlines, including starting, second-year, tenth-year, and captain's pay. They published pass and jump seat privileges, and also included information on flight hours, duty rigs, pay guarantees, days off, per diem rates, recall rights, and profit sharing.

FAPA had a computer data base for storing all your flight time, the type of aircraft flown, airplane ratings, education and so forth. They would match this data with potential airlines that were hiring pilots. FAPA started conducting pilot hiring seminars in conjunction with airline companies across the U.S.A. The second such seminar in March of 1987 was held in Atlanta and I attended. Unlike the majority of other job seekers who attended, I did my homework and was well prepared. Virtually all of the job seekers showed up, picked up a job application and dropped off their resume with the representative at the various airline companies.

I did some work up-front. I obtained the various job applications and learned the names of the individuals who would represent the airlines that interested me. So at the seminar I had a completed job application, a personalized cover letter for each company, a resume, photo copies of my pilot licenses, medical paperwork and copies of three letters of references. All were arranged neatly in a large brown envelope.

Professionally dressed in a grey suit, I approached each airline representative, introduced myself and personally hand-delivered a completed pilot application package. As the representatives flew back to their headquarters they had my complete application package—the only one they had received at the seminar with photo copies of all necessary documents.

At this Sunday seminar I met the chief pilot of Atlantic Southeast Airlines, Inc. (ASA) and he said he would call me on Monday.

The next day, dressed in that same grey suit, I showed up at the office of the chief pilot of ASA (located in Atlanta) a half-hour before he had arrived to start his work day. He saw that I was highly motivated to get a pilot job with ASA, and he offered me a job as a First Officer flying Embrea EMB 110 aircraft. I would be responsible for flying passengers to and from Dallas International Airport under FAR Part 135 operations.

Midnite Express had provided me the opportunity to increase my multi-engine pilot flight time to 600 hours, my total pilot flight time to 1,780 hours, and my pilot-in-command time to 1,640 hours; but it was time to move on to a bigger airplane and a bigger company and better pay.

The Embrea EMB 110 Bandeirante was the largest airplane I had ever flown. In fact, the FAA requires two pilots to operate the aircraft: a captain (the PIC, the pilot in command) and a first officer (the SIC, the second in command)—me.

Two 750 HP Pratt and Whitney turbo prop engines enable the EMB 110 to fly as fast as 248 knots, as high as 22,500 feet, and as far as 1,000 nautical miles. The aircraft max take off gross weight was 13,000 pounds, with a wingspan of 50 feet and a length of 50 feet. (See photo number four page 154.) There were 500 EMB 110 aircraft built.[17] The EMB 110 was configured to carry 19 passengers and two flight crew members. Guess who was the flight attendant? Yes, me.

After training in Atlanta, I drove the 1966 Chrysler Newport Miss Black Beauty to Dallas. How did that car make the trip? I'll never know. She was tough. It was my second time in Dallas, but my first time going to Dallas with a job in hand. Summers in Dallas can be brutally hot with temperatures that may rise up to 117° F. The terrain is flat with warm, dry air blowing from the north and the west, while warm and humid air can blow in from the south, causing temperatures to rise.

An approaching cold front can be seen from miles away and looks like a tidal wave (like the tidal wave on the old *Hawaii Five-O* TV show), kicking up a dust storm or forming a tornado. Women-wise, Dallas was better than Atlanta. There was nothing to do outside of Dallas, so when the women turned of age, like 18 to 20 years old, they all moved to Dallas. Maybe that's why the Dallas Cowboy Cheerleaders are able to obtain the best selection of girls for their cheerleader squads. Texans speak much slower and differently than New Yorkers. In New York, the girls say, "You can." In Texas, the gals say, "You all can." We had so much fun barbecuing, playing water volleyball, and making margaritas that pilot roommate friend Bob Ycraz and I rarely left our thriving apartment complex.

When I first got to urban Texas, I drove to a convenience store to buy some beer. There was no beer, so I drove to the next one. There was no beer there, either.

"Where's the beer?" I asked.

The clerk explained that this was a dry county. No one but no one can buy or sell alcohol of any kind in a dry county.

After getting directions to the next wet county, off I went. Believe it or not, there was a long line of cars parked outside the package store located in a wet county. Apparently, most Texans make a big alcohol run once a week instead of buying small portions on a daily basis.

In June 1989, Flying Tiger Line, Inc. (FTL), an airline not a circus, invited me to a job interview in Los Angeles, California. The interview process consisted of five parts. First, Beth Mentor, an employment specialist with a psychology degree, interviewed me on a one-on-one basis for about an hour. Beth asked me why I took 54 college credit hours in one year. Like a politician, I turned the question around and answered the question to my advantage. "I observed that the airline industry was rebounding and that there would be a need to hire more pilots so I wanted to get a competitive advantage over my peers by increasing my qualifications at a faster rate."

Then, I was interviewed by a three-pilot board for around an hour and a half. Captain John asked me if I ever had an emergency. The

C 402 nose gear failure landing was the best emergency story I could think of, and I told that story. At the end of the story, I kept silent, looked at the pilot board members, and held my ground. One of the other pilot board members wanted to know what happened afterward.

I paused. I wanted the job. I didn't want to come across as an "I Doctor." Do you know what an "I Doctor" is? You've probably met those guys with a PHD who say, "I did this, I did that, I was it, I am the best, I am the greatest," et cetera.

It's always best if you have someone else toot your horn.

So I pulled out a copy of the letter written by Robert Milton, the CEO of Midnite Express, and handed it to the pilot board members.

"Impressive," said one of the pilot board members. After that I was put in a B 747 simulator for a 30-minute check. The simulator ride included a takeoff, some vertical S turns, a non-standard holding entry and holding followed by an ILS approach to a landing.

I had never flown a jet before, so I asked the simulator pilot evaluator for a few pitch and thrust settings and flew the B 747 just like any other airplane: Attitude, Trim, Cross Check, and adjust the Pitch and Power accordingly. The next part was to complete the Minnesota Multiphasic Personality test, a personality psychological profile. The final part was a thorough medical exam, the next day.

Then I was on my way back home to Dallas wondering how I did.

*Did I wear the right color tie?*

## Turbulent Landing in San Angelo

On May 13, 1987, Captain Phil and I operated the Embraer EMB 110, tail number N404AS, with 19 passengers from Lawton Regional Airport, Oklahoma (KLAW) to San Angelo Regional Airport, Texas (KSJT). San Angelo weather forecast was predicting gusty winds, cumulonimbus clouds, and thunderstorms in the area for our estimated time of arrival. As defined by National Oceanic and Atmospheric

Administration, which provides the National Weather Service, a thunderstorm is a local storm produced by a cumulonimbus cloud and always accompanied by lightning and thunder, usually with strong gusts of wind, heavy rain, and sometimes hail. Severe thunderstorms can produce funnel clouds, tornadoes, and wind shear. Wind shear is a rapid change of wind direction and wind strengths with clouds of different levels moving in different directions. The updrafts and downdrafts can produce microbursts. A pilot considers wind shear severe when an airspeed change is greater than 15 knots, or a vertical speed change is greater than 500 feet per minute, or the aircraft's pitch attitude changes greater than five degrees. Some microbursts can exceed the performance capability of all aircraft, and even the best pilot would not be able to escape.

En route to San Angelo, I was thinking about Delta Flight 191, an L-1011 aircraft that crashed in Dallas/Fort Worth with 134 fatalities on Aug. 2, 1985 because of thunderstorms, wind shear, and microburst. According to the International Civil Aviation Organization (ICAO) statistics from 1970 to 1985, at least 28 aviation accidents with 700 fatalities occurred because of low-level (near the ground) wind shear.

In the cockpit, we have a weather radar instrument that helps us see and avoid severe weather. The radar transmits beams out in front of the aircraft to detect precipitation and reflect that information back to the cockpit for the pilots to interpolate. The pilot uses the Antennae Tilt, Range, Gain and Radar Mode features to operate the radar. While flying as a captain on the C 402 for Midnite Express, I had accumulated valuable flying experience using radar, however, I had been flying the EMB 110 for less than a month, and I was not the captain. I was the first officer. The radar displays colors that reflect humidity in the air, but not necessarily turbulence. The radar is good at detecting moisture, rainfall, and wet hail, but it is not good at detecting ice crystals, dry snow, clear air turbulence, dry hail, or wind shear.

Thunderstorms are categorized in levels one through five, with five being the most severe. So, if a pilot was familiar with the flying in the northeast United States (like New York) and familiar with viewing a Level Three or Level Four thunderstorm on the radar scope, he would adjust his flight path and avoid the thunderstorm cells. If this same pilot was flying in the southwest United States (like San Angelo) and viewed a Level One or Level Two thunderstorm on the radar scope, he might not adjust his flight path, thinking the thunderstorm cells were small and did not contain much severe dangerous energy.

However, he would be wrong, because thunderstorms in southwest usually contain dry moisture, and the radar is not good at detecting this. Therefore, viewing a category Level One or Level Two thunderstorm in the southwest could be as dangerous as a Level Three or Level Four in the northeast.

San Angelo was about thirty minutes away and our radar scope did not show much severe thunderstorm activity. Each individual cell in a thunderstorm can last approximately 30 to 60 minutes and has three stages: the cumulus stage, mature stage, and dissipating stage. It is the microburst produced in these stages that can bring down an aircraft because the numerous updrafts and downdrafts can cause the aircraft to lose airspeed. The most severe, deadly microburst can usually last only six to eight minutes, but it can be severe enough to where the best pilot in the world cannot recover.

As we approached San Angelo, thunderstorms loomed to the southwest. The radar display did not look that bad. The tower-reported winds were not that bad. We had just received a PIREP (PIREP stands for pilot report and provides notice of actual weather conditions encountered by another pilot while in flight) from a Learjet pilot who said that landing on Runway 36 was not that bad.

We turned onto final and set up for the ILS Runway 18 approach. During the approach, first we encountered heavy rain and wind gusts and we saw some lightning strikes.

Then we encountered turbulence.

The runway was in clear view, but from five miles away, that humongous thunderstorm spit and spewed hailstones in our direction. The hailstones were like Rambo's bazooka shooting hail at our innocent and defenseless Embraer 110.

Rock-'n-roll.

The aircraft was getting bounced around like a wine cork in rough ocean waves. There were no conversations going on in the back—all of the passengers were shittin' bricks, peeing in their pants, or praying for their lives.

The captain, though barely, commanded aircraft control.

"I can't believe we're doing this."

Yank and bank—the captain fought Mother Nature with the Embraer 110 aircraft's pitch and power. I did everything possible as a first officer to support the captain. With purpose and care, Captain Phil landed firmly on the soaking wet runway. We encountered a little hydroplaning, but we were able to maintain steering control and taxied to the arrival gate.

As we came to a full stop, that unpredictable evil thunderstorm positioned directly above us.

God must have been pissed off.

Strong, gusty winds, heavy rain, and hailstones pounded the San Angelo airfield. All the passengers thanked us, especially the captain, for getting everyone safely on the ground.

In the aviation industry, you will often hear the phrase: "That's why he gets paid the big bucks" meaning he, the captain, earns a high salary to compensate for his expert skills and critical decision-making skills that make it possible to transport passengers and the plane safely from departure airport to destination airport.

We also have a vested interest, too.

We want to live, too.

## "Top Gun"

On March 3, 1969 the U.S. government formed an organization called Top Gun to teach the lost art of aerial combat, to ensure that U.S. Navy pilots were the best fighter pilots in the world.[18]

Seventeen years later, the movie version *Top Gun* was released. Tom Cruise (born Tom Cruise Mapother IV) played the main character, Lieutenant Pete Mitchell.[19]

Mitchell's call sign name was "Maverick."

My call sign name was "Seagull." I'm sure you remember how I got that name.

Tom Cruise, who was only eighteen months older than me, was only twenty-four years old when he starred in Top Gun, the highest grossing film of 1986.

In 1987 pilot friend and apartment mate Bob Ycraz and I rented *Top Gun* (on VHS) and watched the movie for the first time, the second time, the third time and many more. With the rewind, pause, and fast forward options, we watched portions of the film 20 or 30 times. We began incorporating many of the lines from the movie into our working flight operations of flying Bandeirante EMB 110 turbo props. These were the lines of the movie we liked most.

> Maverick: *I feel the need...*
> Maverick, Goose: *...the need for speed.* (It does feel good to go 600 miles per hour.)
>
> Maverick: *Talk to me Goose.* (Sometimes on long flights, especially night flights, it is good just to have the other pilot talk to you. Talking to each other can make the difference from being half awake to half asleep.)
>
> Maverick: *It's just a walk in the park, Kazansky.* (Yes, sometimes flying can be as easy as walking in the park, especially when there are no emergencies, no maintenance issues, no

weather problems, no traffic delays, no physical or mental fatigue issues and a whole slew of events that could or may happen.)

Stinger: *And if you screw up just this much, you'll be flying a cargo plane full of rubber dog shit out of Hong Kong!"* (This was actually our job at flying Tigers. We were carrying rubber ducks and everything out of Hong Kong.)

Viper: *I like that in a pilot.* (What do you like in a pilot?)

Maverick: *She lost that loving feeling.* Goose: *I hate when she does that.* (This is a fallacy because men know nothing about women and their loving feelings. Women are the most intelligent creatures on earth. Women know when they have that loving feeling—all they have to say is *yes, no* or *maybe*.)

Maverick: *Crashed and burned on the first one it wasn't pretty.* (This is what I was thinking during my first aviation emergency landing in Ormond Beach, FL in an aircraft with smoke pouring out of the avionics.)

Maverick: *I'm going to need a beer to put these flames out Yo! Great Mav, real slick.* (Aviating jets can create a great deal of stress on pilots and sometimes a beer can help release that stress.)

Air Boss Johnson: *Two of your snot-nose jockeys did a fly-by on my tower at over 400 KNOTS! I want somebody's butt; I want it now, I've HAD IT!* (This reminds me of the FAA, just when we are having fun they want to penalize us.)

Goose: *Do you have the number for that truck driving school, truck master I think it was, I might need that.* (After that nose-gear-up landing in Mobile, I thought I would need the number for selling pretzels on a street corner in New York City.)

## Aviation School (Age 25–26)

Hollywood: *Gutsiest move I ever saw, Mav.* (Afterwards, some of those pilot maneuvers seem like a gutsy move but while executing those pilot maneuvers it is not the guts, it's the motor skills.)

Maverick: *Jesus Christ, and you think I'm reckless? When I fly, I'll have you know that my crew and my plane come first.* (This is true for me too. Safety is the most important concern during every flight operation. First, safety and then legality. I believe safety and legality is mandatory in my cockpit).

Carole: *Hey, Goose, you big stud.* Goose: *That's me, honey.* Carole: *Take me to bed or lose me forever.* (Reminds me when I was a big-time flight instructor at ERAU loving life while teaching college students how to fly airplanes. The next day I saw the space shuttle Challenger explode with seven people aboard.)

Goose: *We're head-to-head. I can't believe we're doing this.* (We were going head-to-head with severe thunderstorms on our flight into San Angelo's airport as I said to myself, "I can't believe we're doing this.")

Charlie: *You're one of the best pilots. What you do up there is dangerous, but you've got to go on.* (Every six months airline pilots are required by Federal law to take a flight simulator check ride, I call this "Yank and Bank School." It consists of multiple, complicated emergency tasks. Every pilot makes mistakes, sometimes at the very beginning of the check ride but you've got to go on.)

Charlie: *When I first met you, you were larger than life. Look at you. You're not going to be happy unless you're going Mach 2 with your hair on fire and you know it.* (I tried to explain this to my sons—that flying in the air at 600 miles per hour is much different than driving on the ground at sixty miles per hour. A jet pilot's scan and motor skills operate at a much faster pace than most automobile drivers.)

Viper: *The simple fact is you feel responsible for Goose and you have a confidence problem. Now I'm not gonna sit here and blow sunshine up your ass, Lieutenant. A good pilot is compelled to always evaluate what happened, so we can apply what he's learned. Up there, we gotta push it. That's our job.*[20] (After each flight a pilot should evaluate what happened. Were there opportunities for improvement? What do you think you did right or wrong and how could you have performed better? After each flight I usually ask my First Officer three questions. "Did we operate safely and legally?" Could we have been more reliable and efficient?" "Do you have any questions?")

## Questions Asked by Non-pilots

1. **The auto-pilot does everything—right?**
   Answer: "The auto pilot is helpful for many things during the flight, but you'd be surprised how much of the time we are flying without the auto pilot turned on."

2. **What is that loud sound after landing?**
   Answer: "That loud powerful force noise is the reverse thrusters. The reverse thrusters help the aircraft slow down by redirecting the thrust of the jet engines."

3. **How do you find the airport? How do you navigate?**
   Answer: "These airplanes are equipped with the best navigational systems you can possibly imagine. It's complicated but there is an explanation in my book."

## Aviation School (Age 25–26)

4. **Do you fly in bad weather?**
   Answer: "When it's safe to do so."

5. **How long have you been flying?**
   Answer: "I've wanted to fly ever since I saw the very first space shuttle launched into space and I took my first flight while enlisted in the Air Force at age twenty."

6. **Did you fly in the military?**
   Answer: "I flew while in the military but I did not fly for the military."

7. **How fast are we going?**
   Answer: I always say "600 mph" and sometimes, depending on the winds, that is the correct answer. People have experienced traveling in an automobile at 60 mph so I say "multiply that by ten."

8. **"How high are we?"**
   Answer: "Not high enough, but probably 35,000 feet."

9. **Do you ever hear funny stories by passengers or other crew members?**
   Answer: "We hear only the best stories, but you will have to show me your pilot credentials for me to reveal one of those stories to you."

10. **"While in uniform, do you get cautious looks from the general public?"**
    Answer: There are times they are eying every move I make. While in the airport at the gate, they are probably thinking, "Is he the pilot of my flight and what is he doing here? Shouldn't he be in the cockpit?" While in uniform and my ID badge obviously displayed, I have been asked, "Are you a pilot?"

One time I was standing outside JFK Airport in my Flying Tigers pilot uniform when a posh lady came up to me and gave me a two dollar tip. She thought I was the sky cap and I was supposed to get her bags.

I've been asked: "Do the cargo pilots use the same runways as the passenger pilots?" My response is simple. "Do you drive your car differently when you're carrying friends or family versus carrying groceries or heavy lumber or a delicate lamp?"

Another time while sitting in a passenger seat in uniform, the person next to you always wants to talk to you about something. One time, this lady gave me a song and dance and then admitted she was scared of flying. I said, "So am I." That was the end of the conversation.

## Moving Up / Moving On

Flying for Atlantic Southeast Airlines was my shortest aviation pilot job, lasting only 100 days.

One Friday evening I received a call from Flying Tiger pilot Gary Stearns and he offered me a position as a Boeing 747 Second Officer with the Flying Tigers Airline, Inc. (FTL).

At first I thought it was one of my friends playing a practical joke, but this was the real deal.

This was fantastic news but I kept the secret for a few days until I received the official offer letter in the mail. With the letter in hand, I exuberantly gathered a few friends and we went out to celebrate. There was widespread envy, jealousy, and curiosity among my peers at Atlantic Southeast Airlines. After all, I had only been employed with Atlantic Southeast Airlines, a regional airline, for about three months. That, and I was leaving to go fly a Boeing B 747 jet with a major airline.

My name became popular, as you might imagine. Many other pilots approached me to ask about how I pulled it off. I jokingly told

## Aviation School (Age 25–26)

those pilots that "the airline just dropped their hiring standards and I wore the right color tie that day." But the real reason was my persistent pursuit and motivation toward advancing my career. I had a goal—and I stuck to it.

Major airlines generate billions of dollars in revenue every year. National airlines are smaller than the major airlines and regional airlines are smaller than the nationals.

In 1987, the average age of a new-hire pilot at a major airline was 32 and the average total pilot flight time was 3,800 hours. Ironically, the average age for a new-hire pilot at a national airline was 35 with an average total pilot flight time of 6,300 hours.

At age 26, I had a total pilot flight time of 2,030 hours including 606 hours of multi-engine time including 250 hours of turbo prop time and 250 hours of second-in-command time.

On July 7, 1987 along with 23 other new-hire pilots, I started basic indoctrination class for Flying Tigers.

The Flying Tigers airline was started in 1945 by Robert W. Prescott and a group of pilots who were formerly members of the First American Volunteer Group (AVG) of the Chinese Air Force in 1941 through 1942. The 1st AVG were comprised mainly of volunteer U.S. pilots who went to help the Chinese fight against the Japanese in 1942. This AVG pilot group was famously called the Flying Tigers because of their uniquely painted P-40 aircraft and their extraordinary kill-to-loss ratio.

Over seven months, the AVG fighter squadron shot down more than 300 Japanese fighter planes over Burma, China, Thailand, and French Indo-China while losing only 12 of their P-40 aircraft in combat.[21, 22]

After the war, Bob Prescott and a handful of these pilots raised $89,000, including the financial backing of Samuel B. Mosher, and they purchased 14 World War II Budd Conestoga aircraft from the U.S. military. They started a daily, scheduled all-cargo service under the name of the Flying Tigers Line, Inc. (New York stock symbol FTL).

In 1949, the Flying Tigers purchased 18 Curtiss C 46 aircraft, and in 1950, the airline purchased a large fleet of Douglass DC-6 freighter aircraft. In 1957, in another wave of expansion, the Flying Tigers bought 15 Lockheed Super Constellation aircraft, allowing them to fly non-stop transcontinental schedules.

In 1965, the Flying Tigers acquired Boeing B 707s, and in 1968, Douglass DC 8s. Flying Tigers eventually purchased Boeing B 747 aircraft and Seaboard World Airlines, allowing Flying Tigers to provide worldwide air freight service.[21, 22]

On my new hire date of July 7, 1987, Tigers (short for Flying Tigers) had six DC 8s, twelve B 727s, and thirteen B 747s. Shortly after being hired, the B 727 fleet expanded to sixteen aircraft, and the B 747 fleet expanded to twenty-one aircraft. Two B 747s were configured to carry passengers used for Military Airlift Command (MAC) charters. Tigers operated the B 747 passenger MAC flights with 498 passengers and 17 crew members on board. Rarely did any airline carry more than 500 people on board in 1988 (or even in present day for that matter).

Flying cargo can be more difficult than flying people because the aircraft is routinely flown at the aircraft's maximum gross weight. There were many times we departed with the maximum takeoff weight of 820,000 pounds and landed (after fuel was burned off) with the maximum landing weight of 630,000 pounds, carrying tigers, racehorses, racecars, cows, chickens, whales, oil rigs, computers, et cetera.

When hired by a major airline, the airline pilot must comply with the Federal Aviation Rules (FAA regulation Part 121). Most airline pilots join the Air Line Pilots Association (ALPA) Union, which negotiates a contract with the airline company, and the pilot must also comply with that contract. The Air Line Pilots Association was started in the 1930's.

*The 1930s was a decade of great significance for airline pilots across the United States, Canada, and beyond. It was the decade when a professional union of pilots was born to protect the interests of airmen during a decade marked by "pilot pushing," horribly unsafe flying conditions, and a company mentality that pilots were an expendable commodity. Fly at all costs, under all conditions; just make sure that the mail is delivered on time.*[23]

In 1931, Captain David L. Behncke, a pilot for Boeing Air Transport, met with 24 other pilots considered "key men" in Chicago, to officially launch a new pilot organization to protect pilot rights.

Among other items, the pilots approved the name Air Line Pilots Association and adopted a motto (Schedule with Safety). More than half of the 24 "key men" would later perish in aircraft accidents.[24] Since the 1930's, ALPA has been the leading aviation safety advocate protecting the safety interest of airline pilots and passengers in the United States and around the world. ALPA had created its own engineering and air safety department and was instrumental in creating:

- Air Traffic Control Center
- Standard T Instrument layout in the cockpit
- NTSB National Transportation Safety Board
- GPWS Terrain Awareness Warning System
- Fasten Seatbelt signs in the aircraft
- HAZMAT standards
- Master Minimum Equipment list for aircraft
- Improved Standard Taxiway signage
- Standards and procedures for ground deicing
- Color Aeronautical Charts for depicting high terrain
- ALPA and ERAU International Aviation Security Academies
- (And many more aviation safety-related enhancements to air travel)

The Federal Aviation Regulations (FARs) stipulate such regulations as: the pilot must pass a first-class medical exam every six months, pass a simulated check ride every six months, and pass a flight check ride every year. In addition, if you fly too fast, if you turn to the wrong heading, if you level off at the wrong altitude or if you do anything that is considered careless and reckless by the Federal Aviation Administration, you can be heavily fined or even lose your license. And your job.

Pilots are the most regulated professionals—more so than in any other professional career. There may be around 900,000 doctors and 1,000,000 lawyers in the U.S.A., but there are only about 100,000 airline pilots in the United States of America. We are an elite group of professionals. We work above planet earth, in the air. Our jobs involve serious business. You can't pull over into a cloud and check the oil.

The pilot's contract is negotiated between the pilot group and the airline company. The pilot's contract contains written legal language that spells out pilot pay provisions, travel expenses, relocation expenses, vacation, training, hours of service, seniority, scheduling, crew rest, retirement, and so forth.

The primary goal of my job is to fly safely and legally—and then attempt to be reliable and efficient.

This is the ALPA code of ethics that pilots live by:

## Code of Ethics

*An Air Line Pilot will keep uppermost in his mind that the safety, comfort, and well-being of the passengers who entrust their lives to him are his first and greatest responsibility.*

*An Air Line Pilot will faithfully discharge the duty he owes the airline which employs him and whose salary makes possible his way of life.*

*An Air Line Pilot will accept the responsibilities as well as the rewards of command, and will at all times so conduct himself*

## Aviation School (Age 25–26)

*both on duty and off as to instill and merit the confidence and respect of his crew, his fellow employees, and his associates within the profession.*

*An Air Line Pilot will conduct his affairs with other members of the profession and with the Association in such a manner as to bring credit to the profession and the Association as well as to himself.*

*To an Air Line Pilot the honor of his profession is dear, and he will remember that his own character and conduct reflect honor or dishonor upon the profession.*[25]

Yeah, I know in reference to the first code I fly mainly cargo. The passengers I carry on my jet are usually other pilots riding on the jump seat and not paying passengers.

But when you drive an automobile with passengers or a car with groceries, as I said earlier, do you drive any differently? With small children or a precious, fragile lamp you may drive more cautiously. With a full passenger load of adults—or full load of heavy lumber—you may be restricted to driving the van or SUV at slower speeds. However, a license to operate is a license, no matter what you're carrying in the back. My motto is: "safety and legality are mandatory. Reliability and efficiency are goals too, but they are optional."

On January 22, 1988 I obtained a Flight Engineer license with a Turbojet Rating on the Whale, the Boeing B 747 jumbo jet airplane, the largest commercial airplane in the world. So I left New York at age 18 with a high school diploma and a driver's license. At age 26, I returned to New York with a couple of college degrees, a handful of pilot licenses and a major international airline pilot job as a second officer pilot on the B 747 jumbo jet airplane. Part of me wondered a simple question: *who the hell did I fool to get this job?* The other part knew that I had studied hard, worked hard and had performed well.

Over 98 percent of the population has no concept of what it is like to fly a jet around the world. So here is an attempt to describe—or provide a taste—of my around-the-world trip in 10 days at age 26.

The itinerary was New York to Brussels (Belgium) to Dubai (Arabia) to Hong Kong to Tokyo to Anchorage to Chicago and back to New York. (See photo number five page 155.)

Captain Spock was called "junior" by the other senior captains because when Spock was 23 years old he was the youngest B 747 international captain at the time. In his forties on this flight, I remember him as being a smart, ambitious investor. He had purchased a Navy ship and was converting it into a commercial yacht. He had also purchased a large tract of land and was subdividing the land into trailer home lots. Finally, he had also purchased 10,000 shares of Flying Tiger's company stock.

First officer Kirk lived in Alaska part time. He was an airline pilot and a bush pilot. He owned and operated a plane that could be configured with floats to land on Alaskan lakes and it could be fitted with skis to land on snow-covered mountain strips. Kirk had a license to hunt brown bears and his passion was to shoot a trophy Kodiak, the largest land-based predator. Kirk vividly described many close bear encounters and potential rifle shots that he did not take because the bear was less than ten feet tall. As I absorbed these stories, I became overwhelmed in the presence of these larger-than-life jumbo jet pilots.

I kept my mouth shut.

I owned a small lot of land in Florida and I fished for 20-inch fish.

The three of us with our distinctive personalities and backgrounds bonded and we crewed the B 747 jumbo jet airliner to Brussels. Brussels is a truly European city with its own currency—the Belgian Franc. Brussels has beautiful medieval and gothic buildings like the Guildhalls on the Grand Place. Also every street seemed to have a butcher, a hairdresser, a pharmacy and a restaurant. Spock and Kirk had been flying to worldwide international cities for years and knew the best places to eat. We consumed the best mussels in Brussels and washed them down with the best Belgian beer. We ate Belgian waffles for breakfast and departed to Dubai.

Dubai is a Middle Eastern city in the United Arab Emirates and it's located on the Persian Gulf, adjacent to the Arabian Desert. We ventured to the fish market in the early morning before the extremely hot temperatures peaked. Afterwards, we strolled to the Gold Souk where over 200 retailer's trade in jewelry. Their currency is called the Dirham. This is not the place where you check out the babes. The women wear long black robes with headscarves that cover their neck and part of their head. Most of the women had their faces covered, exposing only their eyes. In this part of the world religion has laws outlining ways in which women live their lives on a day-to-day basis. We heard the "call to prayer" horn alerting people that it was one of the designated five times a day to turn toward Mecca and pray to Allah.

I observed a man with his left hand cut off and after an inquiry I learned he was found guilty of stealing with that hand. The locals explained to me that they still occasionally have hangings on the third Thursday of the month. This was definitely a new strange culture and, to me, it seemed archaic. After consuming fantastically cooked kabobs and pita bread, we returned to the hotel for a swim. The outdoor temperature rises so high in Dubai that it is the only place I know where cold water is pumped into the lap swimming pool to maintain a comfortable temperature.

We flew from Dubai to Hong Kong. We executed the Hong Kong Checkerboard approach and I remember being totally amazed, overwhelmed, and enlightened. (More in an upcoming chapter on the Hong Kong Checkerboard approach.) The sensation is that you are flying into a mountain in order to see an airport runway. We were now halfway around the world. Hong Kong is 13 hours ahead of New York City's time zone.

Hong Kong is a bustling Asian city with a touch of an English western influence. The currency is the Hong Kong dollar, which was pegged to the U.S. dollar. At that time Hong Kong was one of the best places in the world for shopping, particularly electronics. I bartered a great price on a large Delsey suitcase.

In Hong Kong, there were always loads of people in the streets. It was not uncommon to see families with small children walking the streets late at night and it wasn't uncommon for two or three families to share one apartment. And to think I had it tough when I shared a bedroom with my brother while growing up.

Hong Kong was fun and after eating and shopping we always ended up at the Ned Kelly's Last Stand, one of Hong Kong's oldest bars. This establishment served Australian Foster's beer on tap and the live band always closed with that most famous Frank Sinatra song, "New York, New York." All humans—white or yellow, man or woman, native or foreign—joined together to dance and sing that blockbuster song as we closed the pub. I felt that Hong Kong wanted to be like New York City. Hong Kong became one of my favorite international layover cities.

We blasted off from Hong Kong to Tokyo, a truly Asian city with a strange currency called the Yen. Japan has a long history of purebred culture. The women were pretty but they all looked the same: five-foot, slim, white, black hair and dark eyes. They bowed to men. Yes, Japanese tradition calls for their women to fully devote herself to the needs and success of her husband. Contrary to the USA, it is not uncommon for Japanese women to hold open the door for a man, refill his sake cup at dinner, serve the man his food first and, yes, bow to him.

In Hong Kong I lodged in an executive high-level suite facing the Kowloon Bay. In Tokyo the hotel was constructed with small matchbox rooms facing a Koi pond. The bathroom door had to be closed in order to use the closet door or the room's exit door.

## Aviation School (Age 25–26)

This tight configuration presents a problem for captain Not-Y, who sleeps naked. As the human male ages, just a few Sapporo beers can trigger your bladder to urge you to pee at 3 a.m. Captain Not-Y arose from a dead sleep to rid himself of unwanted liquids. He opens the bathroom door, stumbles in and the door closes.

However, he is not in the bathroom.

The exit room door closes and he is now in the hallway, totally naked, and locked out of his room. And he still had to pee.

Well there were various stories of the reactions of a few shocked Japanese guests and the obliging hotel staff of that naked, six-foot and fairly well-built white guy, a Flying Tiger pilot. I'm not saying don't go to Tokyo, drink beer, and sleep naked. I'm trying to say identify which door to utilize to pee in those minuscule hotel rooms.

We departed Tokyo for Anchorage. Tokyo is 18 hours ahead of Anchorage. That means when it is 3:00 a.m. in Anchorage it is 9:00 p.m. in Tokyo on the same calendar day. What I experienced on this particular eight-hour flight occurs during certain times of the year with the right jet stream winds. As the jumbo jet traveled through so many time zones, I observed Mother Nature's beautiful sun rise and set during the same flight—a very short day, I said to myself.

Anchorage was my favorite layover city. Even with the U.S. dollar as the currency and English as the language, it seemed like a foreign place that was not Western, European, Middle Eastern, or Asian. A salmon fish burger was less expensive than a hamburger. Milk was more expensive than beer. In the winter, there are only a few hours of daylight and that was only if there was not an overcast snowstorm. In the summer, it never really turns dark; the sky dims for a few hours. Just a few blocks from the hotel you can fish for salmon and watch whales in the bay. Walk a little further out of town you can often see deer roaming around. And for the brave-hearted who stroll a little further, certain times of the year you'll see bears.

After Anchorage it was on to Chicago. With the howling wind blowing from Lake Michigan, Chicago was colder than Anchorage.

And to think (feel) just a few days ago I was in Dubai, a destination where the temperatures are so hot that water in the swimming pools needs to be cooled down. The least favorite part of my job is doing a pre-flight walk around of a 228-foot B-747 jumbo jet at four a.m. in the winter in Chicago.

From Chicago, we flew into JFK—back to New York. At age 26, I flew around the world in ten days. Life is great, only in America can you leave home at eighteen with a driver's license and return at age twenty six with a pilot's license.

## "The Whale"

Some aviators called the jumbo jet Boeing B 747 "the whale," others called it "the queen of the skies," because the B 747 was the largest aircraft in the world for many decades. Three flight crew members were required to operate the aircraft—a captain, a first officer, and a second officer (I was the second officer, sometimes referred to as the flight engineer).

The B 747 was known for being the first wide-body airliner, the largest and heaviest airliner, and the first to use fuel-efficient high bypass turbofan engines. The B 747 opened up international travel to millions of people and allowed shipment of commercial cargo worldwide. The B 747 had a wingspan of over 195 feet, was over 230 feet long, and over sixty-three feet high. The max takeoff gross weight on the -200 model was 820,000 pounds; the max landing gross weight was 635,000 pounds, enabling the B 747 to carry over 500 people on board, or over 250,000 pounds of cargo freight. (See photo number six page 156.)

I have operated flights with 515 people on board, and flights with 256,000 pounds of freight on board. The B 747 could fly at a speed of over 500 knots and a distance of over 7,000 nautical miles. The basic 747-100 model entered service with Pan America in 1970. The -200 model version was developed shortly after, allowing higher aircraft weights, longer range, and more powerful engines. Initially, the 747-100 model was equipped with 4 Pratt and Whitney JF9D turbo fan engines that produced 48,000 pounds of thrust. The later -200 model produced 54,000 pounds of thrust. At Flying Tigers we operated twenty-one B 747 jets, including the -100 and -200 models. Nineteen of the B 747s were cargo-configured versions and two were passenger-configured versions. We flew people and freight all over the world. Over 1,990 Boeing B 747 100/200 jets were built through 1991.[26] Other B 747 model versions are still being built today.

A previous English girlfriend Debbie traveled from Liverpool to Long Island to visit me. We had a good time together but after a week she concluded that I was not ready to settle down yet. She left disappointed and went home.

## Almost Died: Age 26
## Warrior gang attack on a New York Subway

The 1979 movie *The Warriors* told a story about a gang that is framed for killing a gang leader who was trying to unite all the gangs in New York City. During the entire movie, all the gangs and police were after the Warriors as the Warriors tried to get from the Bronx back to their home turf in Coney Island.

Little did I know that one day I would have a chance to relive one of the classic scenes in this film?

Air Force friend Tom Youhey and I were bar-hopping and clubbing around Manhattan in dress suits. We ran out of money and it was time to go home. Remember, always buy a subway token before you go out and put that token in your sock. So around 4 a.m. we were standing on a subway platform waiting on a subway train. Trains in New York City don't run that often at this wee hour before dawn.

I was standing at the side of the bottom of the stairs that lead down to the train platform. Tom was in a position around 30 feet away in plain daylight—at least, in New York City night light. All of a sudden, a gang (just like one of the gangs looking to kill the Warrior gang in the movie) started running down the platform stairs.

It took about two minutes for the whole 50-member gang to flood down the stairs onto subway platform, which was otherwise vacant except for the two of us. Just as the last gang member entered the platform, the subway train arrived and the whole gang stormed on board.

Tom and I were frozen in our tracks, visualizing for two minutes how they were going to kill us. If you have money to give to the gang, that is good. If you're broke and do not have money to give, then the gang members may get pissed off and kill you.

This gang had other plans and left in a hurry on the subway train that had just arrived. Without verbal communication Tom and I waited for the next train.

And lived.

## World Travels

The Tiger pilot group was a unique bunch.

After landing in a city—any city—anywhere in the world, the philosophy was simple: "Let's have the greatest time of our lives because this could be our last day" (or night) on planet earth.

After a day or two in that city we would start up the Boeing (the B 747 or the Whale), and take it to another city, and another city, and eventually to Gotham City. We imagined the Batman's Gotham City was supposed to be New York City. Because we were based at John F. Kennedy International Airport in New York City, flying the plane to Gotham City was like flying the plane home, even though very few pilots lived near their base.

Tiger pilots lived all over the U.S. and other countries and they commuted to and from home to JFK to fly the B 747. Home! Yes, halfway through a typical twelve-day trip, I wanted to go home to rest and recuperate and take a time out from the fun times. After being home just a few days, I yearned to go back to work with the other

Tiger pilots to fly somewhere in this world and have fun or, in other words, to make more memories.

In the B 747, I have flown around the world east-bound eight times and west-bound twice. I have from over North Pole from Anchorage, Alaska (ANC-PANC) to London, England (LHR-EGLL) and back to Anchorage. I've flown that route a few times. I have flown to Bahrain, Arabia (BAH-QBBI) to deliver Desert Storm war supplies. I've flown from Naha, Okinawa Japan (OKA-ROAH) to U Tapao, Thailand (UTP-VTBU) with 498 Marines for war-game exercises.

I've flown from Brussels, Belgium (BRU-EBBR) to Dubai, United Arab Emirates (DXB-OMDB) with zoo animals, including a few four-month-old baby tigers that were invited into the cockpit for photo opportunities.

I've flown from Anchorage (ANC-PANC) to Tokyo, Japan (NRT-RJAA) with 256 pregnant female cows.

Many of those B 747 flights had an aircraft take-off weight of 820,000 pounds and a landing weight of 630,000 pounds, including 200,000 to 250,000 pounds of cargo freight.

These are some of the cities I visited when touring around the world: Brussels, Belgium (BRU); Berlin, Germany (TXL); Frankfurt, Germany (FRA); Cologne-Bonn, Germany (CGN); Munich, Germany (MUC)' Stuttgart, Germany (STR); London, England (LHR); Prestwick, Scotland (PIK); Amsterdam, Netherlands (AMS); Paris, France (CDG); Basil, Switzerland (BSL); Zurich, Switzerland (ZRH); Milan, Italy (MXP); Guadalajara, Mexico (GDL); Mexico City, Mexico (MEX); Toluca, Mexico (TLC); Panama City, Panama (PTY); Dubai, United Arab Emirates (DXB); Anchorage, Alaska (ANC); Guam, Mariana (UAM); Taipei, Taiwan (TPE); Tokyo, Japan (NRT); Seoul, South Korea (ICN); Okinawa, Japan (DNA); Manaus, Brazil (MAO); Rio De Janeiro, Brazil (GIG); San Juan, Puerto Rico (SJU); Sidney, Australia (SYD); Singapore (SIN); and Hong Kong (HKG).

Oh, yeah, Hong Kong and the famous Hong Kong Checkerboard Approach. An Instrument Landing System (ILS) approach terminates at a runway center line, plus or minus 30 degrees. An Instrument Guidance System (IGS) approach is a variation of the ILS approach. However, the IGS approach terminates off the runway center line.

The Kai Tak International Airport in Hong Kong had an IGS approach to runway 13, famously known as the Hong Kong Checkerboard Approach, and this approach was one of the most unusual and dangerous airport approaches in the world.

The airport was located between the Victoria Harbor Bay and Hong Kong city limits, and the runway was surrounded by city buildings and mountains. So basically, the captain would fly the B 747, guided by the IGS runway 13 approach, toward a large checkerboard pattern. The checkerboard which was colored in a red and white pattern and it was located on a hill surrounded by buildings. While flying this approach, if you flew through the bad visibility and you could identify the checkerboard, then the real fun—or challenge—began. Once the visual reference point of the checkerboard was established, the captain would have to look right about forty degrees off the nose of the heavy jumbo jet to spot runway 13. If he did not see the checkerboard or runway, then he would have to execute a missed approach go around, and try again—or land someplace else. If he could spot the runway, then the captain had many tasks to accomplish in quick order—line up with the runway 13, lower the landing gear, set flaps for landing, correct for crosswinds if needed. If he landed long, the jet could run into Victoria Harbor Bay (others have done this). If he landed short or off center line, he would crash into the airport's property or city buildings (others have done this).

Because of many crashes and mishaps, the Kai Tak Airport and its very strange checkerboard approach has been replaced with the new Chep Lap Kak International Airport.

## Almost Died: Age 27
## Near-drowning in Bondi Beach in Sydney, Australia

In March of 1988, screw scheduling—I mean crew scheduling—called to tell me they were buying my next 10-day trip from me.

They weren't trying to screw me.

They wanted to use my trip to train a new B 747 second officer. The result? I would earn my wages for the 10-days but I would not have to work.

Great. I thought: *What shall I do with my time off? Maybe I'll go to Sydney, Australia to celebrate St. Patrick's Day.*

So I secured an Australian Visa, withdrew some cash and drove to JFK to ride the jump seat on a Tiger's B 747 flight to Sydney. Even though March was the end of Sydney's summer, the weather would still be in the lower 80° Fahrenheit.

Perfect.

Or maybe not.

One day while I was hanging out at Bondi Beach, I decided to go for a swim. I had been swimming since I was about six years old. As you will recall, I swam on the Catholic Youth Organization (CYO) team for about eight years. I'm a great swimmer compared to most others, but only good when compared to great swimmers. Although I won my first gold medal in a backstroke swimming event at the young age of eight, there were no records with my name on them. Nonetheless, I believed that I could surely swim a few miles in the ocean.

Wearing my black swimsuit (some Australians wore nothing), I jumped off the hot white sand and headed into the cool, crystal water. I started the Australian Crawl (also known as the Freestyle). I set a course to swim parallel to the coast and I put my head down for the workout, swimming hard like always.

Bondi Beach is really a big cove located between Marks Park Point and Roy O'Keefe Reserve Point, which opens up to the Tasman Sea, which is part of the Pacific Ocean. Bondi Beach is also home to a powerful riptide and I was slowly, without knowing it, being sucked out to sea. I was in deep, deep water and when I looked up, I realized I was a long way out to sea...

With Bondi Beach as the only reference point, it was too difficult to determine how far out I was—one, two, or more than three miles. On my left, I could see I was out further than the furthest surfers—and the surfers had their boards as floating devices.

I had no such flotation device and I was tired from my long swim.

*Oh shit! What was I gonna do?*

I tried not to panic. What were my choices? I was only 27. I did not even have a wife or child, but I wanted to live. I had no choice but to swim.

Putting mind over matter and using all the will power I could muster, I concentrated on my mental attitude to counteract the physical exhaustion. My body wanted to quit, but I wouldn't let my mind give up.

In order to avoid straining any much-needed muscles and to stretch out the endurance of all the energy remaining in my body, I mixed up my swimming styles. I employed two variations of the back stroke (left and right side stroke), breast stroke, some Australian Crawl, a lot of floating on my back, and a lot of treading water.

*Keep your mind focused on land.*

*Don't think about the Jaws movie.*

*Don't think about stopping or drowning.*

*Is there a God? God help me, or Jesus, Mary, or Joseph, or the Holy Spirit, anyone or any being.*

*My soul is not ready to be judged yet.*

*This is still better than hell.*

*My parents know I am in Australia, but no one knows I am in the Pacific Ocean and in trouble.*

*Focus—I will not die—I will succeed.*

*My body aches, and I am tired from breathing, but barely breathing with exhaustion is better than not breathing at all. What's the alternative?*

*How do these marathoners, triathletes and decathletes do this?*
*Go on, go on—keep going.*
*Finally, after treading water for the last time, I felt my foot touch sand underneath the water.*
*Land.*
*Yes I made it!*
I walked to shore.

Do you know there are man-eating Great White Sharks in Bondi Beach? In fact, today, underwater shark nets are installed for the summer months at Bondi Beach. The next day, I celebrated St. Patrick's Day in Sydney. Then I flew to New York City to land just in time to celebrate St. Patrick's Day again, but in New York City.

That year, I celebrated St. Patrick's Day in two separate cities, countries, and continents.

And almost died.

## One Drink

When hired at a major airline, the new pilot is assigned a seniority number. In my class of 24 new-hire pilots, the oldest person in the class was assigned the next pilot seniority number. Then, in descending order, the youngest person was assigned the last pilot seniority number. So, if the airline had 700 pilots and hired 24 new pilots, the oldest of the new pilots would get seniority number 701 and the youngest new-hire pilot would get pilot seniority number 724.

Every year, the seniority list is adjusted to account for pilots who retired or are deceased. This results in active pilots acquiring a new, lower seniority number, thereby increasing a pilot's overall seniority. *Your seniority number is the most important number in airline life* because bidding on flight schedules, aircraft equipment, domiciles, training dates, and vacation days is based solely on seniority. Seniority number 1 gets first choice. Seniority number 724 gets whatever is left.

On the evening of Aug. 24, 1988 I was driving with my cousin Redward, my friend John and we were heading from Redward's summer bungalow in East Marion to Claudio's Restaurant Club in Greenport, Long Island. Redward suggested we stop at Skippers Restaurant for a drink. I did not want to stop at Skippers. Because I was the driver, I should have gotten my way. However, I lost the vote—two to one.

It is amazing how one drink can change your life. It is amazing how you have this preconceived image of the perfect woman that you will meet one day, and then one day you meet a completely different person and you fall in love.

Skippers was a small restaurant located on a golf course and it included a small pub section with a seating capacity of about ten people. Irishman Tom Murphy was the bartender that night. Irishwoman Ann Murphy, Tom's wife, and Bernadette Carmel Wallace were socializing as we walked in.

Ann and Bernadette had planned on meeting the night before but had canceled because Ann was not feeling well. Their postponed get-together, it turned out, might have been fate.

Bernadette had a soft, baby-skin complexion. She had shoulder-length goldilocks blonde hair, a pretty smile, a healthy Irish body and sparkling blue eyes ("Blue Eyes," by Elton John always came to mind).

Those eyes did me in. I had to make a move.

All I had to do, I told myself, was just walk up to her, softly and delicately grab her hand, look into her eyes, and project my happiest smile. I would say, "Hi, my name is Francis" and wait for her verbal and or non-verbal reaction. If all signals were go, I would say, "You're gorgeous." If things were still going well, and if it felt right, I would give her a soft and delicate kiss on the cheek.

As a man, If you are dirty, smell, and are poorly dressed it won't help your quest, but your best smile projected onto her eyes is your best offensive weapon.

So is a drink.

Bernadette was so gorgeous that I was too shy to say anything directly. So, I decided on the indirect approach. I spoke, instead, with her friend Ann.

After a few, quick strong drinks I courageously uttered a few direct words to Bernadette and she responded with kind, soft and friendly words. She could have been royalty—Lady Diana. That is the how, when, where, what, who and why of the start of our relationship.

## Witnessing Tragedy in Dallas

At the end of August 1988, I jump-seated down to Dallas, Texas to visit friends at my old apartment complex. On Aug. 31, around 9 a.m., Delta flight attendant friend Wanda knocked on my door.

"There's been a plane crash at the airport. Let's go," she said.

We arrived at the Dallas/Fort Worth airport in just a few minutes and approached the airport perimeter fence adjacent to runway 18L. There was the crashed B 727-232 jet (Delta Airlines flight #1141, Aircraft #N473DA).

Firefighters were still extinguishing the fires, and passengers that survived were emerging from dark, smoky and smelly clouds and making their way to emergency vehicles. Two of the four flight attendants and twelve of the 101 passengers died.

Seeing this crash was emotional and it affected us in both personal and professional ways—aviation was our professional career. *We make our money above planet earth, and it is serious business.* You know, you just can't pull over to a cloud and check the oil. In fact, sometimes you are only permitted to talk about your job while you're doing your job.

How did that crash happen?

FAA regulations require flight crew members to maintain a strict, sterile cockpit. A sterile cockpit means that once the aircraft starts moving, pilots are not to engage in any conversation that is unrelated to flight operations. This applies to any operation on the airport property and all flight operations up to 10,000 feet in altitude. This sterile cockpit also applies to the last 1,000 feet of any climb or descent.

The investigation of this crash found that while taxiing to runway 18L, the flight crew was talking extensively and that their conversations had nothing to do with the operations of that flight.

The investigation found two main causes for the crash. The crew's failure to extend the flaps and slats to proper takeoff configuration was attributed to inadequate cockpit discipline. The other problem was the plane's takeoff configuration warning horn, designed to alert the crew if the engines are throttled to takeoff power without the flaps and slats being correctly set, was not operating correctly.

The airplane did not gain sufficient speed to climb in a flaps-and-slats-retracted condition, causing a loss of lift. The continued high angle of attack combined with a lack of lift resulted in a configuration where disturbed air flowing over the wings disrupted the air flow into the engines causing compressor stall. Failing to gain altitude, the jet struck an antenna array 1,000 feet beyond the runway—and crashed.

The flight lasted only about 22 seconds from lift-off to impact.[27]

# CHAPTER 6
# 1989: Hell of a Year

1989 was a hell of a year.

I built my first house in Port St. Lucie, Florida and purchased my first primary residence in Key Largo, Florida.

Twenty-five friends and relatives travelled to Castlecomer, Ireland, where Bernadette and I were married during a short, 12-hour wedding day. We held a reception in New York City as well.

Bernadette got pregnant on our honeymoon.

We moved into our home in Key Largo.

And Flying Tigers Airline and Federal Express Corp. merged.

But let me back up for a moment. I've getting ahead of myself.

The corporate merger—and my personal merger, the marriage—had their roots in the events that happened in 1988.

The airline merger talks started in December of 1988 when 17-year-old Federal Express Inc. announced that it would acquire the 43-year-old Tiger International, Inc. Federal Express offered $880 million. The offer was made on Dec. 17.

I did not know it at the time, but my days with Flying Tigers were numbered.

Eight months later, on Aug. 8, 1989, I operated flight number 76 aircraft number N822FT from Columbus, Ohio (KLCK) to JFK International Airport (KJFK). This was my last flight as a Flying Tigers Airline Pilot. The official merger had been completed the day before and my next flight would be as a pilot for Federal Express. I think it's worth noting that "merger" was a kind, gentle word that didn't capture the confusion and uncertainty among pilots and workers from both companies. It was us and them. Us: the Flying Tigers, had about 1,000 pilots, and they called us the Silver Pilots. Them: the Federal Express had about 1,100 pilots, and we called them the Purple Pilots. How would the pilot lists be merged, and what would be my new *seniority number*? Normally, airline pilot mergers are stressful, and I should have been more concerned, but I had just bought a house, built another house, and was about to get married in Ireland (we'll get to that story soon).

## Proposal

Four days after first reading about the merger announcement, on Dec. 21 1988, a Pan Am B 747-100 was about a half-hour into a scheduled flight from London's Heathrow airport to New York JFK airport when an explosion occurred in the forward cargo compartment. The plane was flying over Lockerbie, Scotland. The airplane tore apart and plummeted to earth. All sixteen crew members and 243 passengers died. Eleven people on the ground were also killed. It was hard to imagine such an awful accident—but it was no accident. It would later be determined that two Libyan nationals had planted a bomb on the plane.

On Dec. 24, Bernadette and I left Seaford, Long Island and boarded the Long Island Railroad on the way to New York City. Bernadette Carmel was all dressed up in her unique, regal European style. I dressed up, too, but nobody would ever accuse me of setting any fashion trends.

On the way, I looked for pay phones along the way—when we boarded at Seaford, when we transferred at Jamaica and at the end of the ride, at Penn Station. I was eager to telephone Ireland and speak with Joe Wallace, Bernadette's father. I finally got him on the phone. Bernadette knew I was talking with her father, but she was unaware that it was no ordinary chat.

I was asking her father for Bernadette's hand in marriage.

We entered The City, viewed the holiday windows at the Saks Fifth Avenue department store and then walked to Rockefeller Center to see the skating rink, the angels, and the Christmas tree. Then, we headed to St. Patrick's Cathedral and visited every display. The area behind the altar was roped-off. Apparently this area was rarely closed except for special occasions, like Christmas Eve. After chatting quietly with the guards, they let us into the closed area to view the remarkable holy statue of the beautiful Blessed Virgin Mary, Mother of Jesus.

Nerves—how do they really work?

Why they are fired up and they were doing a job on me.

But I did it anyway.

Reaching into my pocket, I pulled out a clear, white-yellow ¾ karat, four-prong diamond ring. While looking into Bernadette Carmel's beautiful blue sparkling eyes, I proposed.

"Will you marry me?"

"Ha?—what?" she asked.

God, the look on her face—the shine, the sparkle, the big joyous smile.

She said "yes!"

We paid our religious respects to the Mother Mary and departed the Cathedral. We strolled a few blocks and then hopped on a horse-drawn buggy to cruise around the famous Central Park. It was an extremely romantic moment and we celebrated with a bottle of Moet & Chandon Imperial champagne and absorbed the spectacular New York City Christmas Eve scenery.

We made our way to a top-rated Italian restaurant. Bernadette probably remembers the restaurant's name; all women remember these details.

Over the coming holidays, we shared our engagement news while spending Christmas Day with my father's side of the family and 54 relatives. New Year's Day was spent with my mother's side of the family and 27 relatives.

It is good to have a balance of family pleasure and business but sometimes work-related events can influence that balance.

On Feb. 19, 1989, a Flying Tiger B 747-200F aircraft, flight number 66, en route from Singapore to Kuala Lumpur, Malaysia, crashed shortly before landing. The crew descended below the glide path and crashed into a hill after receiving ambiguous instructions from air traffic control. All four crew members were killed.

Just five days later, on Feb. 24, 1989, Flight 811 was on a scheduled international trip from Honolulu, Hawaii to Auckland, New Zealand. About sixteen minutes after takeoff, the United Airlines B 747-100 aircraft was climbing through about 22,000 feet when the forward cargo door on the right side blew out. The resulting explosion and decompression led to the loss of parts of the fuselage and the cabin interior, including a number of seats and passengers. Some of the ejected debris damaged the two right side engines, and the crew had to shut them down. The crew was able to return to Honolulu and land about fourteen minutes after the decompression. All eighteen crew members survived, but nine of the 337 passengers were killed.

It was not a good stretch for aviation accidents.

On July 19, 1989 a United Airlines DC-10 crashed near Sioux City, Iowa as a result of a hydraulic system failure. One hundred eleven of the 298 passengers were killed. The crew performed an emergency landing in a corn field after an engine failure severed all the hydraulic fluid lines.

As pilots, we study and discuss what happened. We learn from the pilots who are able to deal with catastrophes and save some lives, as was the case in Honolulu and Sioux City. But there are some situations, like Lockerbie, where there's just nothing to be done.

After I complete a flight trip I try to temporarily forget these events and all work-related business so that I can concentrate on other business.

In 1989, I had a contractor build a three-bedroom, two-bath, one-car garage house on the land I had purchased in Port Saint Lucie,

Florida. This was the greatest financial asset I have ever owned. The bank own 80 percent of the property by mortgage, but it felt like mine. The dwelling was used as a non-owner occupied rental.

After traveling throughout Florida's southeast coast, I ended up in Key Largo, talking to realtor Roger Barren, who could have been a double for the actor Chevy Chase. Roger and I boarded his boat and surveyed homes for sale via various waterways. We found a three-bedroom, two-bath furnished home located at mile marker 105 on a canal adjacent to the John Pennekamp Coral Reef State Park, in Key Largo. I thought it would be a perfect house for us to live in and I bought it.

Key Largo in Monroe County is located around 100 miles north of Key West and fifty miles south of Miami International Airport. Key Largo is located in the sub-tropical zone; temperatures ranged around the high 60° F in the winter and the low 80° F in the summer with very little humidity. From my residence in Key Largo, I would commute to work at JFK International Airport and then fly all over the world.

One memorable flight occurred on March 28, 1989. Back then and even today very few airlines transported more than 500 people on a jet. Captain Billy, First Officer Larry, and I flew flight number 2121 in a B 747-100, aircraft number N890, from Anchorage, Alaska (PANC) to Kadena Air Base, Okinawa Japan (RODN). We carried 492 passengers and 17 crew members for a total of 509 people on board.

Passengers? On a cargo plane?

Yes. Flying Tigers operated 21 B-74 jumbo jets. Of those, 19 were configured for transporting cargo and two were configured for transporting passengers. The two passenger airplanes were used for charter flights—mainly military personnel. Therefore, I had to be prepared to operate of flight that carried up to a quarter million pounds of cargo freight or up to 500 passengers. (See photo number seven page 156.)

## School and Schooled

One of the main differences in operating passenger flights is to maintain comfortable temperatures throughout the various zones of the jet. (Cargo doesn't tend to complain so much.) Usually if one of the 14 flight attendants enters the cockpit and complains that zone three is too cold, it usually means that one passenger has said he or she is cold and needs warmer air. I would adjust the temperature accordingly. However, if another flight attendant came into our office (and that's what the cockpit is—an office) and expressed that it was too hot in zone five, that usually indicated that she was busy working hard and sweating. Most of the time I ignored this request. In fact this coming and going and the running commentary—"it's too cold in zone two, it's too hot in zone five"—became a distraction to my other duties.

The Captain, First Officer and I devised a fantastic scheme.

I labelled an inactive switch (we called it the Dummy Switch) the "TEMP. SW." Whenever, one of the working girls came in to complain about how hot was in zone "XYZ," I authorized my special flight-operation permission to adjust the temperature herself using that special "TEMP. SW." I made her promise to keep this a special secret between us because the Captain may become furious if he found out when, in fact, the Captain was discreetly laughing all the way to Japan. We had our laughs and they were happy to adjust the "TEMP. SW" up or down as often as they wanted to. These were great memories.

Another memorable flight occurred on April 19, 1989 when we transported almost a quarter million pounds of cargo freight. Captain Jeff, First Officer Belton, and I flew flight number 1021 aircraft number N813FT from Keflavik International airport (BIKF) to Anchorage, Alaska (PANC) carrying 239,590 pounds of freight. Our max takeoff gross weight that day was 819,731 pounds.

Two memorable flights occurred on Aug. 17, 1989. Bernadette was on one flight and I was on the other. Bernadette boarded an Aer Lingus jumbo jet B 747 flight to fly from JFK International Airport with a quick scheduled stop in Shannon International Airport and then on to Dublin International Airport, Ireland. At the last minute, I obtained the jump seat (a pilot privilege where a pilot can get a free flight ride) on a Pan Am B 747 jumbo jet flight to fly from JFK International Airport to Shannon International Airport, Ireland. While riding in the cockpit, the captain transmitted an air-to-air message to the Aer Lingus captain to inform Bernadette to depart at Shannon International Airport. It was not difficult for the flight attendant to locate Bernadette—she was the pretty blonde carrying a wedding dress and sitting in seat 6A. During the plane ride across the pond (the Atlantic Ocean), the Pan Am pilots and a few flight attendants were jokingly trying to talk me out of getting married.

"You don't like to fight? Then why are you getting married?"

"Why do men die before their wives? Because they want to."

"Make sure you get the whole 'I do list' before you get to church."

My mind started wandering on the thoughts of marriage.

"What do men want? To be loved." Men want to have sex so that they can pass on their genes to offspring. Men will give love to get sex. But men not only want a good-looking sexy woman, they want a woman that is kind, giving and a compassionate caretaker amongst other things. Yes, men want someone similar to mother who will cook, clean and take care of them.

"What do women want? To be loved." Women want to have sex to produce a healthy offspring. Women will give sex to get love. But women not only want a handsome physically-fit masculine man with power and money, they want a man who is respectful, nurturing, an emotional supporter and a caretaker amongst other things. Yes women want someone like father who will provide and support her and her future offspring.

So I was thinking maybe before you marry that significant other person, maybe you should list all the things and traits you despise most about that person. Assume that the potential partner will never improve in those areas, will never change, and may get worse. Now ask yourself, "Can I live and accept that person with those perceived faults?" If the answer is yes, then get married. The problem is that "opposites attract"—opposite personalities, religions, morals, politics, ideas about raising children, spending and saving habits, and so forth. Opposites attract, you get married, and then you have to learn to live with each other. Initially, love blinds those faults that you perceive in your spouse. You then have children (yeah, God really set things up right). When married with children you do everything you can to keep the marriage together and to raise your children. But I didn't have any children and I wasn't married—yet. After the flight lands, I knew I would find Bernadette because I had strong, loving feelings for her. I wanted to love and be loved.

Upon meeting at Shannon Airport, we rented a car and drove 17 miles on the wrong side of the road to her parents' house. If you are ever planning a trip to Ireland, do not rent a large automobile with an automatic transmission—instead, rent a small midsized automobile with a manual shift because most of the roads are very narrow, winding and hilly. Gasoline is very expensive in Ireland and manual transmissions always get better mileage than automatics.

We spent more than a week preparing for the legal and religious commitment day, except for that one day I took off with brother-in-law-to-be, Mike O'Brendan. Mike was Anne O'Brendan's husband. Anne was one of Bernadette's sisters and her very best friend. After Mike helped me write the music to the song I wrote for Bernadette, we decided to visit the Dunmore Caves. Shortly after arriving at the Dunmore Caves, we realized that this tourist site wasn't worth visiting. It was only 11 a.m., but we decided to visit the next best thing, the Dunmore Cave Pub.

While indulging in the Irish tradition, I recalled the Coors Brewing Company non-tour beer story to Mike and told him I had read that Kilkenny Brewery might offer a beer tour. So, bottoms up, out the door, and away we went to Kilkenny.

We participated in the whole brewery tour. I learned a lot, and at the end of the tour we were offered one free Kilkenny Irish Red beer each. Apparently, Bernadette's family and the O'Brendan family were both well-known in Kilkenny and the men in charge of the pub let us stay until closing. Needless to say, we drank more than the one authorized pint. We finally walked out of the brewery across the street to another pub that Mike wanted me to visit. For one reason or another, we stopped and visited every pub located on our way while leaving downtown Kilkenny.

We went arrived back in the town of Castlecomer around 10 p.m.

"It's almost last call," said Mike, explaining that the pubs would be closed in an hour, and it didn't make sense to go home yet.

So we were having the time of our lives and doing some true male bonding as new male relatives. When in Rome, do like the Romans. When in Ireland, socialize while under the influence of Guinness Stout in gratitude and respect of Sir Arthur Guinness.

Sir Arthur Guinness was born in Celbridge, Co' Kildare, Ireland in 1725. Arthur Guinness began brewing ale beer at the St. James Gate brewery in Dublin, Ireland in 1759. In 1778, Guinness began to brew Porter beer—a dark beer containing roasted barley. This brew was known as "Porter" beer because of its popularity with the porters and the dock workers of London. In 1759, at 34 years old, Arthur signed a 9,000-year lease on Dublin's St. James Street to build what is today's Guinness Brewery. In the 1820's, the word stout was added as an adjective to qualify the noun porter, and "Extra Stout Porter" was considered stronger and more full-bodied porter beer.[28]

Mike O'Brendan and company of newly-made Irish friends were trying to get me into heaven.

> "When we drink we get drunk,
> When we get drunk, we go home,
> When we go home, we go to sleep,
> When we sleep, we commit no sin,

When we commit no sin, we go to heaven.
So let's all get drunk and go to heaven."
—*Unknown*

This new group of Irish friends was providing historical education while I was feeding my body with a healthy dose of barley in the form of Guinness Extra Stout.

Life was great.

What could go wrong?

*Women!*

Mike's wife Anne and her sister Bernadette stormed into the pub. There was a lot of yelling and nagging; I only coherently remember: "You've been drinking over twelve hours!" and "I don't want to be married to a person like that."

Those two Irish sisters were steaming mad.

I think the wedding was called off.

Did they know that 25 of my family and friends were en route to Ireland to see me get married?

Sometimes, it's easier to bond with another male than with any female. But my female was Bernadette Carmel and her love, affection, lovemaking, sweetness, kindness, thoughtfulness, and the attraction of the beauty of the female itself won the day. It will win most of the time. She won—the wedding was back on. (Besides, the couch is no place for a man.)

On Aug. 24, 1989, all the men met me at an authentic pub in Kilkenny. Those stories will not be told here.

Bernadette Carmel Wallace, born in Castlecomer, Ireland in 1957, is daughter to Joe Wallace, born in Castlecomer, Ireland in 1926. Joe Wallace's parents, Walter Wallace and Margret Nolan, were born in Ireland. Walter Wallace's parents, Edward Wallace and Julia Judy were born in Ireland. Bernadette Carmel Wallace is daughter to Teresa Kavanagh, born in Clough, Ireland in 1929. Teresa Kavanagh's parents, Paddy Kavanagh and Annie Mealy were born in Ireland. However, Wallace is a family name of Scottish descent and Bernadette would be getting a new family name of Irish descent—Donohue.

On Aug. 25, 1989 Bernadette gave up her family name. It started when the 1956 Rolls Royce that belonged to Sam Sneed (the actor from the English TV show "The Avengers") rolled up to the entrance of the Church of the Immaculate Conception carrying Bernadette. The Gothic style church with Italian handmade "stations of the Cross" statues was built in 1852. Bernadette entered the church as special singer Joe O'Neil graciously sang. Father O'Toole religiously and legally married Bernadette Carmel Wallace to Francis John Donohue, Jr. There were 25 family members and friends from the United States to witness (or maybe guarantee) the ceremony.

A side note to all engaged men: Get the "I Do" list before and read it thoroughly before you say "I Do." Soon after you marry you will notice that the "I Do" list has miraculously grown into the "To Do" list, the "To Re-Do" list, the "You Should Have Done" list, and the "Why Didn't You Do" list.

If she says *why didn't you do the To Do list and the Re-Do list?* then respond *I should have done that. I'm sorry. I'll do that. You're right. I Love You.*

A man selects a woman to have offspring with and expects that woman will not change. Think again. She will change.

A woman selects a man to provide for her offspring and she expects she will spend the rest of her life trying to change her man.

Remember those words of promise: "I, Francis John, take you, Bernadette Carmel, for my lawful wife, to have and to hold, from this day forward, for better, for worse, for richer, for poorer, in sickness and health, until death do us part"— through all good times and bad times.

After Joe O'Neil sang the Ave Maria song, we departed in that same Rolls Royce for the Kilkenny Castle. The driver drove right around to the back, where the front entrance was located. We were all dressed like royalty—the men that day were all dressed in top caps and tuxedos—and French and Italian tourists rushed off their tour buses, flashing their cameras at the royal wedding party.

They didn't know any better. We looked and dressed the part and we were entering the great Kilkenny castle. Bernadette looked like Lady Diana. She was a princess on her wedding day. The flashbulbs popped and we played right along.

The Kilkenny castle had been built around 1213 and had had numerous owners (there was even evidence that an O'Donohue was once an owner) until the Butler family bought the castle in 1391. The Butler's transferred ownership to the Irish Castle Restoration Committee in 1967.[29] Our specially selected photographer Sean Oliver was instrumental in obtaining special permission to allow our wedding party to enter the Kilkenny castles' great room to photograph the wedding party. After being photographed inside and outside of the castle, we entered the Kilkenny Hotel to start the wedding reception.

The Irish love to sing, and my Aunt Blinda knew this, so my aunt made multiple copies of various popular Irish songs so all the visiting Americans could join in with the party. Without Bernadette's knowledge, copies of "My Lovely One" were also distributed to everyone. I had written this song for my wife, and we sang it to her at the wedding reception.

Generally reserved and slightly shy, Bernadette was very surprised and her face blushed a bright red color, which highlighted her beautiful white wedding dress.

## My Lovely One

O I love to love my lovely one.
O I love to love my only one,
O I love to love my Bernadette
The only one for me.

Her hair is golden blonde, and shiny,
With her gorgeous sparkling blue eyes
They blind me,
Her skin is so young, clean, and beautiful,
With that glowing smile she brings happiness to all.

O I love to love my lovely one.
O I love to love my only one,
O I love to love my Bernadette,
The only one for me.

I met her in Skippers at four,
Blinded to see my future wife,
I tripped while staggering through the door,
And fell into her lonely life.

O I love to love my lovely one.
O I love to love my only one,
O I love to love my Bernadette,
The only one for me.

Can I tell you a secret? I love you,
But I think the whole world can see through,
And every night—God I pray,
Be closer to her when I'm away.

O I love to love my lovely one.
O I love to love my only one,
I love to love my Bernadette, the only one for me.

    I never did, and should someday; record this song for publication and distribution.

    My Uncle Rohn orated the Irish Blessing for us.

**An Irish Blessing**

May the road rise to meet you,
May the wind be always at your back,
May the sun shine warm upon your face,
May the rains fall soft upon your fields,
And, until we meet again,
May God hold you in the hollow of His hand.

—*Unknown, although some attribute it to St. Patrick*

The next morning, after the 12-hour wedding day, Mr. and Mrs. Francis J. Donohue, Jr. drove to Ventry, a small village in Dingle in the West of Ireland to start the honeymoon. We traveled from Dingle to attend the "Rose of Tralee," then to Listowel, Kilrush, Galway and many other towns before concluding the honeymoon at the Bun Ratty Castle Medieval Banquet in Shannon.

I'm a rambler, I'm a gambler,
I'm a long way from home;
And if you don't like me,
Just leave me alone.

I'll eat when I'm hungry,
I'll drink when I'm dry,
If moonshine don't kill me,
I'll live till I die.
—*From the "Moonshiner" song*

Then, we flew from Shannon International Airport Ireland to John F. Kennedy International Airport to attend the 100-person New York wedding ceremony and reception. I know: I always was a pain in the ass.

Not only did I have to get married in a foreign country, but I had to have two ceremonies and receptions—one in her country and one in my country.

After the New York reception, not many of my relatives wanted to fly on commercial air planes anymore. Maybe because at the reception they met my pilot colleagues: John of American Airlines, Mark of Trans World Airlines, Bill of Continental Airlines, Bob of USAir, Robert of United Airlines, and so forth. You get the picture—I think? A few days later we drove home to our furnished home in Key Largo, Florida to live happily ever after.

Yeah, right.

Mr. and Mrs. Donohue moved into their new home in Key Largo, mile marker 105. Shortly after, Bernadette revealed to me that she was with child. Our conception of this child was dated a few days after the wedding—hence, a honeymoon baby was on the way.

## The Berlin Wall

On Nov. 9, 1989, jubilant East and West Berlin Germans began tearing down the 96-mile, 28-year-old Berlin Wall. The Berlin Wall was erected by the Communist East German government to prevent the German residents of Communist East Berlin from escaping to the German Democratic West Berlin. Hundreds people died trying to escape. The Berlin Wall symbolized the Cold War divisions between East Communism and West Capitalism. Among many other changes in Eastern European and the Soviet Union, the persistent will of the East Berlin people ended in their rights, and freedom, being restored. Human motivation and will power for basic rights are unstoppable.

The formation of the United States of America in the early 1700's is a good example of this, and today we have a great country—the best country on the planet Earth.

Shortly after the Berlin Wall came down, Captain Jean, first officer Bob, and I flew from JFK New York to Dover, Delaware and then on to Frankfurt, Germany. We had a three-day layover in Frankfurt and decided to turn it into a little vacation. That night, we went out to eat Schweinehaxen (pork with cabbage and potatoes) and of course, German beer. The next day, the three of us took a Pan Am jump seat to Berlin. We crossed the dilapidated Berlin Wall into East Berlin. We spent the night in West Berlin, and the next day, we took a jump seat to Stuttgart, Germany. After a day in Stuttgart, we took the midnight train back to Frankfurt and went to get a late night snack, a near-fatal mistake.

I ate a Brockwurst sausage, drank some milk and went to sleep.

## Almost Died: Age 28
## Passed out and choking in Frankfurt, Germany

Did you ever have a dream? Dreams have several scales of awareness. At times, you may be unaware that you have dreamed. And occasionally a dream may be recalled in sharp detail and other times it is vague. You may experience a dream that is so lucid that you think the events are real—it's so vivid that you cannot initially distinguish between the reality of the dream and the reality of the awake life. In your dream you see, hear, feel and touch. The effects or feelings that we experience in our dreams can persist after we are awake and can seem as real as anything in the awake life.

In this dream, I had to piss but the bathroom was miles away and I was so tired that I began to crawl and eventually stopped to rest or re-sleep. But there was something ferociously alive in my stomach and it was trying to escape by trying to squeeze through my throat. It was too big to get through my throat. As I tried to open my mouth, my tongue tasted its nastiness. Just then my breathing system stopped and I started to panic for air.

"It won't get out."
"I cannot breathe."

"I do not want to die."
"What is this nasty creature?"

I had drunk some bad milk and some good alcohol, and I woke up on the bathroom floor around 4:00 a.m., choking on my own regurgitation. When you are choking you are cutting off the airway to your trachea. If you vomit and choke on the big chunks, you can die from suffocation. The choking actually woke me up, as I was passed out. As my eyes started to blink open I crawled up to the top of the toilet bowl to let the creature—the vomit—out. After smelling that terrible smell I started to realize that I was transitioning from a nightmare dream to the reality of awake life—*somewhere, sometime, somehow*. I stood up on my own two feet, turned the bright bathroom light on and stared at myself in the mirror. Next, I washed my unusually pale white face with cold, refreshing water, took some Lamotal (an oral anti-diarrheal drug) and drank a bottle of warm water.

If you ever suspect that you may vomit in your sleep, do not sleep on your back, staring at the ceiling. If you do vomit while sleeping in this position, there is nowhere for the vomit to go and you might choke and die. Sleep on your side so that the puke will drain out of your mouth as you sleep. Rock guitarist Jimi Hendrix died at age 27 in London in 1970 from choking on his own vomit after drinking wine and consuming too many sleeping pills. All I consumed was some bad milk, a little good beer, and a German bratwurst sausage. Thank you, thank you, and thank you. I lived and did not die.

# CHAPTER 7
# FedEx® Career

**Silver versus Purple**

Every airline and its pilot group have a distinct culture.

The FedEx pilot crew (the Purple Pilots) and the Flying Tiger crew (the Silver Pilots) were the two most distinctive pilot groups that ever existed. However, the challenge in 1989 was to merge, to become one culture.

A physician and medical consultant hired by FedEx to evaluate the two pilot groups unofficially said that the Purple pilots were like "the church choir" and that the Silver pilots were like "the Hells Angels club." Most of the Purple Pilots were novices to the airline industry. The Purple Pilot group only had a 15-year history in the airline business. Most of the Silver Pilots were much more experienced and the company itself had a 45-five year history.

The Purple Pilots were a non-union group and consisted of mostly ex-military pilots, mainly Navy, Marines, and some Air Force. They were regimented and individualistic.

The Purple Pilots, on the other hand, were used to abiding by the company requests—follow the general or colonel and don't ask questions. One pilot stated to me, "Whatever Fred Smith says is okay by me." Another pilot remarked: "If Fred wants a domicile in Anchorage, he will get one."

Up to this point, most of the work rules for the Purple Pilots was dictated by the company and not negotiated, like most of the other airline pilot groups. The Silver Pilots were an ALPA Union group and consisted of a varied group of mostly civilian pilots. They were fun, friendly, and group oriented.

"When we land in XYZ city, let's have the best time of our life together because it could be our last day." I was a Silver Pilot and that was our attitude.

The Silver Pilots were dubious of company intentions. If the company wanted an Anchorage, Alaska domicile, then the pilot union group would investigate and negotiate.

"What do they (the company) want, and what do we (the pilot group) want?"

The majority of the Purple Pilots were based near their headquarters in Memphis, Tennessee and flew domestically (within the United States). In the 1980's, you could buy a really big house in Memphis and drive to work on the average pay of a Purple Pilot.

The majority of the Silver Pilots flew internationally and lived all over the United States. Most Silver Pilots lived where they wanted to and commuted by plane to their home base to begin work. I initially commuted from Key Largo to John F. Kennedy International Airport and temporarily lived in Memphis for one year (1991). The standard of living—and the cost—was higher in New York and California than it was in Tennessee. Most of the Purple Captain Pilots promoted the use of the aircraft autopilot to direct the jet's flight path, even during the departure and approach phase of flight. You'd hear suggestions like this from Purple Pilots: "Practice using the autopilot so that if the weather gets bad, you will be efficient at using the autopilot."

Most of the Silver Captain pilots promoted the use of hand-flying during departure and approach. Our belief was this: "Practice hand-flying so that if the autopilot fails, you will be proficient at hand-flying the aircraft."

The Purple Pilots did not have probation for new-hire pilots. So if a friend of a friend got hired, and if he or she was a bad pilot or a bad character, then that pilot stayed and did not get fired.

The Silver Pilots had a one-year probation period for all new hires. So, if a hiring mistake was made, the company could fire that pilot and not suffer with the poor hiring decision.

While on layovers, the Purple Pilots generally paid their own way, except that because the Second Officer carried the coffee jug, the Captain and First Officer would take turns tipping the limo driver on behalf of the Second Officer.

All Silver Pilots did their own tipping to the limo drivers; however, the Captain gave an extra tip to the limo driver for providing attitude=adjustment beverages for the crew while being transported to the layover hotel.

It was not uncommon for the Captain to buy dinner for the crew.

One time in Taipei, Taiwan (TPE), the limo driver did not have cold beer for the crew. The Captain uncharacteristically scolded the driver. It was the first time I saw a grown man cry. Driving a limo in Taipei in the 1980's was a good-paying job, and the driver feared that he might lose it. Besides, it was a 45-minute drive to the hotel. Well, the driver stopped, we purchased beer, the driver kept his job—and he earned a tip. The Captain and First Officer always bought drinks and sometimes meals for the Second Officer because the Second Officer was on probation and could not afford to buy drinks.

These are just a few examples of how extremely distinctive these two pilot groups were—and they had to merge and get along.

Fred Smith, the founder and chief executive officer of Federal Express (renamed FedEx in 1994) first got the idea of developing a new logistics system while living in New Haven, Connecticut during his college years. While Fred Smith was a charter pilot at Tweed New Haven Airport, he observed the logistical challenge of flying large computer parts around every time a computer broke down. While at Yale University, Fred wrote a term paper on the idea of using a hub-and-spoke overnight logistics system to solve the challenge of moving cargo. His professor was not impressed with the idea and issued him an average grade on his term paper.[30]

After serving in the U.S. Marine Corps, Fred continued to develop his idea of a new cargo delivery service. In 1971, Fred incorporated Federal Express. Using $4 million dollars of his own money and $80 million dollars from investors, he started developing his idea. On April 17, 1973, Federal Express officially began operations with the launch of 14 Falcon aircraft based at Memphis International Airport and delivered 186 packages to 25 U.S. cities. In less than two years, Federal Express made its first monthly profit of $20,000 by delivering over 13,000 packages per night.

In 1978 Federal Express was listed on the New York Stock Exchange under the ticker symbol FDX and by the end of the 1980, two years after the passage of the Airline Deregulation Act of 1978, Federal Express became the nation's leading cargo carrier.

By 1983, Federal Express became the first U.S. corporation to achieve annual revenues of $1 billion in less than 10 years. In 1986, Federal Express's volume exceeded 1 million packages per night. In 1990, Federal Express became the first service company to win the "Malcolm Baldrige National Quality Award." In 1994, Federal Express changed its name to FedEx and launched its worldwide website: fedex.com.[31]

FedEx continually expanded the size of the company through growth and acquisitions. In fiscal year 2013, FedEx delivered more than 4 million packages per day and more than 10 million pounds of goods to the United States and to more than 220 countries worldwide, utilizing approximately 4,500 pilots. FedEx produced over $42 billion of revenue that year.

September 6, 1990 was my last flight on the B 747 flight as Flight Engineer. In over three years I had accumulated 1510 hours as a Flight Engineer on the jumbo Boeing B 747 jet.

On December 13, 1990 I upgraded to Boeing B 727 First Officer pilot position. The B 727 jet was the first jet airplane I ever flew. I was twenty-nine years old.

The Boeing B 727-100 jet aircraft was developed in 1965 and shortly after the 727-200 jet version was offered. The -200 model was basically the -100 model with the fuselage stretched 20 feet, allowing increased passenger and freight capacity.

The B 727-200 entered service with Northwest Airlines in December 1967. One thousand, eight hundred thirty-one (1,831) B 727 of all model versions were built from 1967 through 1984 when production ceased. The B 727 had a max gross takeoff weight of more than 200,000 pounds. It could carry more than 200 people or more than 50,000 pounds of freight. The wingspan of the B 727 stretched more than 100 feet and its length measured more than 150 feet. It stood more than 34 feet high. The B 727 included three turbo fan engines. Each engine produced more than 16,000 pounds of thrust, enabling it to fly a distance of more than 2,000 miles and a speed of more than 500 knots.[32] Three crew members were required—a Captain, a First Officer, and a Flight Engineer. I was the First Officer. (See photo number eight page 157.)

The B 727 aircraft was a fun plane to fly. It was like a high-speed go-cart.

"If you could see it, you could land on it," was the motto of B 727 pilots. The motto meant if you could see the landing runway from level altitude, then you were capable of descending at a steep rate, slowing down and landing.

With the use of speed brakes, wing flight spoilers would deploy, allowing the aircraft to be piloted at a high rate of descent and/or slow down very quickly. We had a requirement to be stabilized on final approach. This would mean the flaps would be fully extended, the final checklist would be complete, the landing gear would be down, and we would have the on-approach air speed and engines out of idle before touchdown. Our goal was to have all this done by ten feet above the ground.

We flew high-speed climbs out of Paris France (CDG) climbing at a speed of 350 knots or more, and then flew high-speed descents into Basel Switzerland (BSL) at the same speed. We would fly at that pace until we were around 30 miles from the field and about 3,000 feet above ground and then slow the aircraft down to be stabilized before touchdown. Then we would taxi in, set the parking brake and shut down the engines. Someone would say, "Last one out loses." That was the most fun part of flying the B 727 and sometimes challenging.

Flying into Vnukovo International Airport, Moscow (VKO-UUWW) in 1986 was challenging. Flying out of Milano Malpensa Airport, Italy (MXP-LIMC) was sometimes challenging—at times you would have to climb in circles to get enough altitude to cross the beautiful Swiss Alps.

Flying the arrivals and departures in and out of Paris, Charles De Gaulle Airport (CDG-LFPG) was challenging using the B 727's old navigation technology, especially when the French controllers spoke English to us but spoke French to the French pilots. Instead of saying "Bonjour" (meaning good day or hello in French), sometimes I would just say "Bon Jovi" (you know the guy who wrote the song, "You Give Love a Bad Name").

Flying into Guadalajara (GDL-MMGL) and Toluca, Mexico (TLC-MMTO) could be challenging at times; you had to *tell* the controllers what you wanted to do and not ask them what you wanted to do; the language confusion could result in a clearance to fly into a mountain. *We make our money above planet earth and it is serious business.*

Pilot Beware.

Thinking about the serious business of flying a big jet, I wrote the poem "Half Awake or Half Asleep."

**Half Awake or Half Asleep**

Are you half awake?
No, I feel half asleep.
I love it when I'm half awake,
I kick the autopilot off for flight's sake.
I can smoothly pitch and bank,
I aviate like the number one rank.

All radio transmissions and receptions I can make,
Executing all motor and decision skills without one mistake.
Watch me, watch me, I bet you a steak,
I am the best pilot, and a smooth landing I can make.
I wish I could always live and fly half awake.
Flying in daytime when half-awake is a piece of cake.
I can be dangerous when I'm half asleep,
My performance is not the best when I cannot leap.
I may be off by ten degrees, ten knots, or a hundred feet,
Deviating from standards with a lack of enthusiasm to meet.
I may just turn the autopilot on at 500 feet,
And off after the airplane and runway meet.
Candy, soda, or coffee, whatever it takes to not count sheep,
I must successfully fly the plane and my job I must keep.
I don't enjoy flying above the ground much when I'm half asleep,
But half asleep is better than being underground deep.

On my last B 727 trip to Europe, I spent the day in Rome before heading to Basil, Switzerland where my trip would begin. On the Rome stopover, I saw Pope John Paul II for my second and third time. The second time, while in St. Peter's Basilica, at a distance of six feet, stood Pope John Paul II. With that holy-ghostly look, white face and white-gray hair, the Pope looked into my eyes and blessed me. His gaze was so powerful it felt as if he was looking in my soul. I was frozen for a few moments—*I'll always remember and never forget.*

Later that day, I was present for Pope John Paul's afternoon blessing in Saint Peter's Square. Before boarding the night train that would take me to Basil, I stopped at a popular Italian Espresso bar to buy and drink an authentically-made espresso coffee. However, my espresso did not taste right. In fact, it did not taste good.

*Should I complain?*
*How could I communicate with them?*

Well, it took at least 15 minutes, many hand gestures and a lot of Italian "I don't knows," but what I found out was that my espresso coffee was not ordered with Sambuca.

You see, my Italian brother-in-law had previously made espresso coffee for me with Sambuca included. How was I supposed to know you can actually order espresso coffee with or without the Italian liquor made from elderberries and flavored with licorice?

Everyone laughed.

Immediately, I made Italian friends and made sure my coffee came with Sambuca. Now, I'm not saying, "Don't trust your brother-in-law," but maybe ask him what he put in the coffee.

## A Quick Lesson in Flight

What makes planes fly? Before we take my last trip in B 727, allow me to summarize. If you hum a song during this section, try "Under Pressure," the classic rock song by David Bowie and Queen.

Inventors Hon von Ohain of Germany in 1939 and Frank Whittle of Great Britain in 1941 built the first jet engines. The simplest gas turbine engine for aircraft was the turbo jet. A turbo jet engine is like a horizontal container—a can. The can is open at both ends and includes several sections inside. Air is sucked in through the intake and compressed. Then, the air is heated and burned with fuel in the combustion chamber. The air moves through the turbine rotor, developing power to operate the compressor, and then the air exits through the engine tailpipe to create propulsion. The difference between the inlet pressure and the exit pressure is the thrust force that moves (pushes) the engine and the aircraft it is attached to.

Yes—pressure. It's the pressure differential of the engine that makes a plane move forward.

Newton's First Law of Motion: "A body at rest remains at rest unless it is acted upon by an outside force."

Newton's Second Law: "a change in motion is proportional to the force applied."

F=Ma.

Force = Mass (wt.) x Acceleration.

However, thrust alone from a turbo jet won't get you to cruising altitude of 35,000 feet.

If the captain of the jet aircraft pushes the thrust levers full forward to obtain maximum thrust (and did nothing else), the jet would just race down the runway and run off the end.

What else does the pilot need? Do you hear a song playing?

Pressure.

You need airfoil pressure to give the plane lift.

The basic description of what makes a jet—or any airplane fly—is the pressure differential between the upper surface of an airfoil wing and the lower surface of an airfoil wing.

An aircraft's wing is flat on the lower surface and curved on the upper. Air moving across the top of the wing travels farther, thus faster (lower pressure) from the leading edge to the back of the wing than the air that is moving underneath the wing. Bernoulli's Theorem states that "the sum of the pressure energy and potential energy and kinetic energy is constant through a tube." If velocity decreases, then the pressure must increase. This pressure differential between the lower part (higher pressure) and the upper part (lower pressure) of the wing is called Lift Force. Lift pushes the wing, which is attached to the jet, upward.

There are four forces involved—lift force, gravity force, drag force, and thrust force. But it all comes down, basically, to pressure. It is engine pressure differential and wing pressure differential that moves the jet from Point A to Point B. While the jet is accelerating down the runway, the captain pulls the aircraft's flight control yoke (at the appropriate moment) to change the wing surface to create the right wing pressure differential and lift the jet into the air.

Obviously, there are a lot more complicated things going on in a jet, but that is the basics—pressure.

And sometimes pilot pressure. As a B 727 First Officer pilot I logged over 2,200 hours of multi-engine jet flight time and made about 900 landings.

## Unions and the Pilot Union History at FedEx

Why do you need a union anyway? If a company takes care of its people—the workers—and the workers provide a good *product or service*, then the company will make a good profit, and everyone will be happy—right?

Well, it is the inherent nature of most companies to squeeze more hours out of its employees and to try and get them to do the work for less pay. The owners and stockholders want to make more money so they can buy bigger yachts than the next guys. The more money and power they get, the happier they will be—right?

This is not personal between us and them; it is just business. In "pursuit of happiness" and seeking shorter hours and higher pay, printers were the first to go on strike in New York in 1794. Cabinetmakers struck in 1796, carpenters in Philadelphia in 1797, and shoemakers in 1799.[33]

In the early years of the 19th century, efforts by unions to improve working conditions and pay through negotiation or strike became more frequent. By the 1820's, various unions were formed in an effort to reduce the working day from 12 to 10 hours. Unions popped up all over—the National Labor Union in 1866; the Knights of Labor in 1869; the American Federation of Labor (AFL) in 1886; and the Committee for Industrial Organization (CIO) in 1935. The AFL and CIO merged in 1955.[34]

The Air Line Pilots Association Union (ALPA) was formed in 1931.

As a major cargo and package delivery business, FedEx placed a priority on customer service. The company established a People – Service – Profit (PSP) philosophy. However, taking care of the people was not working for the pilots. The profit was piling up, but the pilots felt left out.

Since FedEx started in 1972 and over the course of twenty six years, FedEx had increased pilot working hours, working duty, days of work, and pilot medical costs. At the same time, it had eliminated profit-sharing plans, refused pay increases, shifted FedEx cargo and FedEx pilot flight time to other air carriers and feeder aircraft, fired pilots, and reneged on many promises.

There were times when the pilot crew force united and obtained increases to their employment package or decreased the degradation process, but it wasn't until 1999 with the FedEx Pilots Association Union and over 90 percent of pilot unity did the pilots get a legalized contract, including significant increases to their employment packages.

Pilots cannot legally negotiate without representation (a union) and therefore, what you get is what the company wants to give you, and that can and did change any time at the company's will. Of course, you will understand from the following brief union history at FedEx that obtaining the first pilot contract was not easy and, to get it, pilot unity was paramount.

*In 1972, Federal Express began to charge $8,800 to each pilot for training to get a type rating in the Falcon aircraft, and 70 percent of the pilots signed authorization cards to be represented by Air Line Pilots Association[35] (ALPA). Company management threatened to shut down all flight operations if ALPA won. The final vote to be represented by the ALPA union failed by a narrow margin.*

*In 1973, The Federal Express Pilots Association (FEPA) was formed.*

*In 1974, management refused to recognize a Pilot Seniority System and changed the pilot's work rules at will. Pilots approached ALPA for representation; ALPA lost the election by a narrow vote after Fred Smith made a personal appeal to the pilots, promising firm work rules, salary review, and a seniority system. Mr. Smith asked for ten years of no efforts to organize a union and he stated that at the end of this period,* if pilots were still unhappy that they should get the best representation available.

In 1975, the initial Flight Crew Handbook (FCH), containing work rules and compensation, was written and published by a committee of the Flight Council. Supposedly, pilots had a vote in approving the work rule portion of the FCH.

In 1978, the senior vice president of flight operations stated to the Flight Council that FedEx pilots would be paid in the top 10 percent of all major U.S. airlines. The idea was that as other airline pilots received pay raises FedEx pilots would receive pay raises and never fall below the top 25 percent of pilot pay.

In 1979, after a pay review showed that the pilots were due for a raise, management refused *and called for a rewrite of the FCH. Management formed its own committee, and without pilot input, rewrote the FCH and instituted the new revised FCH.*

In 1981, pilots were no longer authorized to vote on the work rules. They only had an opportunity to review and comment on the FCH changes. The FCH International Operations section only contained basic FARs. Management stated, "We do not fly internationally, therefore we do not need international rules; we can add them later." Management established the Flight Advisory Board (FAB).

In 1984, DC 10 aircraft began to fly international charters to Europe. Charter operators, such as Emery and Iasco airlines, were added to the quarterly pay comparison to keep the pilots in the promised top 25 percent pilot pay in the industry. Initial management statements included feeder pilots on the pilot seniority list. Later, management stated they would farm out the feeder system work to other pilots. In later presentations to the pilots, the boss man tried to soften his actions by stating that there would never be many feeders and certainly never any large feeder aircraft. Overtime pay, reverse seniority pay, volunteer pay, and per diem pay were included in pilot's salaries for the quarterly pay review. A small number of pilots flying lots of overtime skewed the

*FedEx pilot averages used in the pilot quarterly pay review. Ninety-five percent of the pilots signed a petition voicing their complaints with the new pay review system. Shortly after, at the "Infamous Hangar Meeting" with CEO Fred Smith, Fred characterized the Federal Express pilots as ungrateful and the FAB as incompetent. Shortly after this meeting, Mr. Smith wrote a letter to Flight Operations stating that a 40,000-pound maximum gross weight limit be established for the feeder system aircraft.*

In 1985, volunteer and reverse seniority pay was removed from the pay comparisons; however, pay scales of airlines in bankruptcy were added to the pay comparisons. The FAB agreed to a modified "B" pay scale with parity at four years. Pilots over the age of sixty begin flying as second officers.

In 1987, FAB insisted that the company pick up part of the cost of pilot uniforms, as they were paying for all other employees' uniforms. DC 10 aircraft began flying international charters to Hong Kong, management insisted on revision to the FCH to allow more block time in a given duty period.

In 1988, management raised the FCH weight limit for feeder aircraft up to 50,000 pounds to allow the operation of four F 27 aircraft that Federal Express had already purchased. In an attempt to appease the pilots, the boss man offered a trade-off proposal to the pilots whereby Section I-96 is inserted into the FCH, stating that in the event of a merger or acquisition of another airline, Federal Express pilots will have seniority preference. The FAB had no choice but to accept. Months later, the Flying Tiger airline acquisition was announced and the boss man **reneged on the Section I-96 proposal promise.** The FCH was a contract between Federal Express and each individual pilot, which the company could change at will, at any time. Federal Express pilots had no structure or union to enforce the Section I-96. The Tiger pilots were represented by ALPA and had an ALPA contract and therefore proposed a significantly greater litigation threat to the Federal Express Corporation.

*In 1989, three members of the FAB resigned and started an independent union movement in hopes of giving Federal Express pilots some control over the upcoming seniority list arbitration between the Federal Express and Tiger pilot groups. Without knowledge of the FAB and contrary to their stated intentions, management had constructed a merger list that would result in minimal training costs to the company. Because the Federal Express pilots did not have a union, they could not legally negotiate a contract with the Tiger ALPA pilot group. The "No" group was formed and a "yellow sheet" with the printed names of Federal Express pilots pledging loyalty to Fred Smith was distributed.* **Mr. Smith asked the "Purple" Pilots to "give us a year" to address the pilot issues that had stirred interest in unionizing.** Remember in 1974 Fred asked the pilots to give him ten years. Most of the pilots still wanted to believe Fred Smith and the People – Service – Profit (PSP) philosophy, and therefore, the independent union movement failed. At the time, there were about 1,000 flying Tiger (Silver) pilots represented by the ALPA union and about 1,100 Federal Express (Purple) pilots represented by the company. A vote to allow ALPA to represent all pilots was defeated, resulting in a non-union pilot group.

Well, within that "give us a year," Federal Express did the following:

- Decreased show time to start trips from an hour and 30 minutes to one hour
- Imposed common pay scales for narrow-body and wide-body aircraft
- Extended block hours and duty times
- Mixed schedules for Federal Express and Flying Tiger prior to Seniority Integration
- Suspended employee profit contributions
- Raised medical deductions
- Cancelled the employee stock option plan
- Changed the vacation policy

*In 1990, a seniority list was imposed by an arbitrator. The arbitrator's approach resembled the management's proposal. Without any negotiations or leverage, the Anchorage, Alaska domicile was opened. Moving expense allowances and conditions were imposed by management.* Previously, Tiger management had wanted an Anchorage domicile (an airline term for where crews begin and end their trips) but could not reach agreeable negotiated terms with the Tiger Pilot ALPA union. Prior to opening the Anchorage domicile, Federal Express and Flying Tiger pilots would deadhead or operate from New York, Memphis or Los Angeles to Anchorage on ten- to twelve-day international trips through Anchorage. The three-pilot crews would get one or two day legally required layover rest periods, with pay, in Anchorage. With an Anchorage base, all those required paid layover rest periods would be eliminated and the deadhead portion of trips would be eliminated. Also the plan was to convert the B 747 and DC 10 jet flights that were manned with three-crew-members to the MD 11 jet flights that were manned with only two-crew-members. The pilot crew force lost at least 300 pilot flight jobs in this deal—and got nothing in return except a limited moving-expense package to live in Anchorage. *The first organized newsletter for the pilots was published— called the "Stick Shaker."* The newsletter's intent was to educate the pilots on industry work rules, pay, and a variety of contract issues.

*In 1991, Federal Express was the only major carrier to terminate all benefits for the pilots (and their families) who were activated to fly in the Desert Storm War.*

*In 1992, the courts ordered a rerun union election* because they found FedEx management behaved inappropriately during the 1989 election. *Of the 2,279 pilots, 271 voted for the United States Pilots Association Union (USPA) and 1,015 pilots voted for the ALPA union.* Therefore, ALPA became the union representing the pilots from 1993 to 1996. *Prior to NMB certification of ALPA, the company started the use of wet-leased* (a term for other pilots flying our freight) *large aircraft to carry FedEx freight.*

*In 1994, Federal Express became FedEx.* Between 1993 and 1996, the company divided the crew force by offering up to 200 percent pay to the No Group pilots to fly the extra trips that the union pilots would not fly. With just over 60 percent pilot unity supporting the FedEx ALPA union, no real progress toward a good contract was made. The process proceeded through mediation and self-help, and finally, the ALPA union submitted to the National Mediation Board that they would accept FedEx management's last offer.

*In June of 1996, management's last best offer in the form of a Tentative Agreement (TA) was sent to the pilots for a vote.* The TA was really bad, and the pilots voted it down. Shortly after, the union representation for the pilots changed from ALPA union to the FedEx Pilots Association (FPA) Union.

In 1996, union membership increased to 75 percent. FedEx closed Newark, Oakland, and Los Angeles domiciles (these were strong pilot union membership domiciles) and moved those pilots to the Memphis domicile. A Tentative Agreement was announced.

*In March of 1998, the TA was voted down by 56 percent of the pilots*, mainly because it obtained marginal work rules and quality-of-life issues. It is important to note that the June 1998 pilot flying bid pack was built using the **"optimizer,"** a computerized pilot flight scheduling program. The new flight schedules were terrible and union membership started increasing. *A "Strike Authorization Ballot" was sent out to the pilots. A "No Draft or No Volunteer For Flying" effort was started. Informational picketing began. Fred Smith sent his famous* **"Red Letter,"** *entitled* **"With or Without You,"** *to the pilots. Threats to convert FedEx Air Express to a ground transportation company were made. Supposedly, the FPA president struck a deal with the company, which was known as "The Parking Lot Deal."* In the meantime, union membership unity increased to over 90 percent and *hundreds of pilots began asking FedEx for summaries of their flying hours so they could apply for jobs at other airlines. This action was noted with great concern* *by management and it was believed that these pilots were taking this action individually without any coordination from the union. Negotiations were completed and a TA was sent to the pilots for a vote.*

*In February of 1999, 87 percent of the voting FedEx pilots ratified the first pilot contract at FedEx.* This was a five-year contract and the first contract obtained by the FedEx pilots in FedEx's 25-year history. This wasn't the best contract, but it was a legal contract and a good start. How did the pilots finally get a contract? First, and most importantly, it took pilot unity of more than 90 percent membership. The "Optimizer" was the final blow. Pilots weren't going to take any more pilot-life degradation.

It was good business for FedEx to sign the contract with the pilots. As Michael Corleone tells Sonny "it's not personal; it's strictly business" ("The Godfather").

*In 2000, the FPA conducted a research survey of the FedEx pilots to gauge their desire to affiliate with a national union.*

In 2001, FedEx reported total operating revenue of just under $20 billion and signed a lucrative $7 billion dollar contract with the U.S. Postal Service. This was good for the company and should have been good for the pilots' career progression. However, FedEx offered the pilots a Letter Agreement (LOA), which could substantially decrease their work rules and increase the number of work days. This was like offering someone a 20 percent promotion but requiring that person to work 30 percent more. *The pilots voted for national affiliation and to pursue a merger with ALPA.*

*In 2002, over 90 percent of the pilots voted to merge FPA with ALPA and the merger became the ALPA FedEx Master Executive Council.* Of note, United Airlines declared bankruptcy in 2002 therefore, *the United pilots had to give back 29 percent of their wages and pay in an effort to keep United Airlines from going out of business. Even after a 29 percent pay cut, the United pilots were still earning a higher MD-11 aircraft class pay than the FedEx pilots.*

*In 2002, a negotiation survey was sent to the pilots to gauge what improvements they wanted to obtain in their second contract due to start in 2004. On May 31, 2004, the amendable date of the first five-year contract expired, and management was dragging its feet during negotiations—again.*[36] (Note [35-36] 1972-2002).

On Aug. 27, 2006, after 30 months of negotiations, a new TA was announced. On Oct. 17, 2006, the pilots voted to ratify the new four-year contract. This was the second pilot contract achieved by the pilots with FedEx.

In August of 2010, new contract negotiations began. On March 24, 2011, the new TA was ratified by the pilots. Included in the new TA was a 3 percent pay hike annually for two years, and a 1 percent retroactive pay in the form of a lump sum payment. The TA agreement called for a one-year contract, extendable to two years at the prerogative of the ALPA FedEx pilots. Flight hours and rest requirements were bypassed, pending new FAA regulations which were soon to be released. As of today the pilots are still in the progress of negotiating these issues.

Is it fair for the airline company to require a pilot to fly eight hours per day six days per week? Probably not. Is it fair for an airline pilot to only fly three take-offs and three landings every ninety days? Probably not. With a union representing a pilot group, a middle-ground can be negotiated. The new negotiated contract will define new responsibilities and authorities of the company and the pilot. The pilot and particularly the captain have defined responsibilities and authorities define by the US Federal government.

## The Role of Captain

Although I had achieved command authority as a Captain on the Cessna C 402 airplane at Midnite Express, the Boeing B 727 aircraft was the first jet that I had obtained command authority as a Captain.

On May 28, 1997 I added to my Airline Transport Pilot license the B 727 Aircraft Rating. The Federal Aviation Rules define the responsibility and authority of an airline captain (FAR 91.3 and FAR 121.537).

*-The pilot in command of an aircraft is directly responsible for, and is the final authority as to, the operation of that aircraft.*

*-In an in-flight emergency requiring immediate action, the pilot in command may deviate from any rule of this part to the extent required to meet that emergency.*

*-Each pilot in command who deviates from a rule under paragraph "B" of this section shall, upon the request of the Administrator, send a written report of that deviation to the Administrator.*[37]

An airline captain has the ultimate responsibility for the safety of the airplane and the crew. The captain by authority of the United States Federal Aviation Administration is the person legally in charge of the aircraft and its flight safety and operation. When the captain signs the Flight Plan Release, he accepts responsibility for the pre-flight planning and safe conduct of the flight between the two airports listed on the Flight Plan Release. His signature indicates he is in compliance with Airport Familiarization (FAR 121.443), Special Airports and Area Qualification (FAR 121.697), and Pilot Route Certification (FAR 121.697 a.4).[38]

The Captain is responsible for everything:

The Captain is responsible for ensuring that the aircraft is loaded properly and is capable of taking off from the runway of intent. If there is no computer-generated flight plan release, the Captain is responsible for preparing a manual release. The Captain must be familiar with weather characteristics, navigation facilities, communication procedures, type of terrain and obstruction hazards, minimum safe flight levels, pertinent air traffic control procedures (including terminal area, arrival and departure, holding), all types of instrument approach procedures and the physical layout of the airport in the terminal area, including congested areas and obstructions.

The Captain has to ensure that the flight can be accomplished safely and in compliance with the FARs and any company policies and procedures. The Captain is responsible for immediately notifying the company in the event of any aircraft damage or injury to any person on board.

During the flight, the Captain is in command of the aircraft and crew and is responsible for the safety of all crewmembers, jump seaters, passengers, cargo, and the airplane itself.

The Captain is responsible for pre-flight planning, any delay, and release of the flight. The Captain is responsible for monitoring the accuracy of radio communications, monitoring engine and system operations, alerting the other crew members of malfunctions, maintaining adequate watch for traffic, and maintaining situational awareness. The Captain is responsible for the proper operation of the flight including compliance with all checklists. The Captain is responsible for the operational security of the aircraft, law enforcement officers (FFDO) on board, cockpit security (in particular the cockpit door), and document security. The Captain is responsible for in-flight security decisions that affect the safety of the aircraft and crew.

If at any time the First Officer screws up, then the Captain must physically take control of the airplane. The Captain is responsible to see that all discrepancies that may affect the air-worthiness of the aircraft are reported to maintenance and recorded in the aircraft maintenance log. The proper exercise of the Captain's authority is the basis for flight deck leadership and is critical to safe, legal, reliable and efficient flight operations. Therefore my priority is that it is mandatory to operate each flight in a safe and legal manner and my secondary goal is to operate each flight in a reliable and efficient manner.

In order to meet all of these responsibilities, the Captain is permitted to break any rule or regulation to ensure safe flight operations and the safety of all humans on board. However, he may have to justify his actions. Otherwise, the pilot can find himself (or herself) in major trouble with the FAA, which can void the pilot's license.

*"No pilot may operate an aircraft in a careless or reckless manner as to endanger the life or property of another"* (FAR regulation 91.13 and FAR regulation 121.537.f)[39]. The interpretation of careless and reckless can be very subjective.

Most Captains usually take the first leg, meaning the Captain is the flying pilot and the First Officer is the non-flying pilot, to set an example. I take a different approach. I usually give the first leg away to the First Officer unless I am required for weather reasons to fly the first leg. I do this for two reasons. One, because 75 percent of all accidents happen on the first day of two crew members flying together for the first time, with the Captain being the flying pilot on the first leg. By giving this first leg to the First Officer where he's the flying pilot, it breaks the chain in that statistic. The second reason is that I want to see, on the first leg, "what do I have?" By that I mean, what is the caliber of my First Officer? Is he a really good pilot, is he an average pilot, or is he substandard pilot and I have to keep an extra-close eye on him or her?

That may seem like overkill, but here is an example of a full brief I would give to my First Officer before we start the jet engines.

"Hi, 'Super John Doe' co-pilot, I am Frank Donohue, your Captain."

Security Brief: "Do you have your pilot license, medical certificate, passport, and visa? Are you a federal flight deck officer (FFDO)?"

If he is an FFDO:

"Your mission is to protect the flight deck from any specific threats. I will continue to command the aircraft." The rest of this briefing is detailed, extensive and confidential.

Then, I will discuss the departure and arrival security threats of the day: terrorist threats, special terrain, minimum equipment list items, configuration deviation list items, weather, fatigue, stresses, any abnormalities for the flight, et cetera. If there are any passengers jump seating or air cargo attendants, "give them a full briefing using the appropriate briefing card." Even though the Captain is responsible for the passenger jump seat brief the captain can delegate this task to the First Officer.

Weather Brief: this covers whether the weather is good enough to take-off. Using information received from the airport's Automatic Terminal Information service the captain will have a discussion (the ATIS brief) on the winds, visibility, cloud ceiling, temperature, dew point, barometric altimeter setting, the runway in use and the possible use of engine and wing anti-ice for take-off. Will we need to spray the aircraft with de-ice and anti-ice fluid before take-off? Is there snow on the taxiways and runways? Is there a possibility of wind shear? Are there any other special items for consideration? What are the take-off and landing runways? If we take off and have an emergency, can we come back and land, or do we have to go to another airport?

Departure Brief: How will we depart from the airport? What direction and altitude will we fly and when will we turn and climb? Each airport issues specific instructions through a Pre-Departure Clearance to flight crews on detailing how to depart that airport. I will say things like this to the First Officer: "Let's discuss the Pre-Departure Clearance (the PDC brief) and perform a route check to make sure that the route loaded in the flight management system (FMS) is the same route we have been cleared to on the PDC. We are flight number 1409, aircraft number 749, cleared on XYZ route, and will use transponder squawk code 954."

Flight Operations Manual Brief (the FOM Brief): Airline companies have a Flight Operations Manual for their specific air operation that list specific operating policies and procedures for their airline and their flight crews.

For the FOM Brief, I will say: "We will operate using standard flight operation procedures. You (or I) will fly the first leg. We will take off from runway 36."

I will brief note-worthy items on the airport facilities diagram, airport operations diagram, and airport parking diagram.

Take-Off Brief: If I am flying the first leg, then I will do the Take-Off brief.

I will brief:

- The terrain function selected on for take-off to avoid local mountains or buildings; or the radar function selected on for take-off to avoid thunder storm weather.

- The take-off constraints that we have to comply with for the take-off, such as what airspeed, heading, and altitude we will fly and when.

- Whether we will take off in heading mode or flight management system navigation mode.

- What specific engines are on the jet, the start-up time limitations and the warm-up time limitations. (In very cold weather, you may need longer engine warm-up times.)

- If we will take off using maximum engine take-off thrust, or a degraded, reduced engine take-off thrust. (A degraded take-off thrust puts less stress on the engine components, therefore reducing the chance of an engine failure on take-off and helping prolong the useful life of the engines.)

- The navigation and communication equipment and frequencies we need for this take-off. I will brief in the event of an emergency, like an engine fire or failure, what altitude and heading we will fly, and which runway we plan to land on.

"At the minimum, in an emergency, we want to do the emergency checklist items, get the landing gear down, and land. Safety and legality are mandatory; our goal is also to be reliable and efficient, but it's optional. Any questions? Let's execute good crew resource management (CRM) and do the Before-Start checklist."

## Debriefing

It's ironic, but the debriefing after the flight is complete is usually much shorter than the pre-briefing.

Debriefing: "Did we operate safely and legally? Do you have any questions? What do you think we did right or wrong and how could we have done it better? Were there opportunities for improvement such as being more reliable and more efficient?"

As a FedEx B 727 Airline Captain I logged over 4,000 pilot flight hours and made over 1,400 landings. In August of 2009 I transitioned from the narrow-body Boeing B 727 jet aircraft to the wide-body heavy Air Bus A 300/310 jet aircraft. This new A 310 airplane rating was added to my Air Transport Pilot (ATP) license. With the promotion to the Air Bus A 300 jet, I had achieved the top of the career ladder in my aviation field—a senior wide-body heavy-jet aircraft major airline captain.

The A 300 jet is the largest and heaviest airplane I have had the privilege to command. In fact, when an aircraft is capable of takeoff weights of more the 255,000 pounds, then the FAA certifies that aircraft weight class as "heavy." Any aircraft that is classified as a "heavy" must use the word "heavy" when communicating with air traffic control on or near the airports. The use of the word heavy alerts pilots and controllers of the additional wake turbulence produced by these larger, heavier airliners. Therefore, I would now have to include "Heavy" with my call sign:

"Kennedy departure FedEx 1340 Heavy climbing out of 2,000 feet cleared to 5,000 feet."

The Airbus A 300-600 could be configured with twenty-two LD3 containers in the forward and aft belly cargo holds in order to carry a total payload of over 120,000 pounds of freight. The most I ever personally carried was 99,000 pounds of freight. The A 300 could carry about a total of 275 people (assuming each person weighs 200 pounds and each person has a 100 pound bag—then that only equals a total weight of 82,500 pounds). (See photo number nine page 157 and photo number 10 page 158.)

To command a jet with 275 people on board is a great feat and so is commanding a jet with 100,000 pounds of cargo freight.

But it's a different, great feat.

The A 300 had a take-off gross weight of more than 375,000 pounds, a wingspan of more than 147 feet, a length of more than 177 feet, and a height of more than fifty-four feet. The A 300 could fly more than 4,000 nautical miles at a speed of around 480 knots. Our Airbus jets were configured with Pratt &Whitney's PW400 or JT9 engines or General Electric's CF-6 engines. The CF-6 engines produced 61,500 pounds of thrust per engine. The A 300 aircraft entered service with Lufthansa Airlines in April 1983.40 The A 300 only required two flight crew members—a Captain and a First Officer—and I was the Captain.

In September of 2009, I commanded my first flight as an Airbus 300 wide-body captain with about 90,000 pounds of cargo. I was reminiscing about the time I watched on television the first space shuttle blast off (Columbia STS-1). It was April 12, 1981. I had just completed my third student pilot flight lesson and I went to the RAF Lakenheath Dorms and turned on the television.

Even though I had memories of the first U.S. landing on the moon, this memory of the first manned space shuttle launch impressed and influenced me greatly.

Remember, I decided to be a pilot right then and right there.

When I was a Cessna C 172 Certified Flight Instructor, I had witnessed the space shuttle Challenger (STS-51L) blow up while piloting a Cessna C 172 at 4,000 feet—less than 80 miles from the disaster.

When I was a Boeing B 747 Second Officer, Bernadette and I observed the space shuttle Discovery (STS-31) launch from our car parked on Highway 95 near Coco Beach, Florida. When I was a Boeing B 727 Captain on a layover in an Orlando, Florida hotel, I watched the night launch of space shuttle Discovery (STS-103). Finally, as an A 300 Captain on July 21, 2011, I watched on television the final space shuttle mission STS-135 (Atlantis) land at the NASA's Kennedy Space Center in Florida. Atlantis had completed its final 13-day mission, delivering 8,000 pounds of cargo to the International Space Station.

When would be my last day of delivering cargo? For 30 years I had been aviating air planes on planet earth and for 30 years, U.S. astronauts had flown space shuttles off planet earth.

The Columbia, Challenger, Discovery, Atlantis, and Endeavor space shuttle missions carried people and cargo into orbit; launched, recovered and repaired satellites; conducted research; conducted space walks; and built the International Space Station. The only thing constant in life is change. I guess now is the time to change our space program to something bigger and better.

From 1986–2011, there had also been 25 years of airline changes. In 1991, Pan Am declared bankruptcy. Delta airlines bought most of Pan Am's European routes, and on Dec. 4, 1991 the once-mighty Pan Am ceased operations.

In 1986, Pan Am had been my first major airline choice to seek employment as a pilot and now Pan Am no longer existed.

My second choice, Eastern Airlines, also went out of business in 1991.

Trans World Airlines (TWA) bought Ozark Airlines in 1986 and later TWA was bought by American Airlines in 2001. Airline "mergers"—there's that word again—had been going on for years.

American Airlines purchased Air California in 1987. USAir bought Pacific Southwest Airlines in 1987 and Piedmont Airlines in 1989. Northwest Airlines (NWA) bought Republic Airlines in 1986. Delta Airlines (DL) bought Western Airlines in 1987 and Northwest Airlines in 2010. United Airlines (UA) bought Continental Airlines (CO) in 2011. Continental Airlines bought New York Air and Texas International Airlines in 1986 and Peoples Express Airlines in 1987. Southwest Airlines (WN) bought Muse Air in 1985 and Air Trans Airways (ATA) in 2011. Air Trans Airways had previously bought Value Jet Airlines in 1997. Braniff Airlines came and went out of business three times—1982, 1990, and 1992.

In 1986, the major airlines in the U.S. were Pan Am, Eastern, TWA, USAir, American, Northwest, United, and Delta. There were a number of small cargo airlines like Flying Tigers, Federal Express, DHL, Emery, UPS, Kalita, Airborne, Zantop and others. Within the last 25 years, there were a lot of airline mergers, buyouts, bankruptcies and corporate restructurings. In the U.S. today, the major airlines are American Airlines (currently in bankruptcy and in merger talks with USAir), Delta Airlines, United Air, US Airways (previously branded as USAir) and Southwest Airlines. FedEx and UPS are virtually the only two U.S. major cargo companies. As I'm writing this book, in fact, American Airlines and US Airways merged to create the largest airline in the country.

What an industry.

How would a pilot know which airline company to get hired with 25 years ago? Who would have known that FedEx would evolve into a great major airline, financially sound, still growing, and one of the best airline companies with which to obtain a position as a pilot? Pilots are whores for flying. They love flying so much that many would fly planes for free.

But we do need to eat.

## School and Schooled

C-150 A/C Frank, Jeff and Simon

C-172 A/C ERAU markings

(ERAU service marks used by permission)

C-402 A/C Landing

(Picture used by permission of AirTeamimages.com.)

EMB 110 A/C Atlantic Southeast Airlines markings

(Picture used by permission of AirTeamimages.com.)

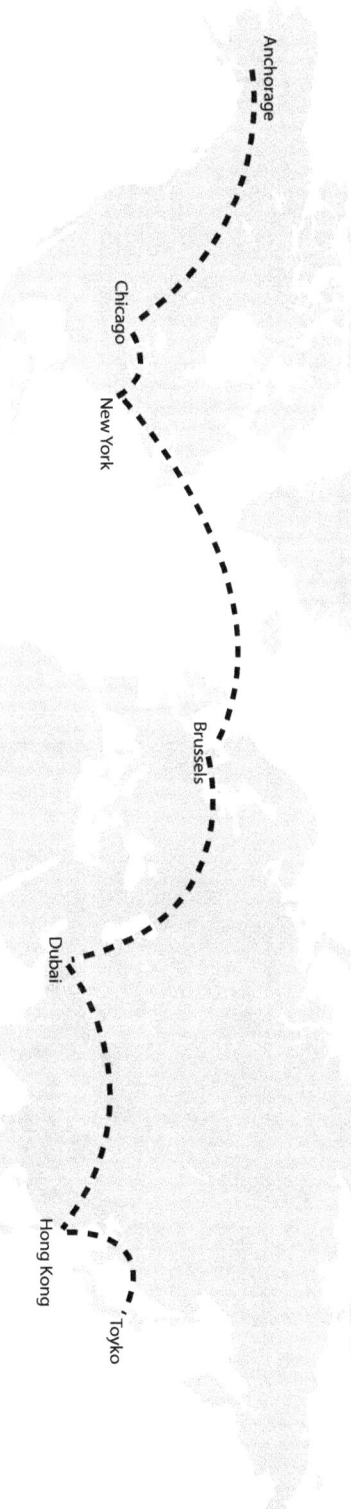

B-747 A/C Landing in Hong Kong

B-747 A/C Passenger configuration

B-727 A/C in flight

A 300 A/C in flight

A 300 A/C (empty cargo fuselage)

CHAPTER 8

# Flight 1340
# Safety — *Live First*

I thought you might like to go for a ride with me, up here in the cockpit.

The following flight happened—*sort of.*

I've changed a few details to protect all involved. I'm writing this book with the goal of showing you how a pilot's mind works and showing you how my life was shaped by becoming a pilot. So I thought you might like to go with me on one specific journey that ends, shall we say, in a moment that just shows "you never know," a moment that shows preparation and training are critical.

Just like life.

So take a seat up here in the cockpit.

Buckle up.

**Take Off**

"FedEx 1340 heavy cleared to line up and wait runway 31 Left."

The transmission is from John F. Kennedy International Airport Air Traffic Control tower, and Charlie, the First Officer of 1340, responds.

"Roger. FedEx 1340 heavy cleared to line up and wait runway 31L."

I reach up above my right shoulder and turn on the taxi lights while simultaneously pressing my two feet on the brake pedals of the Air 300 wide-body heavy aircraft.

I lower my right hand to turn and release the parking brake handle while depressing the brake pedals with my two feet. The jet starts to roll, but with more than 90,000 pounds of cargo on board, I will have to advance the thrust levers to assist the movement of this big jet that weighs over 300,000 pounds.

"Charlie, complete the before-takeoff checklist," I say.

"Takeoff configuration? Normal for takeoff. V speeds?"

I scan the forward instrument panel.

"Checked."

Charlie does the same.

"Checked. Radar?"

"On," I confirm.

"Flight control panel?"

I scan the flight control panel to double-check that the appropriate airspeed, altitude, heading and navigation controls are correctly set for takeoff.

"Set."

Charlie does the same.

"Set," he states. He engages the ignition selector and turns on the runway turnoff and landing lights.

"Ignition selector continuous relight. Before takeoff checklist complete," he says.

I scan left to confirm that final approach path to runway 31L is clear of arriving aircraft. Even if the control tower tells me it's clear, I want visual confirmation.

"Clear Left."

Charlie looks right to view that the runway is clear of all obstacles, especially other aircraft. You can't be too careful.

"Clear right."

I look right and double check. In our line of work, there is a lot of trust. This trust, however, must also be verified.

Kennedy Tower Controller tells me 31L is clear for me to enter, and my first officer tells me runway 31L from his viewpoint is clear to enter. I look left and right to double check and confirm.

Trust but verify. If they are wrong and I do not catch the mistake, another aircraft could land on the one I'm piloting. On me. On us.

My day would change from good to bad.

All is clear as I taxi onto the unoccupied runway, 150 feet wide and over 14,500 feet (nearly three miles) long.

Pushing the rudder control pedals with my feet provides limited control of the jet's steering, but it is the steering tiller installed on all large jets and controlled by my left hand that will steer the nose wheel through the hydraulic system.

This A 300 has a wingspan of 147 feet, a length of 177 feet and a height of 54 feet. The nose wheel gear and main gear are located 13 feet and 47 feet behind me, respectively. Therefore, as I enter the turn onto the runway from my point of view, I will have to overshoot the runway center line to compensate for the aft position of the nose gear. My position in the Captain's seat must actually pass the runway center line before I begin to turn in order to align the jet with the center line. Just as I complete the turn and return the nose wheel steering tiller to the center position, the Kennedy Air Traffic Controller issues us a take-off clearance.

"Fed Ex 1340 Heavy, winds 010 degrees at ten knots cleared for takeoff runway 31L."

Of course, as the airline Captain of this flight, I have the authority to decline the take-off clearance, but instead, I let Charlie respond.

"FedEx 1340 Heavy cleared for takeoff runway 31L."

To my left is the Jamaica Bay and to my right is the airport, a sprawling facility with seven passenger terminals and ten cargo buildings. After pushing the thrust levers to 40% N1 position, I observe that the engines have stabilized.

"Set standard power."

I give the command as I engage the takeoff go-around thrust levers. Each of the two General Electric CF 6 engines is capable of producing over 60,000 pounds of thrust at maximum power for takeoff. However, when conditions permit, it is best to takeoff with a reduced power setting called Standard Power in order to decrease stress on the engine and prolong engine life.

Charlie confirms the engines are stable at the desired thrust setting.

"Standard power set," he confirms.

The sound of the engine increases. The airframe vibrates, shakes and rumbles. You can feel the power building up. The airspeed gauge comes alive and tells me our increasing speed—ten knots, twenty knots, thirty knots. The jet rolls faster and it's my decision whether to reject the takeoff or continue.

I may reject the takeoff for just about any reason, like an unusual noise or vibration, a warning light or sound, any system failure, a tire failure, or even abnormally slow aircraft acceleration.

"Eighty knots." Charlie spits the reading as I check the airspeed gauge.

"Check," I say.

Above eighty knots, we are in the high-speed phase of the takeoff roll. Below this speed I may reject the takeoff for just about any abnormality. Now, I am in a more go-oriented decision mode and will only reject the takeoff for a serious situation that might prevent the jet from flying safely. Wind shear, engine fire or engine failure are good reasons to reject the takeoff at this speed.

"V1." Charlie eyeballs the airspeed indicator and scans the other instruments.

I remove my right hand from the thrust levers and grasp the control yoke where my left hand is located.

"Rotate," says Charlie.

The V1 speed is a numerical speed which varies. V1 varies due to aircraft weight, runway length, wing flap setting, engine thrust used, runway surface contamination and other factors. The simplest definition is that V1 is the takeoff decision speed. Before V1, if something bad happens, I have to choose to continue or abort the takeoff. After V1, if something bad happens, it is usually safer to continue the takeoff because there is not enough runway remaining to stop.

Charlie observes positive rate of climb on the vertical speed indicator and altimeters.

We go.

The aircraft is airborne—doing what it was designed to do.

"Positive rate," he says.

"Gear up," I respond.

Charlie retracts the landing gear lever to the up position.

With my hands on the control wheel yoke and my feet on the rudder pedals, I turn the jet left toward Carnarsie VOR as required for this standard instrument departure.

We are quickly 1,500 feet above the ground.

"Flaps up."

Charlie retracts the wing flaps from the takeoff position to the flight position.

"Slats retract, after takeoff checklist."

Charlie retracts the slats and verifies that the ignition selector, slats and flaps, gear and spoilers are placed in the appropriate position with no warning lights illuminated.

"After takeoff checklist to the line complete," he says.

"FedEx 1340 Heavy contact Departure Control on 125.87."

"Switching to departure on 125.87," he says.

"Kennedy departure FedEx 1340 Heavy climbing out of 2,000 feet cleared to 5,000 feet," said Charlie.

"1340 after Carnarsie cleared direct to Robinsville, cleared to 12,000 feet. Contact New York Center on 135.47."

Charlie reads back the clearance, dials 135.47 for the VHF frequency and sets 12,000 feet in the altitude select window. After verifying the correct altitude is set, I state the new altitude.

"12,000 feet."

"New York Center, 1340 cleared to 12,000 feet."

"1340, traffic at your two o'clock position descending to flight level 210. After Robinsville, cleared as filed, climb to flight level 240, contact New York Center on 135.5."

Charlie reads back the clearance once again and sets 240 in the altitude select window, switching the VHF radio frequency to 135.5. I verify the correct altitude is set.

"Flight level 240."

I join Charlie in scanning for traffic in the sky.

Looking westbound, various shades of the dark and light blue sky is partially obscured by mostly white, puffy cumulus clouds.

There are rays of orange and pink from the sun coloring the ever-changing clouds. Way above us, a jet contrail crosses our view from the cockpit. It is the only man-made feature included in this beautiful scene, provided free of charge by Mother Nature.

We're heading westbound and chasing the sun, but she's outrunning us and darkness is not far off. Although I have not identified the traffic, I fixate below on New York City; a city where more than 8 million diverse people live.

I'm lucky to be up here, in the clouds. And it's beautiful.

"Altimeters 29.92."

We are climbing through 18,000 feet, I set the altimeter.

"29.92."

"After takeoff checklist is complete."

The aeronautical airspace above 18,000 feet is classified as Class A airspace. All pilots flying in the United States set the altimeter to a standard pressure 29.92 inches of mercury. We reference altitudes as flight levels. Flight level FL 240 is the height of 24,000 feet above the average height of sea level.

Our cargo jet accommodates jump-seaters as passengers, so if it is not too turbulent, I check to ensure that Charlie has turned the seatbelt sign switch off. Additionally, I check that the runway turnoff and landing lights have been turned off and that our altimeters are within the variance of plus or minus 200 feet tolerance in order for us to enter into the reduced vertical separation minimum airspace. I check that the aircraft temperature is suitable for the jump seat passengers and the live chickens we're carrying. Finally, I check all systems: hydraulic, electric, pressurization, fuel, et cetera.

While monitoring the fuel, I catch one last glimpse of New York City, far below and disappearing fast.

John F. Kennedy Airport hands us off to Washington Center, meaning they have told us to switch our frequency to another Air Traffic Control Center. Washington Center clears us to flight level 350 (35,000 feet), but I tell Charlie to relay to Washington Center that we are unable to climb to flight level 350 due to our weight.

It is usually more efficient to fly at the highest altitude, but because we are carrying over 90,000 pounds of cargo freight and over 60,000 pounds of fuel, we are too heavy to climb to flight level 350. Washington Center clears us to flight level 310. The autopilot is controlling the jet's flight path now and through a system of electronics, hydraulics and computers, the jet levels off at flight level 310.

I keep my hands on the control yoke and on the auto throttles just in case the autopilot does not do its job and levels off at an incorrect altitude. If the jet levels off below or above where it's supposed to be, the flight crew, particularly the captain, could get a Federal Aviation Administration (FAA) violation including a monetary fine, a pilot license suspension, or worse—loss of pilot's license.

The jet levels off at flight level 310. I scan and monitor a few systems.

My mind runs through a series of questions.

Is the temperature for the chickens appropriate?

Is the temperature for the jump seat passengers appropriate?

Are there any abnormalities with the engine, hydraulics, the electrical system, the fuel system, the pressurization system, or other systems?

Is the flight management system and navigation system performing appropriately?

Do I need to make any adjustments?

I check our estimated time of arrival for Memphis and fuel on board. Time and fuel are important in this business. We want to be reliable and that means delivering the cargo to the customers on time. Fuel wise, flying at a slower speed is more efficient and saves fuel but when we're running late, we must fly faster in order to arrive on time.

It's an ongoing balance between speed and fuel.

## Changing Light

It is now night time—the sun won. The sun is always moving faster on its journey than we can fly.

The brain and eyes play tricks during night time flying, so I concentrate more on the cockpit instruments. On long night time flights, I keep the cockpit lights turned bright for optimal eyesight. Photopic vision, under bright light, helps detect color, details and far away objects.

But since we will be landing in Memphis soon, I turn all the cockpit and instrument lights from bright to dim to allow my scotopic vision to adapt to the dark. Scotopic vision works in low light and helps detect objects, particularly moving objects. However, detail and color are not so good. It may take up to 30 minutes for our eyes to fully adapt to optimum night vision, which we will need for landing.

"Look at that," says Charlie.

"Where?"

"Over there."

Again, Mother Nature provides first class entertainment free of charge. Glowing shades of pale, yellowish-green rays are shooting up and dancing in the dark eerie sky. A collision of electrically charged particles from the sun and gaseous particles from the Earth's atmosphere perform in the Aurora Borealis show, more commonly known as the Northern Lights.

"It's just energized ions and atoms colliding, or at least that's what they told us in school," Charlie explains.

You can explain it scientifically, but there is no explanation for the beauty that Mother Nature frequently displays.

## Co-Pilot

My co-pilot Charlie is a healthy six-footer. He's muscular, black-haired and brown eyed. He's cleanly shaved with a military haircut. From the way his starched, short-sleeved white uniform shirt captures his physique, a woman could idolize his big biceps and presume he has a chiseled chest and a flat abdomen. One of the greatest benefits of my career is that I have to opportunity to fly with pilots of various diverse personalities and backgrounds. There are unique and interesting features of Californians, Floridians, Kansans, New Yorkers and Texans.

"Charlie, how did you become a pilot?"

"I grew up in Texas on a small, not so profitable farm," says Charlie. "To supplement the household income, my father started a small air crop dusting business with one Air Tractor 502 Ag plane. My father took me with him many times and taught me the basic fundamentals of flying—climbs, descents, turns and straight and level. I entered the United States Navy and attended flight school at Pensacola. I learned to fly T-34 trainers at Corpus Christi and learned to fly T-45 Goshawks at Kingsville Naval Air Station. After receiving my wings, I was assigned to fly F-14 Tomcats."

I always enjoy getting to know who I'm working with so I ask, "Where did you go to school, Charlie?"

Charlie tells a story of being in high school and one evening after dinner his father presented him with some papers. "He told me, 'sign these papers. The U.S. Navy will educate you, teach you to fly and pay you at the same time. It's a good deal.'" So Charlie ended up attending the U.S. Naval Academy in Annapolis, Maryland.

Charlie is equally inquisitive of my background and I spend a few minutes recapping the many things you have learned about my background by reading this book.

We chat, but we're flying the plane all the time, too—our eyes scanning both the skies and instruments out of routine.

Washington Center switches us off to Indy Center. Indy Center clears us direct to the Bowling Green Fix and to join the LTOWN 6 RNAV STAR to Memphis International Airport.

LTOWN 6 is the name of the STAR associated with the LTOWN fix, a point defined by latitude and longitude coordinates. RNAV stands for "area navigation" and is a method of air navigation that allows an aircraft to fly from point to point. STAR is an acronym for "Standard Terminal Arrival Route" and is a published procedure describing specific instructions for descent, routing and communications for arrival to a specific runway at a specific airport.

Charlie obtains the Automatic Terminal Information (ATIS), computes landing performance data and transfers the information onto a landing performance card. ATIS is the continuous broadcast of essential information at busy airports including weather, active runways, available approaches and other important information.

The weather is perfect.

It is CAVU, meaning that the ceiling and visibility is unrestricted. (CAVU is a pilot's favorite acronym.)

The Memphis ATIS information reads whiskey: time—03:55; winds—010 degrees at 5 knots; visibility—better than ten miles, few clouds at 16,000 feet; temperature—17 degrees Celsius; dew point—12 degrees Celsius, altimeter—29.96 inches; ILS parallel approaches landing 36L, 36C, 36R and 27. Read back all holding instructions and advise you have information Whisky. In aviation, we use a phonetic code. 'A' is for Alpha, 'B' is for Bravo, 'C' is for Charlie, et cetera., and 'W' is for Whiskey. The flight is perfect.

So far.

## Adjustments—and a Problem

Indy Center informs us to contact Memphis Center on 136.25. We check in with Memphis Center. On the primary flight display instrument the projected descent arrow symbol appears. Like other pilots I call this symbol the A.O.H., the Arrow of Happiness. If you are on a long tiring flight and the projected descent arrow symbol appears, you become happy knowing that a descent to destination will begin soon, thus the Arrow of Happiness. The beginning of the end.

However, the center issues us a route and speed change.

"Turn right twenty degrees and slow to .78 mach. Maintain .78 Mach or less."

Jets fly at high speeds expressed in Mach numbers. Mach is the ratio of the speed of any object to the speed of sound. A jet flying at 2.0 Mach would be considered flying at twice the speed of sound.

"Roger right twenty degrees. Maintain .78 Mach or less."

I check the fuel, weather and all the jet's systems again, and then I start to brief Charlie on the Memphis LTOWN 6 RNAV STAR and the runway 36 Right approach. I load the ILS runway 36R approach into the Flight Management System primary flight plan and load the ILS runway 27 in the secondary flight plan. I start to brief Charlie on the particulars of the LTOWN 6 RNAV STAR.

After Bowling Green, we'll fly 240 degrees to the AXXEL Fix and plan on arriving there above flight level 240 and at an air speed of 290 knots. Then, we will cross SPKER between 14,000 feet and flight level 230, turn to 226 degrees to cross at LTOWN between 10,000 and 16,000 feet. Then, we will slow down to be at DAPLE at 250 knots. Cross DASAC between 9,000 and 11,000 feet, cross CLARK above 8,000 feet, and turn to 178 degrees, cross DIGLE above 6,000 feet and cross DINKE at 3,000 feet. After DINKE, expect radar vectors to HADAN for the visual approach backed up with the ILS approach to runway 36R. 36R LOC frequency is 111.35, the inbound course is 360 degrees and the category one barometric decision height is 540 feet.

Runway 36R is 9,000 feet long and 150 feet wide with an approach light configuration system number two and a Vertical Approach Sight Indicator on the right side. The Minimum Sector Altitude for our sector is 2,500 feet. In the event we have to go around the published Missed Approach Procedure for 36R is to fly 360 degrees, climb at 1,000 feet, and then turn to a heading of 070 degrees to intercept the Memphis VOR 117.5 040 degree radial. Then, proceed to OROCU and climb to 5,000 feet, enter the holding pattern at OROCU. If the landing goes as planned, I will exit the runway at taxiway S3, make a right turn onto S, and enter spot number ten entry point to proceed to parking spot 686 on the ramp.

"1340 cleared direct BWG, descend via the LTOWN 6 RNAV STAR, north transition, altimeter 29.96, resume normal speed, and contact Memphis Center 133.7."

The profile descent flight mode annunciator flashes, the auto throttles reduce to idle thrust speed setting and the auto pilot pitches the nose down to start the descent. Passing through 18,000 feet, we reset our altimeters to 29.96, turn the seatbelt sign and the landing lights on, and ensure that everyone has fastened their seatbelts and harnesses.

The in-range checklist is complete, the landing data and all aircraft systems have been checked—everything looks smooth and perfect.

Charlie contacts approach control and tells them we are descending via the LTOWN 6 arrival, north transition, we have ATIS info whisky and we are parking in entry spot number ten. Approach control instructs us to turn left twenty degrees, descend to 3,000 feet and expect runway 27.

Runway 27—great.

Landing on 27 versus 36 right will save us approximately four minutes air time and two minutes taxi time and about five hundred pounds of fuel. Five hundred pounds of fuel equates to seventy-five gallons of fuel, which is a savings of approximately $350.

We comply with the new clearance.

Things are starting to get really busy.

Even though we had a brief discussion that we may land on runway 27, our mindset and aircraft set was programmed to land on runway 36R.

We have lots of changes to accomplish.

I reach down to the center console pedestal and change the LOC frequency to 108.9 and the LOC approach course to 270 degrees. I then reach forward to the main instrument panel and change the barometric category to 500 feet. Charlie retrieves the secondary flight plan information and activates it. He makes several other adjustments to the Flight Management System, acquires an audible in Morse code to verify that we have selected the correct LOC frequency for runway 27. The LOC frequency is audibled in Morse code so that a skilled listener can detect a series of on-off signals to correctly identify a particular LOC. We complete the approach checklist.

Approaching 10,000 feet during the descent, I slow to 250 knots, which is almost 290 miles per hour. As required by FAA law, the maximum speed permitted below 10,000 feet is 250 knots. Approaching twenty miles from runway 27, I slow to 210 knots.

"Slats extend," I say.

Charlie puts his left hand on the slats/flaps handle and extends the slats.

"Slats extended," Charlie responds.

Slats and flaps are electrically controlled by a computer and hydraulically operated by motors. Slats and flaps help increase lift generated by the wings by changing the overall shape of the wing. The additional lift helps support the weight of the jet needed for safe operation and control at slower jet air speeds, as when taking off or landing. We are on an extended right base leg to runway 27.

"Flaps fifteen."

Charlie extends the flaps to the fifteen degree position.

"Flaps fifteen, set."

"1340, the field is at your one o'clock do you have the field in sight?" asks the controller.

On such a clear and perfect night, I have identified the Memphis aerodrome a few minutes ago. However, I look at Charlie.

"Do you have the field?" I ask him.

"Yes."

"Tell approach we have the field."

"1340 has the field in sight," Charlie tells the controller.

"1340, you are cleared for the visual approach runway 27. Contact tower on 120.9."

"Cleared for the visual runway 27 and switching to the tower 120.9. Good evening, Memphis tower. "1340 nine miles out for runway 27."

"1340, cleared to land runway 27."

"Roger, cleared to land runway 27."

I slow the jet's air speed to 170 knots.

"Flaps twenty," I say.

Charlie selects flaps to twenty.

But there's a problem.

The flaps do not extend to the twenty degree position; the indicator tells us they are not where they are supposed to be. Each wing is complex system of movable parts and includes three single-slotted, Fowler-type flap sections.

"Charlie, cycle the slats/flaps handle."

He cycles the handle to the previous flaps fifteen position and reselects the handle to the desired twenty-degree position.

We are hoping that the cycling of the slats/flaps handle will be successful so that we can continue with our normal operations and land.

But it doesn't work.

"What do you think, Charlie?"

"We have to complete the flaps stuck at less than twenty degrees checklist."

"Here's what we are going to do," I say. At this stage of the game, decisions need to be made quickly. "We are going to abort the approach, split up the cockpit duties and try to fix the flight control problem."

We accomplish the go-around procedure. I increase the jet's pitch attitude and thrust power setting. Charlie retracts the slats/flaps and landing gear and engages the autopilot and flight management navigation system. Charlie contacts Memphis tower.

"Memphis tower, this is 1340. We need to abort the approach due to a flight control problem."

"Roger, 1340. Fly runway heading to 3,000 feet and contact departure control on 122.9."

"Wilco 122.9."

'Wilco' simply means that I have received your instructions and will comply.

"I have the airplane and the radios."

Normally, the nonflying pilot operates the radio while the other pilot is flying the airplane.

"You work the ECAM."

ECAM is the jet's electronic centralized aircraft monitoring system. With these two commands, the cockpit duties are divided. Charlie and I are now operating in our own worlds.

There is an understanding that I will aviate, navigate, communicate and configure the jet's flight operations while Charlie executes and completes all the normal and abnormal checklist items. Charlie will update me on the aircraft conditions and the requirements and progress of all checklists he will need to accomplish. On the other hand, I will update him on the progress of the flight. I prioritize my four goals in order:

1. Land the jet safely.
2. Operate the jet legally without violating any federal laws.
3. Continue to provide a reliable service in order to deliver the packages to the customers.
4. Try to accomplish these tasks efficiently because I have a limited amount of fuel, which correlates directly to the amount of flight time remaining.

I check in with departure control.

"What is the problem and how can we be of assistance?" inquires departure control.

"We have a flap control problem, I am declaring an emergency. There are five souls on board, 12,000 pounds of fuel and no dangerous goods. We need fifteen to twenty minutes to run some checklists."

"Roger. Understand you are declaring emergency. Fly the published missed approach procedure, hold over GOWRI, and let us know when you are ready for the approach."

"1340 will fly the published missed approach, hold over GOWRI and get back to you."

The published missed approach is a written, preplanned set of instructions associated with a particular runway approach directing the pilot to follow particular turns and climbs to a designated safe position in the airspace. GOWRI is a holding fix located at a safe position away from terrain and other aircraft.

We are in the Memphis International Airport Airspace. Between 10 p.m. and 6 a.m., because of its use as a hub for FedEx and sorting point for millions of pounds of cargo every night, Memphis becomes the busiest airport in the world. Approximately 150 fifty planes will land, sometimes at an interval of only forty-five seconds between each landing. Our position is a five-letter name called GROWI, located 17 miles from Memphis airport at 5,000 feet. Once we arrive at GOWRI, we will fly a race track pattern.

"Memphis departure, 1340 entered holding at 43 minutes past the hour at 5,000 feet."

"Roger, 1340. Keep us informed of your status. Expect 36L."

While Charlie is executing all the checklist items, I am reprogramming the flight management system and the flight control panel for an approach to runway 36L. Charlie completes the flight control malfunction checklist and provides me with a status report.

"The flaps are stuck at fifteen degrees, the fuel consumption increases, the approach speed increases, the runway landing distance required for landing increases, and certain systems will be deactivated, like the auto throttle system."

Charlie computes and completes a performance landing data card.

"You have the airplane." I give the aircraft control to Charlie. He is now flying the jet, which allows me to be a better resource manager. I brief our situation and then I brief the approach to runway 36L to Charlie.

After executing the in-range and approach checklist again, I contact Memphis approach.

"Memphis approach, 1340 is ready for the approach."

"1340, turn to a heading of 180 degrees and descend to 2,000 feet."

The clearance is acknowledged. Charlie departs the holding pattern, turns to the 180 degree heading, and descends to 2,000 feet.

"1340, turn left to 090 degrees. The airport is at your ten o'clock position."

Charlie is doing a good job flying the jet. He turns the aircraft to the 90 degree heading, and I see runway 36L.

"Memphis approach, 1340 has the field in sight."

"You are cleared for the visual approach runway 36L. Contact tower on 120.9."

Charlie makes a turn to get established on the final approach course, and I contact Memphis tower.

"1340, you are cleared to land runway 36L."

I acknowledge the clearance and turn to Charlie.

"I have the airplane."

Charlie was doing a great job flying the jet but as a Captain, I am responsible for the safety of the jet and all souls on board. I want my hands and feet on the flight controls. I tell Charlie to extend the landing gear. I slow the aircraft to final approach speed. I disconnect the auto throttles and autopilot and I tell Charlie to execute the before-landing checklist.

Charlie checks landing lights on, auto brakes set, spoilers armed, the landing gear is down and the flaps are set. Of course, I scan and verify that all those tasks are completed correctly. This jet has a radar altimeter system that measures the height above ground and at 1,000 feet, the jet's cockpit computer calls out "1,000."

Looking outside toward the runway 36L, I notice the picture is different from what I normally visualize. Because of the flight control abnormality, we are landing with less than normal flaps and we are flying at a faster approach speed. Therefore, I must maintain a higher-than-normal aircraft pitch attitude in order to fly a standard vertical flight path. To compensate for this illusion, I study the aircraft instruments and rely mostly on those instrument readings until I get within a few hundred feet above the ground. At five hundred feet above the ground, the jet's computer calls out "500."

At this elevation, it is mandatory that various performance factors be stabilized and not allowed to vary significantly. Charlie is monitoring my work. He is double-checking that the aircraft is configured correctly, the engine power setting is appropriate, the air speed is appropriate, the vertical and lateral flight path is appropriate and that all briefings and checklists are accomplished.

He is satisfied with the results.

"Stable, cleared to land runway 36L."

I start my transition from looking mainly inside at the cockpit instruments to looking outside at the real world and the runway itself.

I start increasing aileron inputs and rudder inputs to compensate for wind drift and to maintain runway alignment.

"100."

I make slight control and thrust inputs to maintain proper flight attitude and runway alignment.

"50."

I start transitioning my eyes from the target landing point to a point further down the runway.

"40."

With my peripheral vision, I capture the ground rising up. The nearness of the ground will help improve the aerodynamic efficiency of the jet.

"30."

I slowly pull back just a little bit on the aircraft control yoke and just a little bit on the thrust levers, just enough to decrease the rate of descent.

"20."

I am looking down the runway, slowly increasing the aircraft pitch attitude and slowly reducing the thrust power. I adjust the aileron and rudder inputs accordingly.

"10."

I maintain the landing pitch attitude while reducing the thrust power to idle. The main wheels, which are located more than seventy feet behind me, touch the runway surface. Releasing the aft yoke pressure, I lower the aircraft nose so that the nose wheel meets the runway surface.

The jet is no longer airborne.

I engage the reverse thrust, the spoilers deploy and the auto brakes engage.

The jet is slowing down.

I slow the jet to a taxi speed of around 15 knots (about 17 miles per hour) and exit the runway. I command Charlie to do the after-landing checklist, and he complies.

"1340, contact ground control on 121.7," instructs Memphis tower.

"Wilco. Ground control, 1340, clear of runway 36L on taxiway Mike 7."

"1340, cleared to taxi Mike, Zulu, Victor to the ramp."

We taxi to the gate, complete the shutdown checklist, and I debrief Charlie.

The aircraft mechanic approaches me.

"How's the aircraft? Any problems?"

If there were no mechanical problems to report, I sometimes jokingly respond, "Yeah, the attitude is all messed up on the Captain's side. I didn't write it up. In fact, I'll take care of it myself."

No jokes this time. There was a flight control problem with the flaps, so I write up the problem in the aircraft logbook and debrief the mechanic.

Charlie and I hop on the flight crew bus, which will transport us to our flight operation center. Within the next four hours, the packages will be removed from all the arriving aircraft, re-sorted at the hub facility, and loaded back onto the appropriate departing aircraft.

On average, 1.5 million packages weighting about 10 million pounds are off loaded from the fleet of FedEx planes in Memphis. About 10,000 workers will remove the packages, scan each package with a bar-code label system, and re-sort the cargo through a package sorting matrix at a rate of 2,500 items per hour.

Then, those packages will be reloaded onto the appropriate departing aircraft. The fleet of airplanes will deliver those packages to more than 220 countries and territories on six continents. Within the next 24 to 48 hours, over 90 percent of the global economy will be serviced by FedEx.

The crew bus stops, I say to the driver, "That was such a good ride, I'm coming back to get another one."

I get off the bus and walk into the flight operations crew room where there are more than 400 pilots. Pilots are talking to pilots, telling good stories and not-so-good stories.

It always feels good to be on the ground, but particularly after you've had a challenging moment in the sky.

I believe in safety—live first. It is better to tell a bad, embarrassing story than to die and not be able to tell a story at all. I have landed the plane safely on the ground, and that is all that matters.

## Transition

This is where the book transitions from a pilot's autobiography to a self-help book on family, money, religion, the body and soul.

My vision is that this book would provide the details of my career as an aviator and offer survival tools that might help my sons succeed through life.

After witnessing death and after almost dying myself ten times, I know that I would not always be there for my sons.

It's my hope that this book will enlighten them on what I accomplished, who I am and how the lessons I learned might help them get through life—and improve their lives.

As the author and publisher, I have made every effort to ensure that the information in this book is correct, but I do not assume and hereby disclaim any liability to any party for any loss, damage, or disruption caused by errors or omissions, whether such errors or omissions result from negligence, accident, or any other cause.

This book is not intended as a substitute for any professional advice on any subject matter discussed. The reader should consult a professional for advice in any of the topics throughout this book. I am not a child specialist, psychiatrist, certified money manager or planner, a holy religious leader, a physician or a lawyer.

I am just a pilot. But pilots, as I've noted, have a unique skill set that might prove valuable. It's in that spirit that I share the following reflections on a host of issues in hopes that it helps provide the reader with a flight plan to improve your life.

# CHAPTER 9
# Family Schooling

*L*ove your wife and children.

You will never make enough money and you will never have enough time off. Your son will not remember the $100 baseball mitt you bought him, but he will remember the time you spent playing catch.

Love them as much and as often as you can, and then spend as much time as you can with them.

**Funny Lines**

When my wife was pregnant with our first child, I said to her "I don't care what you have, I'm taking a boy home from the hospital, and I'm gonna name him Francis."

When my first-born was about a year-and-a-half old, one day I came home from a trip and walked in the door.

"Hi, Daddy," my son said. He ran into the kitchen and brought me a beer and said "here."

"What's this for?" I asked.

"That's what you always want when you come home."

**Love Line**

I was cutting the grass with my youngest son on the riding mower. The drive belt broke and I sighed. I was stressed out, didn't need to spend time on a repair. My son, sitting in front of me, turned around and gave me a big kiss.

"What's that for?" I asked.

"You're having a bad day, Daddy. You need some loving."

## Scary Times

Your child will test your wits, make you worry to almost death, and you will learn to pray—like the time our child fell on his head. He was acting uncharacteristically lethargic and he didn't want to eat. We wanted to keep him awake because if he fell asleep with a head injury, he might slip into a coma. Well, on the way to the hospital, he fell asleep.

Or like the time when I lifted my son out of the shopping cart to try on a potential new pair of sneakers and, at only two years old, he ran away. It was a fun game to him. I was worried sick, especially when it took me over ten minutes to locate him in Wal-Mart.

Then there are the colds, flus, viruses, ear infections, surgeries, and all of those sports injuries. To top things off, once they start driving automobiles, you will not be able to sleep until they arrive home safe and sound.

Children will scare the hell out of you, bring tremendous worry and make you real mad, but they will also enlighten your heart with the most enjoyable, loving experiences and memories. And let's face it—when you are old and grey and on your death bed, your children are the only people that may care about you.

It is like the balance of life; those with the greatest pleasures also experience the greatest pain. Rose Kennedy's son became the president of the United States and her son was shot to death.

If it wasn't for caffeine and alcohol I would not have made it through parenthood!

## Good Sportsmanship

My oldest was about nine years old, and at the end of a soccer game, the ballplayers would usually line up, shake each other's hands, and say something like, "good game."

In this particular game, which we won with a score of seven to one, the referee came up to me and inquired as to who was the parent of player number nine. Knowing number nine was my son, I said, "What is the problem?"

The referee told me that the number nine player had said to each of the players from the other team, "You suck, you suck." Well, after a few explanations, I made my son run around the soccer field three times for his poor sportsmanship. Win or lose, it is just a game. Thank your opponent, thank your coach, and yes, thank the referee.

One year, we had the best soccer team in the league. It wasn't because we had the best soccer players, but we had the best coach—me. Like most teams, we had a few very athletic players and few who weren't so athletic and many who were average.

But we became a great team.

From the start of the season, I distributed diagrams I drew up that displayed the soccer field and all the soccer positions. There were diagrams displaying where each player should be—when we had the ball, when the opposing team had the ball, when corner kicks were made by each team, when throw-ins were made by each team, when penalty kicks were made, and when the kick-off was made to start the game. During each practice, I would teach one or two new skills, review a few diagrams on the field, and conduct skill-training drills.

From my experience I found that it was important to limit each drill to a maximum of six to eight minutes (or else the kids got bored). I also worked to make the drills fun and make them relevant to the soccer game that they would play each week.

For instance, the Three-on-Two Drill consisted of three offensive players trying to score against two defending players. If offense scored, then they would stay on the field and the two defendants would be replaced. If defense prevented a score or stole the ball, then the defense would choose two of the offensive players to replace. This makes for a fun—and competitive—drill. (I have used this drill in basketball practice as well.)

After the drills were complete, I allowed at least twenty minutes for scrimmage time. The ballplayers loved scrimmage time because it's similar to a game. To start the scrimmage, I would call out each player by name and assign him to a position such as left fullback, right forward, or center midfielder. If that person knew his position and played that position accurately, he was awarded a small piece of candy, to eat later. If that person made three passes during scrimmage, then he was also awarded a small piece of candy.

Note: I did not give out candy for goals scored. By awarding candy to these six-year-olds, it motivated each player to learn the various soccer positions and to play team ball by passing the ball to each other. As the season progressed, I eventually weaned the players off the candy award system.

After scrimmage, we practiced a little penalty shoot-out against the goalie. Every person on the team was offered goalie time so that when game time came, all my players knew their positions, and each player played half of their game time on offense and half of their game time on defense. Each player on the team had to try playing the goalie position for at least a half a game.

As we played various other teams, all my players went to their respective positions, played their positions accordingly, executed their drills from practice, and most importantly, passed the ball. We had beaten every team in the league, and I had made arrangements to play the best team in another league. During that game, we had three goals to their two goals at half time. My son Jared and I agreed to have him play goalie in the second half in order to lock up the final win and keep us undefeated. Then, Johnny approached me about playing goalie. Johnny was the only player on my team who never played goalie during game time. In all of the previous games, Johnny was too afraid to try the goalie position, but now he had the courage and nerve to try. Jared displayed good sportsmanship and relinquished the goalie gloves and the goalie position to Johnny.

We lost the game, 4 to 3. But in my mind, we won the game because Johnny finally experienced playing goalie. Jared and I knew that if Jared had played goalie, we would have prevented those two goals and would have won the game. But sportsmanship was more important.

Both boys played soccer from age five to around age thirteen. Both boys swam on the Alanton Bolts swim team from age five to around age thirteen. Both boys played basketball from age six through their senior year in high school. Both boys practiced Taekwondo for three years. Both boys have been skiing and snowboarding since around age six and surfing since around age thirteen. Francis also played four years of high school football and lacrosse and he also swam and ran some track. Jared also played five years of high school lacrosse and four years of high school track. Jared played seven years of baseball and four years of football. In fact, at one time, during five consecutive Saturdays, Jared played midfielder in a soccer game in the morning, played quarterback in a football game in the midday and played shortstop in a baseball game in the afternoon. In high school, Francis would swim before school to keep in shape to play basketball after school. Jared has been playing guitar since around age thirteen and was involved with the Future Leaders of America in Washington, D.C. Francis competed in Odyssey of the Mind for two years.

My wife, the CEO of the home, and I encouraged and supported these activities. I coached and/or co-coached 12 years of basketball and soccer and a few years of baseball. You ask "how did we make it through all those years?" I say "alcohol, caffeine and prayers!"

In fact, one time, we had to travel to Niagara Falls, New York to participate in the Regional Soccer Tournament consisting of 512 soccer teams. My son asked me if I was ever in a soccer tournament with 512 teams. "Francis, when I was your age, there weren't 512 soccer teams in this country," I told him.

Both boys made many great and memorable plays in various sporting events, and although neither son obtained a college scholarship or wanted to pursue a sports career, we kept those boys in physical and mental shape—and too busy to get into trouble.

Playing sports helped the boys manage their time. They learned when to play and when to do homework. Sports also help develop teamwork and leadership skills for use later in life. Whether you own a company or work for a company, there will be a goal or mission statement that everyone will be working together to achieve—and rules with consequences resulting in success or failure. Sports help develop the motor skills, strategic thinking, and mental discipline to succeed in achieving your personal goals in life. Playing sports helps reduce physical and mental stress, which every human being unavoidably incurs throughout life. Had a bad day? Go for a run or a swim—or play some ball. Believe me, it will help. Physical exercise helps to cleanse the body of the toxins we consume—the toxins from unhealthy foods and bad drinks.

## Friends and Family

You cannot choose your kids' family members—brothers, sisters, aunts, uncles, and cousins will mate and choose mates. You probably shouldn't choose your kids' friends, but you can manipulate the environment in which your children will choose their friends. If your children are in an environment where the other children are hateful and routinely disregard all rules, laws, and commandments, then do what you can to move to a better place or move them into an environment where most of the children love God, themselves, and everyone. You can quote me, *it is better to have no friends than to have bad friends.*

## Spoiling Children

To spoil or not to spoil your children—that is the question. It is our inherent, human nature to give to our children more than what we had when we were at their age. But how do you decide when to say yes and when to say no? When my eldest was still a baby, he would wake up in the middle of the night wanting a bottle of milk. My loving wife wanted to arise out of bed to oblige him his request, and I was grasping my wife's arm to keep her in bed.

"Let him cry a little bit and he will fall back asleep and wean himself off that nighttime milk-bottle snack."

Mothers naturally will do everything and anything to provide for and protect their offspring. Naturally, fathers want to teach and shape their offspring so that they can be independent survivors someday. If one of my sons left his gym bag at home, and as a result, would not be able to participate in gym class that day—then if my wife was home, she would bring the gym bag to school for him. If I was home, I would not bring the gym bag to school for him. Who was right and who was wrong? When do you say yes and when do you say no? Does little Johnny deserve a toy to play with? Yes. Does little Johnny deserve to have all the best toys to play with? I don't know. She says yes he says no. Mother and father should try to meet on the same page because a child will detect dissimilarities and try to take advantage of one of the parents. Maybe parents can compromise and set limits and establish boundaries.

## Discipline

As a parent I had to learn to mold and correct my children to enhance their mental and moral character. Every child is different, and some children require various and aggressive techniques to help them conform. These are some of the discipline strategies I have learned to use with my boys. Maybe they'll help you.

### Use "No" Sparingly
*Use "no" only a few times a day with a different I-mean-it tone of voice. A child who is told "no" a lot will usually get into more trouble than a child who is in child-proof house where he can explore with fewer restrictions.*[41]

### Use a Positive Approach
Stoop down and obtain eye contact before you tell him what you want him to do. Use the phrases "you need to" and "you may not." For example, use "the lamp needs to stay on the table" instead of "don't touch the lamp."[42]

### Distract Him
Offer alternatives; move him away from things he cannot have and closer to his toys.

### Give Him a Choice
For example, "It's time to go to bed. Which bedtime story would you like me to read?" "Do you want lunch outside or inside your high chair?" Either way you win, your child eats lunch and goes to bed.

### Reinforce Behaviors You Like
Positive attention from significant persons makes learning more meaningful and important. Praise works much better than punishment. If he's earning your attention and companionship when he's behaving the way you want him to behave, he'll probably continue doing those things that draw the attention he craves. If he seems to obtain attention mostly through being naughty, he'll probably act naughty more often.[43]

### Provide Reward
Finding ways to help your child want to cooperate is much more logical than setting out to prove who is in charge. Everyone enjoys receiving compliments. Many times the best reward is telling him that he did a good job and you're proud of him (versus "you're a good boy"). By recognizing his ability to do the task and do it well, you help him feel competent. He'll feel able to learn even more.[44] You can say this simple phrase to you children regardless of their age (age 2, 22

or 62), "I am very proud of you for_____." It is amazing how good it feels when someone says this to you.

### Time Out May Help

Time out need not be spent without any activity; it can be time spent resting, or with a quiet activity away from noise and excitement or other stimulation. The goal is not to punish the child, but to help and support him so that he can get back to within the parameter of acceptable behavior.

### 1-2-3 Count Time Out:

*Parent:* "No, son, I am not going to buy you that candy bar—put it back. If you do not put the candy bar back, then when we get home, you will earn six minutes of time-out."
*Child:* "But I want the candy."
*Parent:* "One."
*Child:* "Please, can I have just one candy bar?"
*Parent:* "Two."
*Child:* "Please?"

If the child does not put the candy bar back by the time you say "Three," then he gets awarded the time-out. For most rule-breakers, give the child a minute of time-out per age. (Six-year-old children get six minutes.) Of course, the rules must be explained to the child beforehand, and the parent must stick to their word and execute the punishment if, upon reaching the count of "three," the child does not comply.[45] Sometimes it is best to include the child in deciding on the appropriate consequences for not behaving appropriately. For example, to prevent your child from messing around and not spending the appropriate allocated time to complete homework, you could say, "Crystal Marie, what do you think your punishment should be if you don't finish your homework before game time?"

### Give Warning Before an Activity Change

"We're going to leave in five minutes." Your child wants to know what is going to happen, so to make a smooth transition from one activity to another, provide warning. This gives your child some courtesy and time to prepare. When your child is in the middle of an activity like playing, say to her:

> *Parent:* "Crystal Marie, in five minutes we're going to leave and it will be time to stop playing."
> *Child:* "But, Mom?"

> *After five minutes has elapsed then say:*

> *Parent:* "It is time to leave, stop playing, and let's go."
> *Child:* "Okay, Mommy."

### Child-Proof the Environment

Lack of child-proofing is the basis for many discipline problems with toddlers. If the child spills milk on the floor, then have the child clean up, or at least help clean up. This way the child is able to see how difficult it is to clean up. The child is much more likely to learn from his or her mistakes if the concern and angry feelings are focused on the action. If the anger is focused on the child, and the child is told he or she is a bad person, the child will be crying and miserable. The child will not be receptive to learning. The child will feel alienated, unloved and unworthy. The child will be harder to reach and to teach. Initially, we did not child-proof our kitchen cabinets. One day there was our precious little child in the middle of the kitchen floor with all the pots and pans scattered all over on the floor. Little precious said, "Hi mommy, I am going to help you cook." After this moment, I got on my hands and knees and ventured throughout the house to put cabinet locks on those cabinet doors and to child-proof the rest of the house.

### *Learning from Mistakes*

Focus anger on the action, not the child. Punishment causes a child to turn angry, hurt feelings either inward on himself or outward toward the person who punished him. When little attention is focused on the action—why it is wrong or what should be done about it, then little is accomplished and there is more anger as a result. Anger doesn't help anyone. Understanding what he has done wrong, realizing the real consequences of the act, and then helping to make things right again will do more to help the child behave correctly than any punishment possibly could.

Using discipline strategies to help him behave appropriately will make child rearing much more effective than the punishment to force him to follow your wishes. With your discipline strategies, you not only help him learn self-control, you support his self-confidence. You give him self-respect.

Discipline is not easy. Some children are easy going and they like to abide by the rules. These children can be more manageable to guide through life. Some children are strong-willed, consistently wanting to test the boundaries. These children can be a challenge to guide through life. Parents will have to identify the right technique for each child. Discipline is an extremely important and often difficult part of child rearing. It takes an unbelievable amount of common sense, patience, practice and love. It also takes a deep desire on your part to help your child learn self-discipline as a first step toward becoming a responsible, independent adult. *Discipline begins with your relationship with your child.*[46] You have been developing this relationship since your child was born. If you have a good relationship, he wants to please you just as you want to please him. You want to do things to make him feel good. Above all, good discipline demands an unending supply of love! Stoop down, put your hands on their shoulders, get eye-to-eye contact and tell your child, *I love you more than you can possibly understand. You are precious to me, and I thank*

*God every day that He gave me the opportunity to let me raise you. Because I love you, I must teach you to obey me. That is the only way I can take care of you and protect you from things that might hurt you.*[47]

## Teenagers

Parenting during the "terrible-two's" stage and the teenage stage were my least favorite memories of parenting. When your child enters that period of years in which rapid physical growth and psychological changes occur, their hormone levels, emotions, and attitudes change drastically. They are now teenagers, and they know it all.

I sometimes wonder if teenagers get so fed up with being harassed by their stupid parents that it might be time for them to leave home, get a job, and pay their own way while they still know everything. The verbal battle of what the parent expects from the teenager and what the teenager wants to do can evolve into a daily nightmare.

A more realistic approach, however, might be to have them sign contracts. Getting an agreement in writing is one way of letting the teenager know you are serious. The following are examples of contracts I have used. Parents may need to modify and revise each contract to meet the needs and circumstances of each student and parent.

### HIGH SCHOOL CONTRACT sample

*In this contract between Junior Son, the student, and Mr. Dad and Mrs. Mom, the parents:*

*Junior Son hereby understands that XYZ Public, Parochial or Private High School will provide a college preparatory education, which nurtures the intellect, shapes character, and forms values. Junior Son understands that this provision comes at a great cost and sacrifice of time and money on the parts of his parents and the community.*

*Junior Son understands and agrees to abide by the school discipline policies and procedures; to be dressed and prepared for school at 7:15 AM; and that he will put in the necessary time and effort to obtain grades of "A" or "B" in all subjects.*

*Junior Son understands and agrees that he will be compensated X amount of dollars for each "B" subject grade, Y amount of dollars for each "A" subject grade and an additional Z amount of dollars if the "B" or "A" grade is in an A.P. or Honors class; and furthermore, if he obtains a grade lower than "C" for any reason in any subject, he is entitled to no payment for the other grades and Junior Son will lose all privileges, such as computer, T.V., cell phone, going out, playing sports, and any other privileges his parents choose to withdraw from him.*

*We understand that this contract is a binding obligation. We have read the contract carefully, understand the contract and do hereby agree to these terms.*

_____, Student  (Date)_____

_____, Parent  (Date)_____

Some parents will find it controversial to pay for academic achievement. Teenagers for a variety of reasons need money while they are in high school. Their precious social life can be more important than good school grades and a job for income, but they do need money while in high school. A high school contract offers students the chance to use their precious high school time to apply themselves to achieve above-average grades in return for the money they need. Notice there is no compensation for a "C" grade. According to me, a "C" grade is just average work for a high school student. In my opinion any student that shows up for every class, completes all assigned homework and studies the material on a daily basis should be capable of earning at least a "C" grade or higher in each subject matter. If a student cannot obtain at least an average grade then maybe the parent may have to get more involved and provide support to help that student in obtaining the necessary learning experience required for that particular subject.

Each student (and child) is different. During a conversation on striving for your best with one of my sons, he replied, "Dad, you want straight A's? I can get straight A's if I want to, but I have a life." At the time he was playing five sports, working part time, socializing and complying with the terms of his high school contract. What could I say? Modify the terms of the contract to meet the needs and circumstances for parent and student but remember high school students will need money.

A teenager may say anything to get out of school and anything to get into a car. One option is for the parent to buy that first vehicle. This puts the parent in the position to get a really safe vehicle, which I believe is the most important factor. At age 17, I self-financed and purchased my first car, a 1972 Chevelle Malibu, for $1,000 and purchased my own car insurance under my own name for $460. That Chevelle Malibu was probably not the safest car for a 17-year-old to operate. If the parent does provide that first car, have the teenager sign a driving contract.

One option is for the parent to obtain an umbrella insurance policy, add the new driver onto their auto insurance and have the new driver pay for his portion of the policy. In the driving contract you can stipulate that the driver will be responsible for the cost of maintenance, the cost of gasoline or whatever works for your situation.

### DRIVING CONTRACT sample

*I, Junior Son, agree to the stipulations stated below, granting me the privilege of driving an automobile. If, at any time, I violate this agreement, the driving privilege will be forfeited to the extent and degree of violation.*

*1. Should I get a traffic violation ticket, I agree to immediately tell my parents and to pay for the ticket as well as the difference in the insurance premium for as long as the premium is in effect.*

*2. I agree to pay for the automobile insurance and damages that I incur that are not covered by insurance.*

*3. At no time will I drive after drinking alcoholic beverages, nor will there be any alcoholic beverages in the car at any time.*

*4. I agree to obey all traffic laws including: speed, signs, signals, no texting, et cetera.*

*5. At no time will I ride in a vehicle with a driver who has been drinking alcoholic beverages.*

*6. I will always buckle up and will not drive until all passengers have buckled up.*

*7. I agree to pay for the cost of gas and maintenance on the vehicle.*

*8. I will keep the car that I drive clean, inside and out, and be aware of its needs for gas, oil, et cetera. I have been briefed on the importance of regularly changing the oil according to the maintenance schedule for the vehicle.*

*I, Mr. Parent, agree to the stipulations stated below:*

*1. As the parent, I reserve the right to revoke your driving privileges any time you display bad driving habits, incur a traffic violation, or engage in any reckless behaviors.*

*2. As the parent, I agree to come and get you at any time, without question, if you are in an unsafe or uncomfortable situation—with the understanding that the matter will be discussed at a later time. If for some reason I cannot get you I will pay for a cab service to transport you home or to a safe place.*

*3. Additional Stipulations between Parent and Teenager:*

_____

_____

_____

_____

_____

Teen Driver_____ (Date)_____

Parent/Guardian_____ (Date)_____

## College Years

After surviving through those first-time driving years and those high school years, the 18- or 19-year-old teenager may want to go to trade school or college. Graduating from a college or a university does not guarantee financial success. Bill Gates of Microsoft did not finish college. However, statistics show that an undergraduate will earn an average annual salary of almost double that of a high school graduate. The cost for college tuition, books, room, board and fun can be very expensive and a financial challenge for most people. Some feel the financial contributions of savings, loans, grants and scholarships should include the student, the parent and the university. If there is a will there is a way and a motivated student can find a way to finance higher education. I believe any motivated person can work for minimum wage and self-finance a two-year degree at a local community college school. Then that motivated person, with the help of loans and grants, can transfer to a state college to obtain a bachelor's degree. As a parent wanting my sons to obtain at least an undergraduate degree, I started saving funds for them from the time they were born. For over 18 years per child, my wife and I sacrificed certain "wants" to save towards this goal.

We explained to each college-bound child that we would contribute the equivalent amount of the cost for tuition, books, room and board for a four year program at a state school. If they choose to attend an out-of-state university or a private university—or if they took longer than four years to obtain an undergraduate degree—that was fine by us. However, they would have to finance any difference in cost. The college student would also be obligated to finance their college cost for auto insurance, fuel for their cars and extracurricular activities. Daddy and mommy will not pay for college parties.

It is beneficial to create a contract that fits the needs and situation of the parent and student. For instance, in this contract varsity basketball and lacrosse were examples of previous success that our sons had in high school. If the student is not doing well and cannot comply with the contract, then take him out of college. The better option is to bring your child home and put him to work until he figures out what he wants to do with his life.

Remember in 1984 I was twenty three years old when I got the opportunity to go to ERAU as a full time student. At age eighteen I was not mature enough to attend a university and I surely would not have completed fifty four college credit hours in that first year.

### COLLEGE CONTRACT sample

*Dear Junior Son, Our Son and College-bound Student:*

*Junior Son, we hope you understand that college will broaden and deepen your knowledge in a range of subjects and develop higher-order skills such as critical thinking, writing, and researching. College is a place where you will learn more about things that interest you and help you to lay the foundations for a personal philosophy of life. College education will enable you to get training for a specific career, make more money, and secure a well-paying job. On average, high school grads earn around X thousand dollars per year, undergraduate college grads earn almost double, about 2xX thousand dollars per year and graduate college grads earn almost triple around 3xX thousand dollars per year.*

*In this contract between Junior Son, the college student, and, Mr. Dad and Mrs. Mom, the parents:*

**Junior Son understands that this provision comes at a great cost and sacrifice of time and money on the parts of his parents, and that his parents will give Junior Son this gift of the cost of a college education under the following terms:**

*Furthermore, Junior Son, we do not believe it is fair as part of our college gift to you for us to pay for grades lower than a "C" grade or equivalent. Junior Son understands and agrees to abide to University of XYZ's school discipline policies and procedures; to be prepared for each college course; to manage his time appropriately; to live as a responsible adult; to not incur any financial debt, including credit card debt; and to put in the necessary time and effort to obtain grades of "A" or "B" in all subjects.*

*Therefore, Junior Son understands and agrees that if he obtains a grade lower then "C" for any reason in any course, he is financially responsible to pay for that course. The cost for fall semester is X dollars per credit or approximately XYZ dollars per course. Junior Son will have to obtain a job, a student loan, and/or sell assets to pay for any and all courses in which he does **not** receive at least a "C" grade or equivalent. We know you are capable of at least average work. We believe and hope that if you find a field that you have a passion for and put the hard work and effort into that field, like you did for your XYZ High School Varsity basketball or lacrosse team, you will be **very** successful.*

*We understand that this contract is a binding obligation. We have read the contract carefully, understand the contract, and do hereby agree to these terms.*

*Your parents wish the best for you and will always be there to support and help you. We have of lot time, money, and prayers invested in you. Make us proud!*

*God bless and good luck in college.*

*Junior Son, student:* _____
*Date:* _____

*Dad:* _____
*Date:*_____

*Mom:*_____
*Date:*_____

## College Talk

When your child is ready to leave home for the military or college, you will not be able to discuss everything, mainly because the collegiate-bound student may only comprehend two or three subject-matter sentences. You can talk with him about: leaving home; what to take to college; living on campus in a dorm; roommates, sex, drugs and alcohol; which classes to take; what major to choose; when and how to study, proper sleep and nutrition; money management; time management; choosing friends; keeping in touch with the family, et cetera, but it is too much for them. Narrow your preaching down to a brief, appropriate speech.

"Son, have your fun, but remember you're going to college to get an education (not just a social one, but an academic one), so absorb all the knowledge you can from that school. Manage your time and your life, and define who you are yourself. Your parents wish the best for you and will always be there to support you. We love you. Make us proud!"

## Walk the walk

Don't just "talk the talk," "walk the walk."

Your child may or may not be listening to you, but bet your last dollar your child is watching you. Say "yes, no, please, thank you," hug with meaning, and say "I love you." Go to church early, get on your knees and pray and participate in the ceremony. Demonstrate respect, do not leave church until after the preacher has finished the ceremony. Be charitable and help others by donating time and money. While driving, use your turn signals, don't speed, obey traffic signals and do not text while driving. If you go to a party and you are the driver, do not drink alcoholic beverages. If you want to drink, arrange for a designated driver.

You can talk all you want, but believe me, they are watching you like a hawk and deducting "if Dad can do it, I can do it."

It takes a good eight to 22 years per child to build a good family, and just when you think you have it satisfactorily built, your child leaves home and starts his or her own family.

CHAPTER 10

# Money Schooling

*People who look for easy money invariably pay the privilege of proving conclusively that it cannot be found on this sordid earth.*
—Larry Livingston, as quoted in *Reminiscences of a Stock Operator* by Edwin Lefevre

**Money**

Money is currency, a coin, a dollar bill, a banknote or any token used as medium of exchange and stamped by state authority. Get money to pay for life necessities such as food, water, clothing, and so on. Keep it simple. Live below your means and invest the difference. Formulate and write down a plan that applies to your situation. Plan, save, and invest towards short-term and long-term goals. First accumulate cash, then bonds, then stocks and other assets.

**Cash**

You need to get cash in a bank, credit union or money jar first for any possible future emergencies. Do not live from paycheck to paycheck. First, figure out what your monthly "nut" is. Your "nut" is the minimum amount of money you need every month to survive. If you do not know what your "nut" is, then track and save receipts for each expenditure you make for a month. This is your monthly "nut." It should include the first 10 percent or 20 percent of your gross paycheck to save and invest. Pay yourself first. You cannot afford to pay anyone until you pay yourself first. Your monthly "nut" should include food and water, room and board, utilities, charity, any financial commitments (i.e.: loans, debts, insurance, et cetera), entertainment, and other miscellaneous items. Take that figure times six months (i.e.: if you need $3000 a month to survive, then you must have $18,000 worth of savings ($3,000 per month times six months = $18,000). Put this money in a very safe place like a high-yielding mutual fund money market account or credit union savings account. I have used the Vanguard Group money market account and the Air Line Pilots Federal Credit Union savings account but there are many others to choose from. Do not ever spend this money; this is your emergency money. If you lose your job or have a medical emergency, at least you could live for six months on this money. This is your *emergency fund*, your last resort reserve. If you have to spend some of your *emergency money*, then replenish it as soon as possible. If your monthly debt increases, then you must increase your *emergency fund*. After you accumulate your required emergency cash fund, then pay off all unnecessary debts. You should only borrow money to buy a needed home, an education to increase future income, a car for transport to employment to produce income, or to invest in your own business.

## Bonds

After you get cash, you need to start a bond fund. Figure out what your net worth (NW) is. Your net worth is what would be left over if you sold everything you owned and paid off everyone you owed. If you have a negative NW, stop here until you change your financial situation and get a positive NW. Take your age and divide it by two to get the percentage of the net worth you should put into your bond fund.

For instance, if you have a $10,000 net worth and you are 30 years old, the formula would look like this: Age 30 divided by 2 = 15 percent; 15 percent of $10,000 should be put into a bond fund, this case $1,500. If you are 60 years old, you would put in 30 percent of your NW, or $3,000. And if you are 90 years old, you would put in 45 percent of your NW, or $4500.

On a yearly basis around your birthday, adjust the amount you need to put into your bond fund, adjusting for age and net worth changes. To keep it simple, just put your bond money into a total bond mutual fund or total bond index (like maybe Vanguard's VBTIX or BND).

## Stocks

Once you have your emergency fund, a positive net worth, and a bond fund, then you can start investing in stocks, or stock mutual funds or stock market indexes. Read the book "The Intelligent Investor" by Benjamin Graham. Warren Buffett studied under Ben Graham's philosophy and became one of the all-time most successful investors. There are many other investment books to read—thousands of investment books. However, "The Intelligent Investor" is probably the best book to start with. After reading this book, if you're not willing to be an active investor by putting the time and effort into investing in stocks (which requires research, reading balance sheets and graphs, studying individual companies and their management, financials, products, services and prospects, et cetera) then become a passive investor and buy the whole stock market. *The best way to own common stocks is through an index fund.*[48]—Warren Buffett. You can buy into the whole stock market and the international stock market with a few thousand dollars through a total stock market mutual fund, a total stock market index fund or an exchange traded fund (ETF). Vanguard has a Total Stock Market Index fund (VTSMX or the ETF=VTI) and the Total International Stock Market Index fund (VGTSX or the ETF=VXUS). There are many other mutual fund companies besides Vanguard. I choose to invest with Vanguard 25 years ago because they are a low-cost mutual fund company.

"How much do I invest?" If you are age thirty, then 30/2=15 percent of your net worth goes into your bond fund and 85 percent of your net worth goes into your stock fund. (At 60 years old, put 70 percent of NW into stocks; at age 90 put 55 percent into stocks). On a yearly basis around your birthday, adjust the amount you need to put into your stock fund, adjusting for age and net worth changes.

You can dollar cost average your investment amounts into your bond and stock funds. When you dollar cost average, have the monthly investment amount (i.e.: $50.00 or $100.00 per month) automatically deducted from your checking account. Whenever you get a pay raise, increase your monthly investment amount. If you don't see it in your take home paycheck, you cannot spend it. For example, if you are age thirty, make $50,000 per year and save $500 per month, you may want to dollar cost average seventy-five dollars per month (15 percent) into the VBTIX fund (or BND ETF), $150.00 dollars per month (30 percent) into the VGTSX fund (or VTI ETF) and $275 per month (55 percent) into the VTSMX fund or (VXUS ETF).

If you prefer to pick stocks yourself, you can simplify your investment strategy by researching and following ten companies and investing in five companies. One company may disappoint you, two or three companies may do average or above-average, and one company may surprise you. All it takes is one or two companies to grow a small investment into a large amount (i.e.: AAPL, BRK, FDX, GOOG, MSFT, et cetera).

I recommend you dollar cost average into these two index funds for a few years until you get a *base investment fund* of say $25,000, $50,000, or $100,000. In the meantime, you can research and invest on paper without actually having to invest real money. After you have your emergency fund and your base investment fund, you can venture into picking your own stocks or buy *other assets* such as real estate, commodities, gold, coins, artwork, diamonds, oil, farmland, et cetera, or maybe start or buy your own business. But just like playing poker, never invest more than 10 percent of your total assets on one idea.

The goal is to stay in the game. You always want to have some portion of investment money to invest in an idea. If you put all your money in one idea and that idea doesn't work out, you get wiped out and don't get to play anymore. *However, you must invest!* Investing is the only way the average guy can get ahead in the long term. Keep in mind it can take years of financial discipline to build up a large investment fund base, and in just a short time, one stupid mistake can wipe you out. If you don't understand the investment, cannot find a good idea, or cannot sleep with your investment idea, then just take your money and put it in a savings account until the proper time when a good investment comes along. Do not trust or invest with anybody except maybe your brother, father, or very close relative or friend. *No one takes care of your money like you do.* If you ever invest your money with someone else, you must thoroughly investigate that person, get references, and find out how they get paid. Do they get a commission from you and will they lie and steal for that commission?

## Love and Money

*A wise man should have money in his head, but not in his heart.*
—Jonathan Swift

Do not let money destroy your relationship with your spouse, children, siblings, family or really close friends. Give back some portion of the money you make to charity and the poor. Like Jesus in the Bible, give to the church and charitable organizations. Money will never solve all your problems. Money will not make you happy. Buying capital goods and services will only satisfy your short-term happy fix. Money buys food, clothes, and utilities, and it puts a roof over your head; *anything and everything else is extra.* You create your own happiness. There are many people who have no money and no assets, yet are very happy in life and with their life. Believing in a God and loving that God, loving yourself, and loving everyone will make you happy. If you give love, you will receive love, and everyone likes to be loved. Anyway, this is about money; religion is another subject matter.

## What I learned from these books

### *The Intelligent Investor* by Benjamin Graham

Ben Graham described that there are two types of intelligent investors, the defensive investor and the enterprising investor. *The defensive (or passive) investor will place his chief emphasis on the avoidance of serious mistakes or losses. His second aim will be freedom from effort, annoyance, and the need for making frequent decisions. The determining trait of the enterprising (or active, or aggressive) investor is his willingness to devote time and care to the selection of securities that are both sound and more attractive than the average. Over many decades an enterprising investor of this sort could expect a worthwhile reward for his extra skill and effort, in the form of a better average return than that realized by the passive investor.*[49]

If you choose to become the intelligent *defensive* (or passive) investor then with just a few thousand dollars you can invest in a low-cost total stock market index fund and you can dollar cost average your investment amounts monthly into that fund. This was discussed above and I recommend everyone to invest this way. If you choose to become the intelligent enterprising (or active) investor then you will have to *thoroughly analyze a company, and the soundness of its underlying business, before you buy its stock. You must deliberately protect yourself against serious losses and you must aspire to "adequate," not extraordinary, performance.*[50]

This type of active investing requires spending a tremendous amount of time evaluating the price and value of a business and its stock. It is like buying a pair of $100 pair of jeans. You discover a store going out of business and selling those $100 jeans for $40, so you buy many pairs. After you discover that there are only a few $100 jeans but there is a great demand for them. Because the demand for those jeans has increased while the supply of those jeans has decreased, the price has jumped to $140. Wisely, you sell all your jeans at a $140 and earn a $100 profit on each pair. The key is that you must know the true value of those $100 jeans and you must buy when the price low and sell when the price is high. You may have to wait a long time to buy at the right price and you may have to wait a long time to sell at the right price.

Walter Schloss, who followed Graham's investment philosophy said: *"if a business is worth a dollar and I can buy it for 40 cents, something good may happen to me."* [51]

Graham said: *"In the short run the market is a voting machine, but in the long run it is a weighing machine."* [52]

Above I have recommended that you establish a base fund (the passive investor) before you venture into becoming an active investor. Becoming an active investor can be very lucrative and make you rich. However, it requires a lot of time and commitment and you have to love this type of work. In some aspects, everyone can become an active investor on a small scale with just a few stocks or a business.

**Warren Buffet Letters**

Warren Buffet was a student of Graham's teachings and Buffet has become one of the world's most successful investors. Buffet, with his partner Charles Munger, looks for what he calls *"franchise" companies with strong consumer brands, easily understandable businesses, robust financial health, and near-monopolies in their markets. Buffet likes to snap up a stock when a scandal, big loss, or other bad news passes over it like a storm cloud. Buffet wants to see managers who set and meet realistic goals; build their businesses from within rather than through acquisition; allocate capital wisely; and do not pay themselves hundred-million-dollar jackpots of stock options. Buffet insists on steady and sustainable growth in earnings, so the company will be worth more in the future than it is today.* [53]

Warren Buffet has never authored a book, however, every year Buffet writes a letter to Berkshire Hathaway's shareholders. Many of Buffet's quotes can be found in *The TAO of Warren Buffet* book by

Mary Buffet and Davis Clark. Buffett's first two rules of investing are: *Rule No. 1: Never lose money. Rule No. 2: Never forget Rule No. 1.*[54]

Buffet likes to buy entire businesses through negotiations or to buy part interest in those businesses through the stock market. Like Graham, Buffet had a similar saying on daily stock market prices: *Investing is a lot like baseball. Every day, Mr. Market pitches you businesses at different prices. Waiting for the fast pitch, or the right price, will yield you big returns. Fortunately for the investor, there are no called strikes in investing. You can wait and wait until Mr. Market serves you the businesses you want at the prices you want.*[55]

Use stock and market fluctuations to serve your approach to investing rather than to instruct your investing. Having the patience to wait is a critical element in taking advantage of Mr. Market's mood swings. Buffett preserves his capital in down markets and he has no problem holding lots and lots of cash until he sees a good opportunity at the right price. Buffet likes to buy companies or its stock on the cheap and then monitor and hold those companies. Sometimes he never sells a stock holding. The best way to study Buffet's investment philosophy is to go to the Berkshirehathaway.com website and read all the letters and annual reports he has written on a yearly basis to his shareholders.

**The Richest Man in Babylon by George Clason**

Keep 10 percent of your gross income for savings and start now. Control expenditures. Multiply savings and compound savings. Guard savings from loss. Stay debt free and own your own house. Insure a future income for retirement and family. Increase the ability to earn and keep learning. Invest with experts. Do not invest if you are unfamiliar with the subject or the investees are unproved in profession. Do not invest in impossible earnings advice by schemers or con artists. Use caution when investing—better a little caution then a great regret. Be determined, take action and be consistent.[56]

**Beating the Street by Peter Lynch with John Rothschild**

The average person can outperform Wall Street by doing his own homework and research. Each person has an investment edge and *you can outperform the experts if you use your edge by investing in companies or industries you already understand.*[57] For example, if you are a pilot in the airline industry, stick with the airline industry and do not try to invest in the pharmaceutical industry. *In every industry and every region of the country, the observant amateur can find great growth companies long before the professionals have discovered them.*[58]

There are many small companies that are overlooked by the big fund managers. But you have to do the research, such as check quarterly and yearly statements, look for cash flow and potential to increase earnings and call the companies. Find out what Wall Street doesn't know yet. Ask questions like: *What other companies do you admire? Which of your competitors do you respect the most? Name your most impressive competitor.*[59]

By calling the company and asking questions you may find out important good news or bad news that Wall Street has not yet learned. In my opinion this is one of the main reasons Peter Lynch was so successful managing the Magellan mutual fund. Lynch constantly and thoroughly researched the stock companies to the point that he knew the companies better than most Wall Street experts. By the time the other experts became aware of the new growth story, Lynch had already purchased stock in that company as early as three to five years before everyone else caught on.

The amateur investor can spend a few hours a week following eight to ten stocks and purchase four or five of these companies. Take and record notes on these stocks and a brief summary on whether to buy, sell or continue to hold these company stocks. Know your handful of companies so well that if the stock market corrects and drops 10 percent, you will have the guts to buy more stock at a lower price. *The real key to making money in stocks is not to get scared out of* them.⁶⁰ *Do not get scared out of your stocks during market corrections. Everyone has the brainpower to make money in stocks. Not everyone has the stomach.*⁶¹

Lynch also wrote that if you are going to buy mutual funds, you only need to buy a maximum of five mutual funds and a money market fund, such as a capital appreciation fund, a value fund, a quality growth fund, an emerging growth fund, a special situations fund, and a money market fund. As previously mention, I believe a money market fund, a total bond index fund and a total stock market index fund should suffice but I am not a great fund manager like Lynch.

### *Bogle on Mutual Funds: New Perspectives for the Intelligent Investor* by John C. Bogle

John Bogle founded the first index mutual fund, the Vanguard 500 Index fund in 1975. In this book, Bogle discusses various fund categories: income, index, international, growth, industry-specialized, long- and short-term bond funds, et cetera. He discusses the pro and cons of sales charges, high-low expense ratios, management track records and tax considerations. Bogle says *performance comes and goes, but costs roll on forever.*⁶²

Minimize fees and taxes. Consider carefully the added cost of advice. When it comes to predicting the stock market, Bogle has said *nobody knows nothing and everybody knows everything.* The market is smarter than you and me. Very few people can consistently beat the S&P 500 stock index benchmark, especially after you back out the cost you pay to invest or trade. Instead of trying to beat the stock market, match the performance by selecting a low-cost index fund. Therefore, over time you will outperform 85 percent of most fund managers by just buying a low-cost S&P 500 market index fund. The total stock market index has more diversity than the S&P 500 market index. Over time, the performance difference between the two is negligible. After reading this book I have been a big fan of the Total Stock Market index fund.

**24 Essential Lessons for Investment Success and How to Make Money in Stocks by William J. O'Neil**

This book provided the CAN SLIM formula for selecting and investing stocks. O'Neil has identified these seven common characteristics of stocks which have performed well historically.

C – Current Earnings per Share
A – Annual Earning per Share
N – New Products, Service, Management, Price Highs
S – Supply and Demand
L – Leaders or Laggards
I – Institutional Sponsorship
M – Market Direction [63]

Interestingly, O'Neil says to sell your stock position if your stock drops 5 to 7 percent from your buy point and Peter Lynch says to buy more of stock positions you own if the stock market is down 10 percent.

"What should I do?"

There are so many different types of investment styles. You have to choose or develop an investment philosophy that you are comfortable with and stick to that style of investing.

Here is one investment trade philosophy:

There is no way to tell which trades will be big losers or big winners. The only control you have is to take small losses and not sell your winning trades with the hope they will develop into big winning trades. Sell a stock trade if it develops into a 7 to 15 percent loss and option trade if it develops into a 20 to 30 percent loss. It is the big winning trades that enable you to achieve a high rate of return and a high reward to risk ratio (a reward to risk ratio may be defined as the total profits divided by total losses). Maintain portfolio diversification and obtain constant profit flow with reduced risk. Trade several different strategies like option spreads, buy writes or covered calls, call and put options, stocks, and exchange-traded funds (ETFs). Vary trade lengths like options that expire in the summer and the winter. Trade stocks in different industry groups and ETFs for different countries.

These are just a few of the many books I have read on investing. When I was young, I used to go to the library, sign out a handful of books on real estate and stock investing and take those books with me on those 12-day international flights. Believe it or not, I learned almost as much listening to the senior pilots and the mistakes they had made.

## Stock Investing

So you have $300,000 to invest. First, you need an emergency fund, then you need a bond fund and then set up a financial base that you can fall back on in case all of your other investments get wiped out. For your financial base, dollar cost average monthly contributions (i.e. $50/month or $100/month each) into Vanguard Total Stock MKT index fund & Vanguard Total International Index fund. Get a $75,000 or $100,000 base. This financial base and your bond fund money are the second to last funds you should ever spend.

Your emergency cash is the last resort and the last of your money to spend. If you have done all of the above, and now you have $300,000 to invest, then pick ten stocks, research them thoroughly and buy five stocks. Invest $60,000 evenly into each stock. These stocks should be diverse in the type of business—industry, size, location, et cetera, they are in (i.e.: technology, energy, retail, et cetera.). You should know these companies very well. In a one to two-minute spiel, you should be able to explain why you are investing in these companies and what changes would have you sell these companies. Know how these companies make their profits.

## Discipline wins; Emotion loses

As in poker, you have to have rules and stick with the rules regardless of emotions. One rule could be to sell losses and keep winners. If a stock drops 8 to 10 percent, sell. If your stock is up big time to 25 or 30 percent, take some profits, maybe sell 20 to 25 percent of your stock position, and let the rest ride. Practice patience. *It never was my thinking that made the big money for me. It was always my sitting. Got that? My sitting tight!*—Edwin Lefevre.[64]

So you get a stock tip from someone. Be dubious. Check the stock charts. There are a large variety of stock charts. The 50-day simple moving average (SMA) chart is a very popular chart that defines the current direction of a stock with a lag by averaging the price data of the stock over a defined time frame. The exponential moving average (EMA) is similar to a simple moving average, except that more weight is given to the most recent data.

In my opinion, the 50-day EMA and the 100-day EMA chart lines provide a more accurate trend with fewer false, trend-changing signals. You can go to "Yahoo.com/finance" and build an interactive chart. Build "50-day EMA over 100-day EMA" chart for a one-year time frame. If your stock's 50-day EMA line is above the 100-day EMA line then you have an uptrend in the stock price.

Now, under the same Yahoo page, go to the Balance Sheet under Financials. Look at the Total Stockholder Equity. The Total Stockholder Equity is the net worth of that company; all the assets minus all the liabilities. If the Total Stockholder Equity is increasing year-to-year and quarter-to-quarter, then proceed. If not, dump the stock prospect. Get rid of all other stock prospects that do not pass both these two test. (During the 2009 thru 2011 years AAPL was a good example; the chart was good and the company was making money for its stock holders).

Now, go research the company and understand the business: How does the company make money? Can it continue to make money and increase profits? Get ten stocks that pass these criteria and buy five that are diversified and in different industries.

Normally, never invest more than 10 percent of your total assets into one stock/investment idea. The goal is to stay in the game. You cannot play/invest if you get wiped out of all your money. Do not trade often; buy and sell rarely and only when you need to. The cost of trading, like commissions and taxes, reduces profits. If you do not feel comfortable in what you are doing, then stay in cash. Making 1 to 2 percent on cash is better than losing 10, 20, 30, or 50 percent on a bad stock/investment idea or a non-disciplined trade.

It can take years to make lots of money and minutes or days to lose it all. If you lose 10 percent, then you need to make 11.11 percent to break even; lose 20 percent, then you must make 25 percent, lose 25 percent, then you must make 33.33 percent, and lose 50 percent, then you need to make 100 percent to break even. Making 100 percent rate of return on your money is hard to do. Always cut your losses short and let your winners run. On the average, professional traders have only 35 percent of their trades that are profitable. This is more about managing a portfolio than about how many times you are right. Learn and enjoy. If done right, one stock can make you a fortune.

Many successful traders follow a disciplined set of rules: How do I decide when to enter a position? What is my exit strategy? How much downside am I willing to accept? Do I have a defined strategy I believe in and am I disciplined in implementing it? When following or using somebody else's trading platform or philosophy, consider the following:

**Reliability** - the reliability or percentage of time you make money
**Relative Size** - the relative size of your prospects compared to your losses.
**Cost** - the cost of trade execution like taxes, slippage, bid-to-ask ratio and commissions.
**Opportunity** - how often you get the opportunity to trade.

**Capital** - the size of your trading or investment capital.
**Position Sizing** - how many units you trade at one time.

## The Bogey

Everyone wants to beat the Bogey—to outperform the S&P 500 stock market index.

The S&P 500 index is the bogey for most investors and investment consultants and is considered the benchmark for U.S. equity performance. It represents 70 percent of all U.S. publicly traded companies. Part of the index's popularity is due to its close association with the largest mutual fund in the world, the Vanguard 500 Index Fund, and Spiders (AMEX: SPY), the first exchange-traded fund (ETF). Over the long term, 85 percent of all money managers (especially when you take into consideration costly fees) do not outperform the S&P 500 index—the Bogey. Warren Buffet's Berkshire Hathaway stock (BRK-A) has been one of the best at beating the Bogey over the long term. Refer to the "Berkshire Corporation Performance vs. the S&P 500" chart located in the appendix section, which was copyrighted and used with permission of Mr. Buffet. The Bogey's compound annual gain per year over 48 years is over 9 percent per year. BRK-A stock's compound annual gain per year over 48 years is over 19 percent per year. Less than 15 percent of all money managers and investors outperform the Bogey over the long term and yet Buffet has outperformed the Bogey by an average margin of 10 percent.

My goal is to be in that 15 percent group that beats the Bogey.

## A few "Best Investment Advice" one-liners:

> *When you do not know a thing, to allow that you do not know it—this is knowledge.*
> —Confucius

**Be humble and ask yourself, "what if I am wrong?"** [65]

- Have core fund to rebuild if your latest investment idea fails.
- Divide your money into three groups: A=50–65 percent treasures, bond, cash; B=30–40 percent blue chip stocks; C= 5–10 percent speculation.
- Analyze downside potential first—do not lose.
- You can lose more money in minutes than you can make in years. Bad news drives stocks down fast and good news rewards slowly.
- Only invest in things you understand.
- Only risk 5–10 percent of your money. Don't bet big on one stock or investment idea.
- Hardly anyone makes money from short-term investing. Avoid short-term trading.
- Avoid the hope without evidence that a spectacular return is just a trade or two away.
- If your stock or the stock market goes down five days in row, sell.
- Keep winners, sell losers.
- Invest 10 percent of all earnings and compound dividends.
- Manage risk sell to a sleeping point. If an investment is worrying you to a point that is preventing you from getting a good night sleep, then sell that investment.
- Buy low price-to-earning (P/E) ratio stocks and high dividend-paying stocks and check on those stocks every ninety days.
- Save pennies and the dollars will take care of themselves.

- Emotions: If it feels good because the whole crowd is heading the same direction you're going, don't do it.

- In investing, you should never feel you know it because if you do, then the market will humble you. The market is smarter than everyone. Listen to the market.

- Few large- and mid-sized companies cannot maintain 15 percent growth over a long time period. Small-sized companies have a better chance of growing 15 percent or more over time.

- Find new dominant trends and industries in that trend group, and then find the dominant stocks in that trend group. Find trends early.

- Accumulate wealth not through salaries, but by acquiring equity.

- Buy companies with high return on equity and low price-to-earning (P/E) ratios.

- Save and invest always and consistently. The more you save, the better you will invest.

- Always have greed when others have fear, and have fear when others have greed. When the crowd is fearful and selling stocks at lower prices you should be greedy and buy stocks at lower prices; and vice-a-versa.

There are so many different types of investment advice and several of these conflict with each other. There are so many different types of investment styles. So, what to do? You have to choose or develop an investment philosophy that you are comfortable with and stick to that style of investing. In dealing with money matters, there a certain financial terms you may need to know. For instance, a debit card verses credit card, a bank verses credit union, a stock verses mutual fund verses exchange traded fund, S&P 500 verses Wilshire 5000, a retirement fund, and all the varieties of insurance, including some that suggest they are smart "investments."

## Build and Be a Business Owner

Use your brains to become a professional (doctor, lawyer, pilot, et cetera) in a field that you enjoy. This way, you can make $200,000 to $500,000 per year, live below your means, and invest $100,000 to $200,000 per year. If you don't want to become a highly-compensated professional, then start and own your own business (using labor leverage to get highly compensated) in a field that you love. Your employees will be your best asset, so keep your employees happy so that they will keep your customers happy.

Start with your idea, creating something different that will stand out. Put together a business plan. Determine whether you need financing. Put together your initial marketing plan. Get visibility for your company, like getting camera time that highlights the products or service your company offers. Build your infrastructure. Move forward, get started, and dedicate your precious time to your new business. Use the web, Facebook, Twitter and all available current social media to promote the business. Make paying for your items or service convenient with an electronic credit card machine.

**Better to lose all when it's only $100
or only $1,000 versus $10 million**

*Losing money teaches you about yourself. Can you come back? Will you come back? Are you driven enough to come back? Will you sell your boat or expensive toy if you have to?* [66]

No one wins all the time. Many successful investors encounter setbacks and failures before they reach their financial goal. You are going to have to work hard to get rich. Focus on things you already know about and things that interest you. Put the time and effort into educating yourself before investing in any stocks, bonds, mutual funds, ETFs, a business, real estate or any other assets. If you're going to hire a money manager to manage your money, then you better put the time and effort into educating yourself about that person or company.

Some people don't want to get rich and money is not that important to them. There were times when I was flat-out broke, penniless, hungry, dirty and tired. It is good to have some money— to eat, put some clothes on your back, put a roof over your head, and acquire a few basic utilities. If you want, once you have your basic needs met, you can give to the poor or help someone else acquire their basic needs. But don't you think maybe it's a good idea to at least learn the basics of money? Start by living on less than you make and building up an emergency cash reserve fund.

> *For age and want, save while you may; no morning sun lasts a whole day.*
> —Benjamin Franklin [67]

# CHAPTER 11
# Religion Schooling

What I know about religion is that you need one.

Religion is a set of beliefs—usually in a super-human being, a supernatural existence, or a god—generally agreed upon by a group of people. A religion usually includes a specific set of practices, rituals, observances, worships, devotional services, prayers, and/or a moral code on how to behave as a human being on this planet earth.

There are thousands of religions and sub-group religions including new religions, extinct religions, and even religions that formed from other religions: Christianity arose from Judaism and Buddhism arose from Hinduism, Babi and Baha'i arose from Islam, and so forth.

Every religion is similar to some or all religions, and every religion is different from some or all religions. Currently the most popular religions in this world in descending order are:

1.) There are over two billion Christians (including Roman Catholics, Protestants, Orthodox Christians, and Anglicans).
2.) There are over one billion Muslims (including Shi'ite and Sunni).
3.) Hindus account for less than one billion followers.
4.) Buddhists have less than half a billion followers.
5.) Sikhs—around twenty million.
6.) Judaism—around fifteen million.

There are agnostics that believe the existence of a god cannot be proven or disproven. Atheist believe that there is no god. There are approximately 200 million atheists—and a large population of approximately one billion who claim no religion at all. [68]

Just as there are various religions, there are several calendars that were used throughout history. In the year 45 Before Common Era (BCE), Julius Cesar added 67 days to the year and introduced 12 calendar months of 30 and 31 days, creating the Julian calendar. Common Error (CE) or Anno Domini (AD) is considered the year of "our lord" or the year Jesus Christ was born, although historians believe Jesus may have been born four or six years earlier.

In the year 1582, Pope Gregory XIII reformed the Julian calendar to the Roman calendar (also known as the Gregorian calendar) because over time the Julian calendar had become in error of about ten days. Today, most of the world uses the Gregorian calendar. While discussing the history of various religions, several of these calendars are used to identify time in history.

In no particular order here is a short description and history of some of the major religions and prophets.

Hinduism is the major religion of India and is considered one of the oldest religions of the world, dating back to around 1500 BCE. Hinduism did not begin with a founder or a particular event but over time evolved from various religious traditions that have existed throughout India's history. Hindus have many rituals, scriptures, and systems of beliefs, and they believe in millions of gods—yet each god is meant to help them reach Brahmin. Hindus believe that Brahmin is the principle and source of the universe. The Brahmin is a divine intelligence that penetrates all living beings including the human soul and all livings things that are embedded in the cosmic cycle of becoming (birth) and perishing (death). They believe in the concept of reincarnation in which, according to the Law of Karma, depending on how one conducts his or her moral behavior one can be reborn to a higher level of existence. The Hindu society has a cast system that consists of five hereditary classes: Brahmin, Kshatriya, Varishya,

Sudra, and the Untouchables. Some of the Hindu books date back to a thousand years BCE. Five of the main Hindu prayers or meditations are:

1.) Moha Mrityunjoya Mantra
2.) Lord Shiva
3.) Lord Ganesha
4.) Sri Krishma
5.) Sri Rama

Mahatma Gandhi was Hindu. The Ganges River is considered the most sacred place for Hindus.

**Buddhism** has its root in Hinduism. Siddhartha Gautama was a Hindu born into the Kshatriya caste in 560 CE in what was then India and is now Nepal. After spending six wandering years living the most simplistic life, including daily fasting and meditation, at age 35 Siddhartha started a new religion known today as Buddhism. Buddhists deny the existence of a human soul, but do not deny the existence of gods. The human person is at the center of Buddhism and meditation is the method through which a person gains the two most important virtues: wisdom and compassion. Buddhists believe that through meditation one can realize that there is no permanence in life and, ultimately, reach the spiritual goal of Nirvana. Saying two of the most common forms of meditations the "Mindfulness of Breath" and "Loving-Kindness" as well as saying the "Om Mani Padme Hum" mantra (a prayer) is a common practice. The Dalai Lama is a famous Buddhist monk. There are many famous Buddhist temples located in India, Indonesia, Thailand, Japan, Korea, Nepal, and Myanmar.

**Sikhism** is a mono-theistic religion (a one-god religion) that contains elements of both Hinduism and Islam. Sikhism was founded in the Punjah region by Guru Nanak in 1459 CE and had ten successive Sikh Gurus, of which Guru Granth Sahib provided the last Holy Scripture teaching. Sikhi believe in faith and justice in one god

(Waheguru) and pursue salvation through disciplined personal meditation on the name and message of god. The Sikhi believe god can be realized through nature and through experiences and through other people; they believe that god has no beginning and no end; and that god created all people equal. Sikhism encourages sharing and giving and defending the rights of all creatures and all human beings.

## Chinese Religions

For civil purposes, the Chinese use the Roman (Gregorian) Calendar but for festivals the Chinese use their own Chinese calendar. The Chinese calendar was probably invented by Emperor Hungli in 2637 BCE, based on astronomical observations of the alignment of the sun and phases of the moon. Our Roman calendar year 2013 is the Chinese calendar year 4711, the year of the snake.

*Chinese religions are a combination of Chinese folk religion, Taoism, Confucianism, and Buddhism*; and have been closely related with the existing Chinese government.[69] The Shang Dynasty of 1500 BCE honored their ancestors, nature gods, weather gods, astrology, and believed the afterlife mirrored earthly life. This was the beginning of Chinese folk religion. K'ung Fu-tzu (also known as Confucius) lived around 551 to 479 BCE, and through his teachings he tried to revitalize Chinese society based on his knowledge of ancient Chinese values and rituals. Confucius tried to instill morality and reduce the chaos that he perceived existed in China at the time. He wrote many of his teachings in the Analects. The Han dynasty (from 206–220 BCE) required the teachings of Confucius as mandatory in all schools. Confucianism is a form of character formation in which one could obtain perfection as the "superior human." Confucianism believes in social order and that humans are naturally good. It emphasizes education and virtues.

The beginnings of **Taoism** probably started around 2000 BCE, but it was Lao-tzu around 500 BCE who is credited as the founder of

Taoism. Lao-tzu wrote the "Tao-te Ching" ("The Way and Its Power"). The Taoists believe that human achievements are foolish. They advise people to live simply, to live in harmony with nature, and to live in harmony with the Yin (the shaded dark bad) and the Yang (the sunny good). Taoists believe in the "go with the flow" mentality, "the way" or "the nature of things." Taoists believe that the actual physical immortality is a reachable goal. Many Chinese Taoists, Buddhists, and Confucian temples were destroyed or taken over by the government during the Chinese Communist revolution.

The **Japanese** were influenced by the Chinese religions. Buddhism flourished in Japan. These beliefs mixed with the Japanese **Shinto** beliefs. *Shinto was a name given to Japanese ethnic religion by the Chinese. The Shinto believed in spirits called Kami and this spiritual force of power existed in all things, especially nature, and was considered "the way of gods."* [70] Shintos believed in harmony, purity and loyalty. Shintos believe that the world is overflowing with Kami—and that all life, all creation and human nature are generally good. The Kajiki and the Nishongi are two of the sacred Japanese writings of eighth century BCE. The emperor was the sacred leader of Japan until the end of WWII. The Grand Shrine of Ise is the most sacred of places for the Shintos.

According to the book of Genesis, god made a covenant with Abraham. Abraham was a great prophet from around 1800 BCE who was recognized by three major religions: Christianity, Islam and Judaism.[71] Abraham was a nomadic tribesmen and a shepherd who traveled extensively from what today is called Iraq to what today is called Palestine. Abraham begot Ishmael with his Egyptian slave servant Hager (he eventually sent them away) and Abraham begot Isaac with his wife Sarah. The three thousand-year-old Jewish religion begins with the prophet Abraham written in the Torah, which is part of the Hebrew Bible (the Tonakh)[72] or what Christians call the Old Testament. This Bible contains 39 books, almost 6,000 words and was inspired by great prophets like Moses, David, Isaiah, Jeremiah, Ezekiel, and many others.[73] Included in the Jewish Bible are 613 laws that Jews must follow, including the famous Ten Commandments that their greatest prophet, Moses, supposedly received directly from god.

The Ten Commandments. —Exodus 20:2–17 (NAB).

1. Thou shall honor God.
2. Thou shalt not honor any other false Gods.
3. Thou shalt not take the name of the Lord thy God in vain.
4. Thou shalt keep holy the Sabbath day.
5. Thou shalt honor thy father and thy mother.
6. Thou shalt not kill.
7. Thou shalt not commit adultery.
8. Thou shalt not steal.
9. Thou shalt not bear false witness against thy neighbor.
10. Thou shalt not covet thy neighbor's house, thou shalt not covet thy neighbor's wife, nor maidservant, nor his ox, nor his ass, nor anything that is thy neighbor's.[74]

The **Jewish** believe in one God who is eternal, who knows all thoughts and deeds of men and who will reward the good and punish the wicked. Accordingly, one should pray to the one God, follow the Written Torah and the words of the prophets, especially the greatest prophet, Moses. The Jewish believe that there is a messiah who will come someday, and the dead will be resurrected. However, in Judaism, actions are more important than beliefs. Jerusalem is their most sacred place.[75]

**Christianity** started around 8–6 BCE with the birth of Jesus and the belief that Jesus was the Messiah, the Christ. The Christian Holy Bible includes two major sections, the Old Testament (the Jewish Hebrew Bible), and the New Testament (God made a new covenant with the people) that included twenty-seven more books and almost two thousand more words. The New Testament includes: the four gospels of Matthew, Mark, Luke, and John, describing Jesus' life and the way to salvation; the history of the new Christian religion; written letters of Paul and others; and the revelation of Apocalypse.[76]

Who was this Jesus guy? *Supposedly Jesus was born in an obscure village to a peasant women and a stepfather over two thousand years ago. He grew up in another obscure village, where he worked as a carpenter until he was about thirty years old.*[77] Then he left home, picked twelve friends, and became a traveling preacher for about three years. Supposedly he performed many miracles. He was a peaceful man and taught people to love God and everyone. Jesus taught the people the "Our Father" prayer and two new commandments:

**The Golden rule** —Mathew 7:12 (NAB) "So whatever you wish that men do to you, do so to them."

**The Great Commandment** —Luke 10:27 (NAB) "You shall love the Lord your God with all your heart, with all your soul, and with all your strength, and with all your mind; and your neighbor as yourself."

*Jesus never had a family or owned a home. He never set foot inside a big city. He never traveled more than 200 miles from the place he was born. He never wrote a book or held an office or did any of the usual things that accompany greatness*[78]

While he was still a young man approximately 33 years old, his popularity changed. His friends deserted him and denied him. *He was turned over to his enemies. He went through a mockery of a trial, was tortured, made to carry his own cross, and nailed to that cross between two thieves.*[79] While he was dying on the cross his executioners gambled for the only piece of property he had—his coat. After He died He was taken down and laid in a borrowed grave. Supposedly three days later He rose from the dead, taught his apostles for an additional 40 days, and then his apostle Peter, as first pope, started what is now the Roman Catholic Church religion (RCC). *Nineteen centuries have come and gone*, and today Jesus is the central figure for much of the human race; approximately two billion people believe in Him. *All the armies that ever marched and all the navies that ever sailed and all the parliaments that ever sat, and all the kings that ever reigned, put together, have not affected the life of man upon this earth as powerful as this one solitary life of Jesus.*[80]

Christians believe *there is a God who sent his son, Jesus, to save the world —John 3:17 (NAB).* Today there are various Christian denominations and beliefs, but the Roman Catholic Christians (RCCs) believe: *In God the Father almighty, Creator of heaven and earth. And in Jesus Christ, God's only Son, their Lord, Who was conceived by the Holy Spirit, born of the Virgin Mary, suffered under Pontius Pilate, was crucified, died, and was buried. Jesus descended into hell; the third day He rose again from the dead. He ascended into heaven, and sits at the right hand of God the Father almighty, from thence He shall come to judge the living and the dead. RCCs believe in the Holy Spirit, the holy Catholic Church, the communion of saints, the forgiveness of sins, the resurrection of the body and life everlasting.*[81] The Pope is the RCCs religious leader and he resides in the Vatican in Rome, Italy. The pope lineage can be traced back to the first pope Peter the Apostle.

This Holy Bible (Old and New Testaments) is a collection of books (and songs) written by many various authors inspired by God and describing God's interactions with people and nations. The Bible can be considered part fictional and non-fictional, which includes poetry, narration, and prophecy. Therefore, when reading the Holy Bible, you need to interpret some texts literally, some texts symbolically, and some texts historically. The Bible has been translated into over 100,000 languages and is always one of the top-ten best-selling books.

Like Judaism and Christianity, **Muslim** is a monotheistic religion. It holds that Muslims were heirs of Abraham. Remember Hager (the handmaid servant of Abraham's wife Sarah) and Hager's son, Ishmael, who were sent away? There is belief that Ishmael and his lineage settled in Mecca, Saudi Arabia. The Arab prophet Muhammad was born around 560 CE in Mecca. Muhammad considered himself the last of the prophets of Islam—the last in line of seven prophets, with Abraham as the first prophet, and Jesus as prophet number six. Muhammad preached complete submission to one true God, a God he called Allah. He cleansed the ancient Ka'aba shrine of idol worship and rebuilt and rededicated it to Allah. He believed the angel Gabriel gave him many revelations, which he memorized and had other people memorize. These recitations became the Oral text of the Quran throughout Muhammad's lifetime. Eventually, after Mohammed's death, the Oral memorized text of the Quran was recorded by Abu Bakr (around 634 CE) and Utham (around 650 CE).

Muslims believe every idea or action must be centered on the oneness of God and that the Quran is the direct word of God. Muslims must express their belief through the duties of the Five Pillars of Islam: profession of faith, prayer, fasting, almsgiving and pilgrimage. Muslims believe attention to God and caring for others are very important duties. Mecca is their most important sacred place. Medina and Jerusalem are also holy places.

**The Baha'i Faith** is one of the newest religions founded by Baha ullah in the 1880's in Persia. Baha'i seems to have emerged from a combination of early religious beliefs, mainly Islam, Messengers such as Abraham, the Buddha, Jesus, Muhammad, and others have been included. This is a monotheistic religion that emphasizes the spiritual unity of God, the unity of religion, and the unity of all mankind. They believe that God periodically reveals His will through divine messengers in order to transform the character of humankind and to develop their moral and spiritual qualities.

**The Mormon Faith** (or the Church of Jesus Christ of Latter-Day Saints) is another relatively new religion started by Joseph Smith Jr. in the 1820's in the United States. Mormonism is a Christian faith that recognizes more of the recent prophets rather than all of the prophets that most other Christians recognize. The Book of Mormon and its interpretation of the Bible are the two primary sources of the Mormon faith. However, they believe that Native Americans are one of the lost tribes of Israel, and believe that someday Jesus will return to Earth and set up a New Jerusalem in America that will reign for 1,000 years.

There are many lesser-known religions, such as African Yoruba, Sonteria, Condomble, Shongo, Voodoo, Australian Aboriginal, to name just a few. There are agnostics who are undecided on whether God exists, and atheists who believe that a god does not exist at all.

"You were raised a Roman Catholic—you're biased." Yes, I am, but I am biased mainly from my open mindedness (and open-heartedness) of accepting any or all other religions and through my investigative reading. I have come to the conclusion that the Roman Catholic (RC) religion is for me. Yes, the Roman Catholic Church has many faults and structured rules. John baptized Jesus, Jesus never baptized anyone, yet the Roman Catholic Church has baptism, which is one of the Seven Sacraments: Baptism, Reconciliation, Eucharist, Confirmation, Matrimony, Holy Orders, and Anointing of the Sick. I like certain parts of the Seven Sacraments.

I like the part of *baptism* in which two adults are chosen to care for the new baby in the event the parents die before the child reaches adulthood. I like the part of confession where you tell someone (it's supposed to be the priest), usually someone who doesn't know you, your sins. Sometimes it feels good to get it off your chest and out of your conscience just to tell someone the things you did wrong. My favorite part is the "do this in memory of me" when receiving the Holy *Eucharist* and wine during communion. By consuming the bread (symbolizing Jesus' body) and the wine (symbolizing Jesus' blood), we remember the suffering He did for us, and remember He's been there, done that, and showed us how to deal with it. Jesus was born with nothing, had nothing, all his friends left him, and then he was brutally killed. He showed us how to forgive, forget, love, and be peaceful.

I like the Pre-Cana part of the Roman Catholic *matrimony* in which the engaged couples spend time questioning each other to get to know each other before they get married. I remember the group leader saying, "Communicate. Verbally fighting is better than not communicating at all." Every human culture has some form of marriage ceremony. Any two humans can have sex, produce a child, and split. But can any two people say to each other "for better, for worse, for richer, for poorer, in sickness and health, until death do us part," and then execute on that commitment? This is a different kind of love—an acquired commitment love—and it's hard, continuous work. Besides, males and females are different and I believe those differences are a benefit to raising children. Finally, I like the part of the *anointing of the sick* when a priest comes to you while you're on your death bed and gives you one last blessing (this blessing is to increase your spiritual and physical health.) Who really knows what happens when you die? Hedge your bets—God may really exist and is about to judge your soul. I think the soul is a scorecard of how we morally live on planet Earth.

There are seven billion human beings and over a billion species from the simplest of living organisms to large mammals on our planet Earth. Earth is just one of the nine planets with the sun in our solar system. We are just one solar system in the Milky Way galaxy of stars. There are billions of other galaxies in our universe. There must be some super-human higher intellectual being who exists—let's call him God (call him Lord or Allah, if you prefer)—but there is only one God. Now read the Holy Bible, Torah, Quran, Analects of Confucius, Tao Te Ching, Trip Taka, Bhagovad-Gita, book of Mormons, et cetera. Now, come on. Some spirit must have influenced those writers to write insights into some type of God. So there must be a God. I hope there is a God or some supernatural being. What is the downside in believing and praying to a God? If there is a God and he or she provides us life twenty-four hours a day, seven days a week, then I will hedge my bets and pray at least an hour a day and honor him or her at least an hour a week. I choose the Roman Catholic religion God only because of what this Jesus guy said. You can throw out the whole Bible and throw all of the religions out the window, but I will accept and believe and attempt to do the two things Jesus said: love God and love all human beings the same. And I will add one more thing: love yourself.

So here are the three things I tell myself:

1. *Love God.*
2. *Love yourself* (if you do not love yourself, change so that you will love yourself).
3. *Love all people* (no matter what, try to love everyone).

If you love God, self, and others, then you will comply with the Ten Commandments, the Quran, and the other major religious doctrines. There will also be peace among all people on planet earth.

"How can I help you?" I need help. Everyone needs help sometimes. Maybe you have a White Knight who will be there all the time to help you. Maybe one day that White Knight cannot help you with your particular problem. Maybe there is no human who can help you. Maybe you need super-human help. Maybe there is a God who can help you. So getting back to "I need help," I want to add my name to that Help Pie with this prayer.

**Help Pie-Request**

Dear God I know you have many requests for help:
Help in healing the sick, removing or reducing pain and suffering, stopping war and crime.
Help to deal with loss of loved ones, healing mental illness, forgiving sins and letting souls into heaven.

Help to improving marriage and family relationships,
and many greater requests for help.
I know you have a great many requests for help from others throughout the world, but please grant me my help-worth
or portion of my help request.

I know the "help pie-request" is large, but please grant me a small portion of help from the "Help Pie Request" list.

So we should pray prayers for help and gratitude. That Jesus guy gave us a prayer (The Lord's Prayer also called The Our Father prayer). Here are two versions of the Our Father prayer:

*Our father, Who art in heaven,*
*Hollow be thy Name.*
*Thy kingdom come.*
*Thy will be done on earth, as it is in heaven.*
*Give us this day our daily bread,*
*and forgive us our trespasses,*
*as we forgive those who trespass against us,*
*and lead us not into temptation,*
*but deliver us from evil. Amen.* [82]

(This version is based on passages from the Luke 11:2–4 (NAB) and Mathew 6:9–13 (NAB).

*Our father in heaven,*
*Reveal who you are.*
*Set the world right,*
*Do what's best—*
*As above, so below.*
*Keep us alive with three square meals.*
*Keep us forgiven with you and forgiving others.*
*Keep us safe from ourselves and the devil.*

*You're in charge!*
*You can do anything you want!*
*You're ablaze in beauty!*
*Yes. Yes. Yes.* [83]

(This is a version from *The Message/Remix* by Eugene H. Peterson)

This prayer by Saint Francis of Assisi is a prayer that followers of most religions of the world would probably feel comfortable saying.

*Lord, make me an instrument of your peace;*
*Where there is hatred, let me sow love;*
*Where there is injury, pardon,*
*Where there is doubt, faith;*
*Where there is despair, hope:*
*Where there is darkness, light;*
*And where there is sadness, joy.*
*Grant that I may not so much seek*
*To be consoled as to console;*
*To be understood as to understand;*
*To be loved as to love;*
*For it is in giving that we receive;*
*It is in pardoning that we are pardoned;*
*And it is in dying that we are born to eternal life.* [84]

Saint Francis, a Christian, was born in Assisi, Italy in 1182. He loved pleasure, wore expensive clothes and spent money lavishly until he received an inspirational dream from God. He changed his life drastically by living very modestly, and giving to and helping the poor. Among other accomplishments Saint Francis started the Franciscan Friars and the Christmas nativity tradition. He loved God, all people, animals and living creators.

Lao-tzu the Taoism founder wrote this:

*If there is to be peace in the world,*
*There must be peace in the nations.*
*If there is to be peace in the nations,*
*There must be peace in the cities.*
*If there is to be peace in the cities,*
*There must be peace between neighbors.*
*If there is to be peace between neighbors,*
*There must be peace in the home.*
*If there is to be peace in the home,*
*There must be peace in the heart.* [85]

Here is a prayer that I wrote, and I say or attempt to say it daily. Actually, I say it nightly before my body succumbs to sleep. I change and customize what's in the box as necessary.

**TRINITY FOR ME**

O my dear God
O my dear Jesus
And the Holy Spirit,
 Thank you for this moment of life.
Thank you for this breath of air.
Thank you for providing water and food for my body,
And thank you for protecting, guiding, and nourishing my soul.
 Thank you for _____.
Please help and/or grant me with_____.
Please protect and guide my thoughts, words, heart, and soul
Towards you during this earthly journey so that after this life
I will be in heaven
Please help me to love God, me, and everyone.
I love you, trust you, believe in you, and hope to be with you.
Amen

The Appendix includes a copy of this prayer for you to use. You can use this prayer (cut out or photocopy it) and customize the contents within the box or write your own prayer. God, thank you for whatever, if You will it, help me with whatever, and I will try to love you, me, and everyone else.

# CHAPTER 12

# Body and Soul

What do we know about the body and soul? After all these years of doctors performing surgeries and dissections on the human body, no one has found the human soul. The soul is that spiritual and moral thought action, emotion and will. The soul may be our scorecard of how we morally live on planet Earth. I believe everyone has a soul. Assuming we have a soul and we can all agree we have a body, here are subject matters that may help us maintain a healthy body and soul. Writing a mission statement, creating daily goals and managing time and stress have helped me. In this chapter you will get *The Ten Healthy Rules*.

**Mission Statement**

Create a mission statement for yourself—a purpose in life. Create a statement and write it down. Then review it periodically. If you do not review and read your statement periodically, you will forget what the hell you were doing in life, or maybe it is time to change your purpose and write a new mission statement.

Here is my mission statement:

I try to:

Pray, fast, and do penitence often. Daily thank God, ask God, and trust God. Pray the "Trinity for Me" and the Rosary daily or at least six times a week. Live a high-quality life and love society. Love all people and serve people and inquire *is there any stresses I can help you with?* Be the best person to every person, every time, all the time. Do as much good as possible, all the time for every person I meet. Make the right chooses in life—be unselfish. Love everyone and be a peacemaker. Love God, love self, and love everyone.

## Daily Goals

It is important to have daily goals because it could be your last living day on planet Earth. Some daily goals are made for you and some daily goals you get to choose for yourself.

Here are my daily goals:

- **Breathe:** Breathe fresh clean air and breathe properly.

- **Sleep:** Sleep eight hours. Aim for 10:00 PM till 6:00 AM; use 12:00 PM to 3:00 PM as the second-chance siesta nap. Get a least a minimum of five straight hours of uninterrupted sleep during any twenty-four hour period. Five straight hours of core sleep during the body's circadian sleep cycle trough is required to regain at least eighty percent performance.

- **Drink:** Drink fluids (water and pure juices and avoid man-made drinks).

- **Eat:** Eat food (fruit, vegetables, nuts, fish, foods from the good list and avoid man-made foods).

- **Pray**: Pray and mediate (thank God for all blessings and ask God for needs or special requests).

- **Love:** Love God and love everyone (help someone and make him or her smile).

- **Exercise:** Exercise the mind and body.

- **De-stress:** Exercise helps to de-stress. Sing, laugh, drink alcohol, tell jokes, or whatever to reduce and manage stress. Talk to someone about your problems or stresses; sometimes just talking to someone helps you get relief and makes you feel better, even though your problem may not get solved.

## Time Management

Construct daily goals and long-term goals. I try to manage my time by prioritizing the aspects of my life, taking care of soul and body (meditate and exercise), being a good friend to family and others, and being a good pilot.

I prioritize in the following order:

- Be a good Christian; take care of my body and soul and pray.

- Be a good family member; be a good husband, father, son, and brother.

- Do my best in my career. Be the best jet airplane Captain. Always command and fly safely and legally, and if possible, be reliable and efficient. Slow down, stop and think, do checklists, and if necessary, take a delay.

- Manage and make money to take care of the needs of life, and be thankful for the extras that may buy the wants of life.

- With my left over time, fish and take care of the garden.

- In summation I say, "Food on the table, a roof over your head and you're healthy, then everything and anything else is extra."

## The Human Body

*Behold, all souls are mine; as the soul of the father, so also the soul of the son is mine.* (Ezekiel 18:4 NAB). Our human life could end at any second without notice by God's will or our will. So by our will we must take good care of our bodies. Remember our soul temporally lives in our body while we live on this earth. *Do you not know that your body is a temple of the Holy Spirit who is in you, whom you have from God, and that you are not your own? For you have been bought with a price: therefore glorify God in your body.*—1 Corinthians 6:19–20 (NAB). To help maintain a healthy human body here are the subject matters I believe that we control. These topics are the building blocks I used to create *The Ten Healthy Rules.*

## Air

Air is odorless, tasteless, and invisible. Air is composed mainly of oxygen and nitrogen and also contains carbon dioxide, argon, hydrogen and small quantities of neon, helium, and other inert gasses. We breathe air and air directly or indirectly supports every form of life on earth. The body must always be able to take in good air and get rid of a bad air. When the body cannot do this, the body will suffocate and we will die. Do not smoke, and always try to breathe fresh, clean air (like air from trees and plants that exchange carbon dioxide for oxygen, mountain air and ocean air.)

Learn to breathe with your diaphragm to obtain normal rhythm directed by the unconscious part of your brain, rather than the unsimultaneous rhythm generated by your chest muscles. During deep abdominal breathing (or belly breathing) your abdomen should expand during inhalation like when a baby breathes—the belly goes up and down, deeply and slowly. To improve your breathing, try one of these techniques:

- Lie on your back and place a book on the belly. Relax your stomach muscles and inhale deeply into your abdomen so that the book rises. When you exhale, the book should fall.

- Sit up and place your right hand on your abdomen and your left hand on your chest. Breathe deeply so that your right hand rises and falls with your breath, while your left hand stays relatively still. Breathe in through your nose and out through your nose or out through your mouth.

- Place a clock with the secondhand counter on your abdomen. Breathe in slowly, feeling your abdomen rise for a count of five seconds. Then breathe out slowly to the same count of five.

- Walk and talk at the same time.

Breathing properly helps establish a state of psychological calm and can neutralize the negative effects of stress. Breathing properly is probably the single best anti-stress medicine. When you bring air down into the lower portion of the lungs (where oxygen exchange is most efficient) the heart rate slows, blood pressure decreases, muscles relax, anxiety ceases and the mind calms. When hurt in sports, or out of breath, or when you are looking for that last wind—breathe deeply.

## Smoking

*"Tobacco use remains the leading cause of preventable death in the U.S. Cigarette smoking and exposure to tobacco smoke account for approximately one in five deaths. Smoking harms nearly every organ of the human body."* [86] Tobacco smoking is a known or probable cause of approximately 25 diseases. When a person smokes a tobacco product they inhale smoke, which contains nicotine and over 500 chemicals. Nicotine is an addictive substance. Tar is another substance that is bad for the mouth, throat, and lungs. Tar can cause lung cancer, emphysema, and bronchial diseases. Another dangerous substance is carbon monoxide, which can cause heart problems. Tobacco contributes to the hardening of arteries, which can cause a heart attack. Smoking can also increase the risk of having strokes. Smoking also increases the risk of oral, liver, kidney, bladder, stomach, cervical and lung cancers, as well as leukemia and emphysema. Other health problems include chronic bronchitis; digestive cancers; gastric ulcers; cancers of the throat, the tongue, the lip, the esophagus, the colon, and the pancreas.

## Drugs

Some of the most commonly abused illegal drugs are: marijuana (cannabis), cocaine and crack, heroin, ecstasy, LSD, poppers, speed, tranquillizers and magic mushrooms. Some common abused legal drugs are: alcohol, caffeine, tobacco, anabolic steroids, gases, glues, aerosols and a variety of pain killers.[87] Some effects from taking drugs are: instant addiction, instant death, instant heart problems, memory loss, damage to nerve endings in the brain, stomach pain, sickness, diarrhea, destruction of family and social life and so on. Addictive drug users resort to crime to obtain funds to buy more drugs. No drug is completely safe; even salt in sufficient quantities can be lethal. Marijuana can act as a stimulant, as a sedative, as an analgesic, or as a mild hallucinogenic drug. The long-term effects of cannabis can lead to respiratory problems, bronchitis, emphysema, heart and vascular disease. Heroin, being an opiate, is a depressant. The short-term effects of heroin are relief of pain and anxiety, feeling of wellbeing and peace, decreased awareness of the outside world and depression of the gastro-intestinal system. The long-term effects of heroin can lead to death. Heroin users frequently overdose and die. Cocaine is a stimulant. It stimulates the brain cortex and central nervous system. Short-term effects are increases in heart rate, arterial blood pressure and respirations per minute. Long-term side effects are sinus headaches, bleeding, or damage to nasal passages. Other consequences include impotence, sexual problems, insomnia, irritability, anxiety and depression. Continued use of cocaine over time can cause difficulty concentrating, unconsciousness, toxic psychosis, and hallucinations. Smoking is bad for the body, certain drugs are bad for the body and too much of any drug is bad for the body. Therefore I say:

> *I. Do not smoke or consume illegal drugs or abuse legal drugs.*

## Water

Pure water is transparent, odorless, and tasteless and consists of hydrogen and oxygen (H20). Water is the most critical and most important nutrient. Death occurs when a person loses 20 percent of total body water. Most people would be able to live only about a week without water. The human body requires about six to eight glasses of water per day. The body consists largely of water; between 50 and 75 percent of a person's body weight is made up of water. Water helps hydrates the body and flushes out impurities. Pure water contains no calories, whereas all other fluids contain at least some calories. Pure juices and milk are good sources of fluids. Diet soft drinks and most man-made drinks are not good sources of fluids.

Drinking sugary fluids and eating *sugary foods lead to a release of sugar into the body's bloodstream. Insulin works by stimulating the cells to sponge up excess sugar out of the body's bloodstream. Once inside the cells, sugar is used for energy, with any excess amount being converted to fat tissue. If you take in too much sugar, your body will have released so much insulin that it will begin to lose its sensitivity to insulin, which means that your cells won't receive as strong a signal to sponge up excess sugar out of your blood.*[88]

Excess insulin is known to cause health problems such as: increase in weight gain, high blood pressure, increase risk for heart disease, possibly of a higher risk for cancer.[89] Remember, always choose to drink water first. All other fluids are second-best for the human body. Drink more water during hot days to avoid dehydration, during cold days to help the body to keep warm and while playing sports to replenish lost fluids from sweat. Some people may need six to eight glasses of water per day. Water is good for the body. Therefore I say;

*II. Drink at least three glasses of pure water per day.*

## Nutrition

Food is one of our most basic needs. Food supplies the nutrients that the human body needs for providing energy, building and repairing tissues and regulating body processes. Water, carbohydrates, fats, proteins, minerals, and vitamins are the essential nutrients your body needs to survive. No single food supplies every necessary nutrient. However, the sweet potato may contain more beneficial nutrients than any other single food item.

Food comes mainly from plants (grains, fruit, vegetables, et cetera.) or from animals that eat plants (meats, eggs, milk, et cetera.). Most people could live only 60 to 70 days without food. How long a person can survive without food depends on the person's supply of body fat. *"Consuming a diet high in refined carbohydrates and fat, along with low-fiber intake, high caloric density, low nutrient density, and inadequate physical activity, are common risk factors for cardiovascular disease, diabetes, obesity, and hypertension among other disease and negative health conditions."* [90]

A healthy diet with proper nutrition can help manage and reduce stress. Avoid mostly all man-made foods and drinks. These are the healthiest, most nutritious foods for the human body: broccoli, cauliflower, spinach, carrots, tomatoes, fish, oranges and grapefruit, garlic, onions, strawberries, sweet potatoes, soy-tofu, peppers, oatmeal, cabbage, avocado, nuts, beans, and peas.

Stay away from man-made junk foods such as: candy, cookies, snacks, doughnuts, fast-food hamburgers, et cetera. Equate a portion of food to the size of a handful of food. Consuming fruits and vegetables is good for the body. Therefore I say:

*III. Eat at least five portions of fruits and or vegetables per day.*

**The Good Food List:**

**Fruits:**
Apples
Apricots, dried
Bananas
Blueberries
Cantaloupe
Cherries
Grapefruit
Grapes, red
Kiwifruit
Oranges
Plumes
Prunes
Pumpkin
Raisins
Raspberries
Strawberries
Avocado
Papaya/Pineapple
Mangoes

**Vegetables:**
Broccoli
Brussel Sprouts
Cabbage
Carrots
Cauliflower
Chick-peas
Chili Peppers
Garlic
Kale
Lentils and Lima Beans
Onions
Peas
Peppers, red bell
Pinto Beans
Potatoes, sweet
Romaine Lettuce
Spinach
Tomatoes
Soybeans/Tofu

**Meats/Fish/Fowl:**
Chicken
Cod
Haddock
Herring
Mackerel and Anchovies
Salmon
Tuna
Turkey

**Grains/Breads/Pasta:**
Barley
Brown Rice
High-fiber Cereal
Oat Bran
Oatmeal
Whole-grain Bread
Whole-grain Pasta

**Dairy products:**

**Cottage Cheese**            **Oils:**
1% or Nonfat Milk             Canola Oil
Skim Yogurt                   Olive Oil

**Other:**
Fig bars, Flaxseed, Red Tea, Green Tea

**The Bad Food List: (mainly man-made foods)**

- Commercially-made cookies, crackers, cakes, and doughnuts
- Candies
- Restaurant fried chicken, onion rings, and French fries
- Margarine and shortening
- Ice cream
- Mayonnaise and salad dressing
- Potato chips and other man-made chips
- Ground beef, red meats, fast-food hamburgers
- Most pizzas
- American cheese (white cheeses are not as bad as yellow cheeses)
- All sodas and artificially sweetened juices and soft drinks

## Cholesterol

If you want to reduce your LDL (low density lipoprotein cholesterol) the bad cholesterol and increase your HDL (high density lipoprotein cholesterol) the good cholesterol, reduce the following:

1) Butter
2) Cheese
3) Ice Cream
4) Meats - bacon, sausage, red meat, beef, lamb, and pork
5) Shortening-pie crust, fried foods, and snacks

And increase the following:

1) Fatty Fish-salmon, tuna, sardines, herring, mackerel, halibut, and trout
2) Oatmeal, oat bran, and high-fiber foods—beans, barley, figs, apples, et cetera.
3) Walnuts, almonds, and other nuts; a handful of nuts per day
4) Olive oil; two tablespoons per day
5) Alcohol (preferably red wine)—one or two glasses per day

All foods have some nutritional value but certain foods are more beneficial to the body. Therefore I say:

*IV. Eat foods from the good list and avoid foods from the bad list.*

## Sugar

Avoid sugar and all foods containing sugar. Sugar has no nutritional value and is directly harmful to your health. The increase in the consumption of sugar, high fructose corn syrup and white flour (all refined carbohydrates) contributes to heart disease, coronary artery disease, diabetes, hypertension, ulcers, gall-bladder disease, varicose veins, colitis, et cetera.

Sugar leads to increased caloric intake and obesity and is the most frequently consumed carcinogen. Cancer cells feed on glucose rather than oxygen, as do normal cells. Some of the largest sources of fat in today's diet are junk foods and convenience foods, such as ice cream, candies, cookies, cakes, corn syrup, fructose, maple syrup and molasses. Refined carbohydrates such as starches, white flour and white rice turn to sugar in the body.

## Caffeine

Caffeine is known medically as trimethylxanthine and is an addictive drug. Caffeine blocks adenosine reception so you feel alert. Caffeine injects adrenaline into the system to give you a boost. Caffeine manipulates dopamine production to make you feel good. As a result, the effects on the human body are: your pupils dilate, your respiratory breathing tubes open up, your heart beats faster and blood vessels on the surface constrict to slow blood flow from cuts.

Also, caffeine increases blood flow to the muscles, blood pressure rises and blood flow to the stomach slows. When caffeine enters the human body, the liver releases sugar into the bloodstream for extra energy and muscles tighten up, ready for action. If you consume a lot of caffeine quickly you feel your hands get cold, your muscles tense, you feel excited and you can feel your heartbeat increase. You may feel jumpy and irritable.

The most important long-term problem is the effect caffeine has on sleep—especially deep sleep. You may be able to fall asleep but you'll miss the benefits of deep sleep. That deficit builds up fast. The next day you feel worse, so you consume caffeine as soon as you get out of bed to feel better. This cycle continues day after day. Even worse, you stop trying to take caffeine and you get tired, depressed and you get splitting headaches as blood vessels in the brain dilate. The negative effects force you to run back to caffeine, even if you want to stop.

Caffeine used in moderation, like one cup of tea or coffee, may provide benefits such as increased memory, help ward off Alzheimer's and may ease depression, among other potential benefits. *However, heavy caffeine use—on the order of four to seven cups of coffee a day—can cause problems such as restlessness, anxiety, irritability and sleeplessness, particularly in susceptible individuals.*[91] Caffeine can be found in coffee (about 100 mg/6 ounce cup) in tea (about 70 mg/6 ounce cup) in colas such (about 50 mg/12 ounce can), in aspirin (about 32 mg/tablet) and candy (about 6 mg/ounce). Green tea contains less than 15–30 mg/6 ounces. Like green tea, red tea contains antioxidants but red tea is caffeine free. Too much sugar and caffeine is not good for the body. Therefore I say:

*V. Do not consume foods or drinks that contain man-made sugars or sugar derivatives or caffeine.*

## Fasting

Fasting may be the single greatest natural healing therapy. Fasting lowers the body metabolism and helps remove toxins and waste from the body. Fasting is the avoidance of solid food and the liquids.

In a larger context, fasting is abstaining from that which is toxic to mind, body, and soul. Fasting can also involve the removal of oneself from worldly responsibilities, complete silence and social isolation. Fasting can last for as little as 12 to 14 hours during evening and sleep time each day or up to three or four days or even a week.

Fasting is a time-proven remedy that goes back thousands of years. From Moses, Elijah, and Daniel to Jesus, the Bible is filled with many who fasted to assist their purification and communion with God. Socrates, Plato, Aristotle, Galen and Hippocrates all used and believed in fasting therapy.

Provided that we are basically well-nourished, systematic under eating and fasting are likely the most important contributors to health and longevity. Fasting clearly improves motivation and creative energy; it also enhances health and vitality and lets many of the body systems rest. Here are some other benefits of fasting: clearer skin, anti-aging effects, reduction of allergies, weight loss, better resistance to disease, better sleep, diet changes, more energy, rest for digestive organs, et cetera.

The physiological effects of fasting include lowering of blood sugar, lowering of cholesterol and lowering of the systolic blood pressure. When we fast, our bodies go into an elimination cycle and toxins are flushed from our body. Detoxification is an important correction and rejuvenation process in the cycle of our nutrition. Fasting is a time when our cells and organs breathe and restore themselves. Refraining from eating minimizes the work done by the digestive organs, including the stomach, intestines, pancreas, gallbladder, and liver. During fasting, the liver can spend more time cleaning up and creating its many new substances for our use.

The breakdown of stored or circulation chemicals is the basic process of the detoxification. The blood and lymph glands also have the opportunity to be cleaned of toxins, as all of the elimination functions are enhanced with fasting. Each cell has the opportunity to catch up on its work. With fewer new demands, the cell can repair itself and dump its waste out of the body. It's just like when you clean out your bedroom or closet of built-up junk.

When you fast, you clean out the built-up junk and toxins within the body. Each day can include a 12 to 14-hour period of fasting during sleep and before getting ready for the day. In the morning you can consume a good breakfast (breakfast meaning that time when we break the fast of the night), intake some water and exercise the body.

When fasting for longer periods of time eliminate alcohol, nicotine, caffeine, sugar, red meats and other animal foods including milk products and eggs. If you need to have one daily meal consume water, juices (especially pure vegetable and fruit juices for essential nutrients and vitamins) and teas (green teas) and even some fresh fruit or vegetables and supplement with proteins such as fish. Occasionally fasting longer then the nightly fasting is good for the body. Therefore I say:

*VI. Fast on Fridays, or at the minimum, one day per month.*

## Sleep

Sleep restores energy to the body, particularly to the brain and nervous system. There are two kinds of sleep—slow-wave sleep and dreaming sleep. Slow-wave sleep is especially useful in building protein and restoring the control of the brain and nervous system over the muscles, glands and other body systems. Dreaming sleep is important for maintaining such mental activities as learning, reasoning, and emotional adjustment.

People deprived of sleep lose energy and become quick-tempered. People going without sleep for two days find lengthy concentration difficult; many mistakes are made, especially with routine tasks. Attention slips at times. People going without sleep for three days or more have great difficulty thinking, seeing and hearing clearly. Some people have hallucinations. They also confuse daydreams with real life and often lose track of their thoughts in the middle of a sentence. Human beings have gone without sleep for up to 11 days, but these people lose contact with reality for periods of time. They become suspicious and fearful of others.

Use these guidelines for sound quality sleep:

1. Go to sleep at the same time nightly in a quiet, dark, and a cool room (your body temperature drops in preparation for sleep).

2. Sleep on your side with a pillow between your legs or sleep on your back with a pillow under your knees (sleeping on your side promotes comfort and helps alleviate certain kinds of back pain).

3. If you wake up in the middle of the night to pee, use a dim light to find the way (bright light at night will decrease your melatonin peak).

4. Avoid caffeine especially after 4:00 p.m. (Caffeine can keep you awake and disrupt sleeping and caffeine can stay in your body up to eight hours after consumption).

5. Limit alcohol to one or two drinks in the evening and don't drink after 10:00 p.m. (excessive alcohol disrupts sleep and prevents the body from entering the deep stages of sleep).

6. Consume proteins for breakfast, snacks, and lunch; and consume carbohydrates in the evening after 4:00 p.m. (proteins increase levels of alertness and energy, whereas carbohydrates causes sleepiness).

7. Exercise regularly (exercise makes you more tired and helps you fall asleep quicker).

8. Get at least two hours of full spectrum sunlight exposure to your eyes (not direct exposure—do not look into the sun) and on part of your skin every day (sunlight helps your body produce melatonin which helps regulate you sleep cycle).

9. Pray, meditate, or read preferably not in bright light for thirty minutes before you sleep.

Sleeping is good for the body. Therefore I say:

*VII. Get a minimum of eight hours of sound-quality sleep per night.*

## Meditation

Meditation reduces stress, anxiety, and aggression. Daily meditation helps to reinforce and integrate your body's rhythms. There are many benefits of meditation. First, it can help most people relax, feel less anxious, and more in control. It also increases self-confidence and feelings of connection to others. It increases self-actualization, emotional stability, happiness and feelings of vitality and rejuvenation. It helps decrease depression, irritability and moodiness. It promotes harmony of brainwave activity in different parts of the brain and is associated with greater creativity, improved moral reasoning and higher IQ. It leads to improved learning ability and memory.

In order to maximize your meditation experience, you should:

- **Ensure privacy.** If you are interrupted, you will break your concentration. Avoid drifting off as you meditate. If you feel yourself nodding off, increase the depth and frequency of your breathing for a few seconds.

- **Don't eat.** Meditate on an empty stomach so your body is not expending energy on digesting, and you will be less inclined to be drowsy.

- **Be refreshed.** To avoid drowsiness, before meditating, wash your hands and face with the cold water.

- **Keep an open mind.** Do not force meditation. It should be a pleasurable experience.

- **Be patient.** If you're restless or distracted, being patient will help you enter your meditation phase.

Experiment with different methods, positions, and locations that work best for you to use. Here are the steps to one meditation technique.

**Step 1**
Allow your back to be straight and head upright. Sit on the floor with your legs crossed and buttocks elevated by a thick cushion. It is important that the back is held straight and the buttocks are higher than the folded knees.

**Step 2**
When you're breathing, breathe with focus; breathe down into the abdomen, letting it swell like a balloon. Take the air in slowly and deliberately through the nose, concentrate exclusively on the act of inhaling. It can help to count from one to ten while breathing in. When ready to exhale, do so from the back of the throat through the mouth. It may again help to count from one to ten while exhaling. It is important to concentrate on fully exhaling, which will cause a noticeable deflation in the abdomen and chest. After repeating this

cycle for about five minutes, allow your breathing to go on autopilot for the duration of the meditation period.

**Step 3**
Heighten your sense of hearing, smell, touch, and taste while keeping your eyes closed. For a few minutes, let nothing available to your senses be missed. Feel and hear the air flow in and out of your body, and feel and hear the blood pass through your blood vessels.

**Step 4**
Clear your mind of all thoughts. It may help to simply imagine looking out into a pitch-black room with your eyes open. Mind-chatter and random imagery are natural parts of the brain, try to avoid this. Resist thinking, let any thoughts or images come and go as if through a revolving door and then evaporate back into the darkness of the pitch-black room.

Meditation is good for the body. Therefore I say:

*VIII. Meditate at least fifteen minutes per day.*

## Exercise

Exercise helps keep the body fit and healthy. Exercise is good for releasing stress, burning calories and increasing cardiovascular oxygen intake capacity. *"Research has demonstrated that virtually all individuals will benefit from regular physical activity.... Moderate physical activity can reduce substantially the risk of developing or dying from heart disease, diabetes, colon cancer, and high blood pressure, Physical activity may also protect against lower back pain and [other] forms of cancer (for example, breast cancer). On average, physically active people outlive those who are inactive."* [92]

Vigorous exercise strengthens muscles and improves the function of the circulatory and respiratory systems. Physical fitness benefits both physical and mental health. It enables the body to withstand stresses that otherwise could cause physical and emotional problems.

"*As of 2005, the American College of Sports Medicine (ACSM) recommendation was to exercise for 30-60 minutes (including warm-up and cool down) three to five times per week.*" [93] To rephrase, stretch and warm up for around ten minutes, exercise for a minimum of twenty to thirty minutes and then cool down and stretch for around ten minutes—and do this at least three to four times a week.

Make exercising fun: dance with a friend, bi-cycle while listening to music, walk some place interesting like New York City or swim in a new place like Bondi Beach. Choose an aerobic or nonaerobic activity that works for you because inactivity may be the single most contributing factor that causes damage to the human body. Exercising is good for the body. Therefore I say:

> IX. Exercise a minimum of twenty to thirty minutes at least three or four times a week.

## Alcohol

Alcohol is a drug and it's a depressant. It acts on the nervous system like an anesthetic. Alcohol causes disturbances in the heart rate. In large amounts, alcohol can be poisonous to the human body, can cause depression and can be fatal.

Too much alcohol consumption over a short period of time can lead to deep sleep, coma or even death. In small amounts (like one or two glasses of red wine per day) it can reduce stress, reduce cholesterol and stimulate the heart. Excessive alcohol consumption can induce sleep disorders by preventing the body from entering the deep stages of sleep and by altering total sleep time. Too much alcohol consumption can cause both temporary and permanent brain injury. Areas affected by alcohol include memory, problem solving, judgment, behavior, understanding of pain and pleasure, coordination, and regulation of body functions. Alcohol abuse can cause fatty liver disease, alcohol hepatitis and cirrhosis.

Consuming too much alcohol regularly may cause you to become an alcoholic, which can ruin your life and the lives of your friends and family. *"For those who choose to drink alcoholic beverages, the U.S. Dietary Guidelines 2005 recommended to do so sensibly and in moderation, defined as the consumption of up to one drink per day for women and up to two drinks per day for men. A standard drink is considered to be 12 ounces of beer, 1.5 ounces of distilled spirit, or 5 ounces of wine."* [94]

A little alcohol is good for the body and too much alcohol is bad for the body. Therefore I say:

X.  Do not consume more than two alcoholic drinks per day.

## The Ten Healthy Rules

I    *Do not smoke or consume illegal drugs or abuse legal drugs.*

II    *Drink at least three glasses of pure water per day.*

III    *Eat at least five portions of fruits and or vegetables per day.*

IV    *Eat foods from the good list and avoid foods from the bad list.*

V    *Do not consume foods or drinks that contain man-made sugars or sugar derivatives or caffeine.*

VI    *Fast on Fridays, or at the minimum, one day per month.*

VII    *Sleep a minimum of eight hours of sound quality sleep per night.*

VIII    *Meditate at least fifteen minutes per day.*

IX    *Exercise a minimum of twenty to thirty minutes for at least three or four times a week.*

X    *Do not consume more than two alcoholic drinks per day.*

## Stress

Stress is a very natural, important part of life and is an unavoidable consequence of life. Stress is the effect our bodies experience as we adjust to the continually changing environment. Stress has physical and emotional effects on us and can create positive or negative feelings. Eustress (good stress) helps keep us alert, motivates us to face challenges and drives us to solve problems. As a positive influence, stress is needed to feel alert and alive. Increased stress results in increased productivity up to a certain point. It is important to find the proper level of stress that promotes optimal performance. Distress (bad stress), on the other hand, is unpleasant, can seriously damage performance and can lead to serious physical and mental illness if not controlled.

The long-term effects of distress can cause physical and psychological problems such as gastrointestinal problems (diarrhea or nausea), depression, or severe headaches. Other long-term effects of distress are insomnia, heart disease and developing bad habits (such as drinking, overeating, smoking and using drugs to cope).

Other negative long-term effects stress can lead to are feelings of distrust, rejection, anger and depression, which can lead to health problems such as headaches, upset stomach, rashes, insomnia, ulcers, high blood pressure, heart disease and stroke.

Stress can come from a range of different sources. Once you understand what is causing your stress, then you can make an action plan to change that stress and/or change your reaction to it. Long-term stress is best managed by changes to lifestyle, attitude, and environment.

Manage Stress by doing these things:

- Become aware of your stresses and your emotional and physical reactions.
- Recognize what you can change and what you cannot change; practice acceptance.

- Reduce the intensity of your emotional reactions to stress.

- Learn to moderate your physical reactions to stress. Slow, deep breathing will bring your heart rate and respiration back to normal. Relaxation techniques can reduce muscle tension.

- Build your physical reserves. Exercise for cardiovascular fitness three or four times a week. Eat well-balanced, nutritious meals. Maintain your ideal weight (I strive to stay within ten percent of the recommended ideal weight for my age, height and gender). Avoid nicotine, excessive caffeine, and other stimulants. Mix play with work, take breaks. Get enough proper and consistent sleep.

- Maintain your emotional reserves. Develop mutually-supportive friends and relationships.

- Manage time efficiently and get organized. Make a list and prioritize what's most important and what needs to be done first. Find the fun in work and make work fun.

## Cancer

Cancer is a major killer throughout human history and has increased as the human race has advanced industrially and technologically. Cancer seems to arise from the effects of two different types of carcinogens. One kind of agent is an agent that damages genes—such as when a single cell accumulates a number of mutations (usually over many years) and these mutations allow cells to develop additional alterations and grow, forming tumors. The cells tend to migrate and carry the disease to other parts of the body. Finally, the illness can reach and disrupt one of the body's vital organs. Tobacco smoke is the single most lethal carcinogen in the United States, causing over 30 percent of cancer deaths and 80 percent of lung cancer.

Diet may be the second-greatest cause of cancer—specifically overeating, consuming animal saturated fats, red meats, food additives like salt and many of today's man-made foods. Normal human cells feed on oxygen; human cancer cells feed on glucose, so reduce your sugar intake.

Obesity is associated with increased risk of a variety of cancers including: breast, colon and rectum, endometrium, esophagus, kidney, and pancreas cancers. So stop smoking, get and maintain a healthy weight, exercise on a regular basis, and eat healthy foods, particularly plant-based foods.

## Safety

Always fasten your seat belt and wear your helmet when applicable, like when bicycling, skateboarding, skiing, et cetera. Wear earplugs around loud noises to prevent hearing loss or damage. Know where the fire exits are located. Be careful playing sports—most injuries occur while involved in some sort of sport. Take care of your back and listen to your body; if your back hurts, stop and rest. Prevent falls, stand tall, and sit correctly. When lifting, wear a thick belt and lift with your legs. Test the water before you jump in: The water may be too cold, too hot, contaminated with deadly chemicals or hazardous waste, or the water may have man-eating sharks or piranhas in it. The "test the water first" advice applies to all areas of life. Say to yourself, "What will happen if?" and if the answer is unsafe, don't do it.

## Giving Thanks

It's always a good idea to take stock of the good things—and to express thanks.

*I am so lucky. I am better off than most people because I have these:*
I have my life today. I can breathe, drink, eat, and sleep. I have my health. I have my spouse and children—family, siblings, parents, and

relatives. I have a house—a great house on a great piece of land—with a good garden. I have a good job. I can make money for my family. I can think and dream.

Thank you for my health and my healthy body. Thank you for my wife, sons, family, and friends. Thank you for my job and ability to make money. Thank you for my intelligence and imagination, sense of humor, compassion, sympathy and love. Thank you for all the various people and Mother Nature on this planet earth. Thank you for my garden, my property, and my house. Thank you for my boat and the ability and opportunity to fish.

I don't have fancy, expensive clothes. I don't have an expensive car. I don't live in a big mansion. I don't take exotic vacations. I am not Mr. Popular (nor do I want to be), knowing hundreds of people and getting invited to many functions. I don't eat at expensive restaurants. I don't have the greatest figure and the greatest looks, nor I am the rich and famous or the sexy-looking and popular type, but I have a brain with an imagination and I can dream about a life. I can imagine people, places and things, great occasions and fun times. I have a heart and compassion. I can love, give love, and be loved. Giving and getting love feels good.

*All I need is persistent effort to keep my soul clean. I have a soul, and all my soul needs is a good body to host the soul while I'm on this planet earth.* So I say throughout life, I will try to work hard to stay healthy mentally and physically. Daily I will attempt to always consume pure, natural, healthy foods and drinks like fruit, vegetables, fish, water, nuts, et cetera. Routinely I will exercise the mind; read and do crossword puzzles or Sudoku games, or trade sophisticated security options, or whatever works to keep the brain sharp. Exercise the body. Keep my soul clean and pray. Do what is right; love everyone and try to help people. If I get cancer, I will fight the battle both physically and mentally. I will not give up. I will still try to exercise and eat right. Taking good care of my body and soul will be my life-long motto.

# CHAPTER 13
# Retirement Thinking

Over fifty years old, and I'm now at least halfway there. A sperm cell attaches to an egg cell and grows into a baby human; an older human raises that child until that child can eat, talk, walk, shit and do other things. The baby becomes a young human who hopefully lives a full life and then, after fifty years of age, the human body and mind start to deteriorate to the point that just before death, you become baby-like again. Your body and mind are so frail that a younger human must take care of you—help you to eat, talk, walk, shit and do other things. Well, before I get to that point, I want to retire—retire from what eats up most of my time, commanding cargo jets.

## Why will I retire?

Well, I may have to retire because of loss of license or loss of medical. I may want to retire. I love my job when I'm half awake, but I don't enjoy it much when I'm half asleep. (Remember the *half awake, half asleep* poem?) If I lose my love of flying, I will retire. I may want to retire because I don't want the responsibility anymore. The money reward may not be worth the time reward anymore. I will miss wearing the uniform, but I will not miss going to the cleaner's, packing and unpacking, and studying for those rare emergencies I hope I will never encounter—like an in-flight engine fire. I will miss all the personnel, the ramp loaders, ramp agents, mechanics, dispatchers, the weather man, the jump seat personnel, corporate travel, and even screw—I mean crew—scheduling, the whole ALPA organization, and many other personnel that make the FedEx flight operations work.

I will especially miss the pilots.

Pilots are a unique professional group.

Just flying jets is usually not enough for them in life; every pilot has another challenge going on in his or her lives.

## Where will I retire?

Maybe I'll consider the ten best places where Americans retire based on the cost of living, healthcare, housing cost, cultural and recreational options as published by Cindy Perryman of AARP (American Association of Retired Persons) on Feb. 3, 2011: Buenos Aires, Argentina; Corozal, Belize; Central Valley, Costa Rica; Longuedoc—Roussillon, France; Le Marche, Italy; Puerto Vallarta Region, Mexico; Granada, Nicaragua; Boquete, Panama; Cascais, Portugal; or Costa del Sol, Spain.

I may want to retire in one of the Blue Zones. Blue Zones are places in the world where people live to over one hundred years of age and stay healthy: Sardinia Island, Italy; Okinawa, Japan; Loma Linda, California; Nicoya Peninsula, Costa Rica; and Ikaria Island, Greece.

Family consideration may dictate where I retire. I was born on Long Island and my wife was born in Ireland—and where will the boys be living?

## When will I retire?

The Germans were probably the first to introduce retirement with pensions in the 1880s, and today, there are many countries that offer retirement to workers of ages ranging from 50 to 80 years old. In the U.S., early retirement age is 62 and the normal retirement age is 67 in order to receive Social Security. The Social Security benefit a retired person can expect to receive in the U.S. can range from around $15,000 to $39,000 a year. If you serve 20 years in the United States Armed Forces, you can retire with 50 percent of your last paycheck.

Airline pilots have a mandatory retirement age of 65; of course, a pilot can lose his FAA pilot's license because of a violation or lose his FAA medical because of a disability such as cardiovascular conditions, blood pressure, cholesterol, et cetera. Soon I will have an opportunity to retire, but will I be able to cover my retirement expenses including: health care or chronic care costs, home maintenance or rent, leisure, gardening, fishing, family, taxes, et cetera?

## What will I do?

I will do charity work—feed the poor. I will be a tourist—travel the world. I have hobbies—gardening and sport fishing. I like feeding the poor. I like to travel. I like gardening and fishing.

Our garden consists of Cool Ridge pineapple guava, pomegranate, blackberry, blueberry, raspberry, various fruit trees, fig trees, apple trees, pear trees, peach trees, kiwi vine, loquat, Jujube trees, citron squat, Ten Degree tangerine and Mandarin tangerine. Yearly, I also plant onions, spinach, lettuce, radishes, green beans, snow peas, sweet potatoes, tomatoes, peppers, eggplants, strawberries, cucumbers, squash, cantaloupe, and watermelon, and a few spices—mint, bay leaf, basil, parsley, rosemary, and thyme.

There are benefits to growing your own fruits and vegetables. For instance, the food tastes better and it's more nutritious than store-bought foods. Growing your own organic foods with no pesticides is safer to eat. It is also more convenient to walk into my back yard to pick the food than to travel to a store. If we should downsize to a smaller dwelling and property, I guess I will start a newer, smaller and better garden.

I like all aspects of salt water: swimming, water skiing, boat riding, and fishing (you've read my *Wish of Fish* poem). The fish species I target most often are striped bass (rock fish), summer flounder (fluke), toug tog (black fish) and sea bass. The other fish species I target are tuna, cobia, blue fish, Spanish mackerel, sheep's head, spade fish, speckled trout, croakers, spot, puppy drum and trigger fish. Of course, I am willing to fish anywhere, at any time for any type of fish. Catching fish is fun and eating fish is so good for you. Fish is the best source of protein on this planet earth for the human body, and fish contain the highly beneficial omega-3 fatty acid. When you are out for the day boating and fishing, you can de-compartmentalize. You can forget about all your worries and stresses and just concentrate on operating and navigating the boat, the sea conditions, locating the fish, rigging and baiting the fishing poles, setting the hook, reeling in the fish and netting the fish. While we're fishing, we only have to worry about boat stuff.

## What have we learned?

Frank lived on Long Island until he was eighteen. He left, traveled across the U.S.A., joined the USAF and moved to England. He traveled across Europe, and then went to Florida to pursue a career in aviation. He traveled throughout the world, and then settled down to raise a family. He learned that taking care of the body and soul and other people are more important than making money. He thinks of himself as smart, motivated, goal-oriented, instructional and funny. If you are motivated and put your mind to it you can do anything you want. At age 26, Frank was a flight crew member operating B-747 jets around the world.

## What will they say about me?

Frank was a religious man. He went to church regularly; served in the Judeo-Christian Outreach Center social ministry, gave time and money to the poor, and wrote the prayer *Trinity for Me*. Frank was a family man, a good husband, a good father, son and sibling. He coached his sons for twelve years in basketball, soccer and baseball; he was a teacher. Frank was a private person, a kind and good-hearted person; he donated blood throughout his whole life. He had a good sense of humor—he was a joker—and he was a strong person (physically, mentally, and spiritually). He was a leader and he raised leaders and independent thinkers. Frank's God-given talents were that he was smart, goal-orientated, motivated, proactive, positive, a hard worker and funny. He was a good pilot, a good fisherman, and a good gardener. You could often hear him say, *Enjoy the day, if not the night*. Some of his other one-liners he would say were:

- *Always remember and you'll never forget.*
- *It is better to have no friends then to have bad friends.*
- *Food on the table, a roof over your head and you're healthy, then everything and anything else is extra.*
- *Safety—live first! It is better to tell a bad, embarrassing story then to die and not be able to tell a story at all.*
- *Many wouldn't but we did, we came back.*
- *Learn from that mistake and don't make the same mistake twice.*
- *Learn two job skills; one with the use of your hands and one with the use of your brain.*
- *We make our money above planet earth, and it is serious business.*
- *You know, you just can't pull over to a cloud and check the oil.*
- *When you get up there, don't forget to land.*
- *Fly safely.*
- *I have Yank and Bank school* (six month flight simulator training school).
- *Money does buy food, clothes, and utilities, and it puts a roof over your head; "anything and everything else is extra."*
- *No one takes care of your money like you do.*
- *Do your best. Regardless of the minuscule job that you may think you may have* (in 1979 Frank was shining shoes),

*do your best,* because you never know how far back someone may check your references.
- *Today's second officer may be tomorrows Chief Pilot.*
- *Jesus and I love you.*

Frank had an answer for everything.

Q: How are you doing?
A: *Better than most but not as good as some.*

Q: When will we get there?
A: *After now and before later.*

Q: Flight crew bus driver, "Where are you going?" (Meaning what aircraft spot number do you need a bus ride to)?
A: *Purgatory.*

After the flight crew bus ride out to the aircraft spot number instead of saying thank you he would say: That was such a good ride I am coming back to get another one.

Q: Aircraft mechanic, "how's the aircraft, any problems?
A: *Yea the attitude is all messed up on the Captain's side. I didn't write it up in fact I will take care of it myself.*

Q: Spouse, "Why didn't you do the To Do list and the Re-Do list?"
A: *I should have done that, I'm sorry. I'll do that. You're right. I love you. I didn't do what I should have done.*

Frank was thoughtful asking:
- *How is life going? Any stresses I can help you with?*
- *Enjoy the day, if not the night!*

## I Made a Deal with God

On September 11, 2001, I commanded a B 727 jet from Indianapolis to Richmond, landed at 5:30 a.m., went to the hotel and went to sleep. Around 11:00 a.m. I awoke and turned on the TV.

"Oh, look. This must be a preview to a new action movie. I wonder who is in it?"

I rubbed my eyes and sat up in the bed to fully wake up.

"Holy Shit! This is not a movie. This is really happening."

The New York Twin Towers and the Pentagon were attacked by airplanes. The Twin Towers were destroyed and the Pentagon was severely damaged, nearly 3,000 people died, the U.S. Air Space was completely shut down except for the Air Force One flight carrying the U.S. president to Offutt Air Force Base in Nebraska.

You never know when your number is up.

Live each day like your last day—because one day will be your last day.

We were grounded for two days; we could not fly.

During this time, I did some soul-searching and made a deal with God. "God, let me live long enough to raise my youngest child through high school. In return I will be the best parent and person that I can be." (A high graduate would then be approximately age 18 years old and no longer considered a minor).

Well, my youngest graduated high school this past June. Damn! Is my deal complete? Am I done? Is the death of my human body due real soon? God works in mysterious ways. You can't make deals with God. It is always on His terms—"Thy Will Be Done." If —and only if —God wills it. Don't make deals with God. Ask God, "If You will it, then please grant it."

## When will my Body Retire?

Wouldn't it be great to achieve the perfect timing to death? Spend all assets to achieve a net worth of zero, not positive one dollar or negative one dollar, and achieve the perfect clean soul. Have at least one known person at my side and receive the sacraments of Confession, Holy Communion, and the Anointing of the Sick, and then die (the Anointing of the Sick, also known as your Last Rights, is a sacrament administered to a person about to die to obtain increased strength with their physical, mental, and spiritual sickness).

## This will be my Act of Contrition:

*O my God, I am heartily sorry for having offended Thee, and I detest all sins, because I dread the loss of heaven, and the pains of hell; but most of all because I have offended Thee, my God who is all good and deserving of all my love. I firmly resolve, with the help of Thy grace, to confess my sins, do penitence and amend my life. Amen.* [95] Jesus, have mercy on me and open the pearly gates to heaven for me. Mary, if all else fails; please sneak me in the back door.

## DEATH NOTICE

Francis John Donohue, Jr. a distinguished Air Line Pilot died (Sunday, Feb. 29, 2114), at age one hundred fifty-two, of unknown natural causes at some place. Frank had been an Airline Captain since 1997 and flying aircraft worldwide since 1981 including the AB-300, B-727, B-747, EMB-110, C-402, C-172 and other aircraft. He held Air Line Transport, Certified Flight Instructor, Flight Engineer, Aircraft Dispatcher and Ground Instructors licenses and was a graduate of Embry-Riddle Aeronautical University. He had a colorful airline career and enjoyed all aspects of flying. Frank was an avid fisherman and enjoyed all aspects of boating and gardening. He was involved in coaching his children in basketball, soccer and baseball. He wrote the pamphlet "Tools for Surviving Life," prayer "Trinity for Me," song "I Love to Love My Lovely One," and book, *School and Schooled*.

Frank was the devoted and loving husband of Bernadette Carmel Donohue of many years and father of two sons, Francis John Donohue, III and Jared Joseph Donohue. He is also survived by two brothers and a sister and grandchildren. Funeral services will be held at some place on someday from twelve to twelve o'clock with celebration at the Holy Roman Catholic Church located somewhere. Please pray for Francis' family to ease their suffering pain during this difficult time and pray that Francis' soul will be accepted into Jesus' arms immediately and sent straight into heaven.

Memorial contributions may be made to his Holy Roman Catholic Church located on some street in some town in some state and his favorite charities, Catholic Charities U.S.A. and the Catholic Relief Services of Baltimore, Maryland. So let's go forth and enjoy our precious lives!

God Bless You for reading this.
Game over.
School's Out.

P.S. (I'm Back! Part I. To Be Continued!)

# Appendix

**TRINITY FOR ME**

O my dear God
O my dear Jesus
And the Holy Spirit,

Thank you for this moment of life.
Thank you for this breath of air.
Thank you for providing water and food for my body,
And thank you for protecting, guiding, and nourishing my soul.
Thank you for _____.
Please help and/or grant me with_____.
Please protect and guide my thoughts, words, heart, and soul
Towards you during this earthly journey so that after this life
I will be in heaven.
Please help me to love God, me, and everyone.
I love you, trust you, believe in you, and hope to be with you.
Amen

### The Ten Healthy Rules

I *Do not smoke or consume illegal drugs or abuse legal drugs.*
II *Drink at least three glasses of pure water per day.*
III *Eat at least five portions of fruits and or vegetables per day.*
IV *Eat foods from the good list and avoid foods from the bad list.*
V *Do not consume foods or drinks that contain man-made sugars or sugar derivatives or caffeine.*
VI *Fast on Fridays, or at the minimum, one day per month.*

VII   Sleep a minimum of eight hours of sound quality sleep per night.
VIII  Meditate at least fifteen minutes per day.
IX    Exercise a minimum of twenty to thirty minutes for at least three or four times a week.
X     Do not consume more than two alcoholic drinks per day.

# Chart

# Berkshire's Corporate Performance vs. the S&P 500

| Year | Annual Percentage Change in Per-Share Book Value of Berkshire (1) | Annual Percentage Change in S&P 500 with Dividends Included (2) | Relative Results (1)-(2) |
|---|---|---|---|
| 1965 | 23.8 | 10.0 | 13.8 |
| 1966 | 20.3 | (11.7) | 32.0 |
| 1967 | 11.0 | 30.9 | (19.9) |
| 1968 | 19.0 | 11.0 | 8.0 |
| 1969 | 16.2 | (8.4) | 24.6 |
| 1970 | 12.0 | 3.9 | 8.1 |
| 1971 | 16.4 | 14.6 | 1.8 |
| 1972 | 21.7 | 18.9 | 2.8 |
| 1973 | 4.7 | (14.8) | 19.5 |
| 1974 | 5.5 | (26.4) | 31.9 |
| 1975 | 21.9 | 37.2 | (15.3) |
| 1976 | 59.3 | 23.6 | 35.7 |
| 1977 | 31.9 | (7.4) | 39.3 |
| 1978 | 24.0 | 6.4 | 17.6 |
| 1979 | 35.7 | 18.2 | 17.5 |
| 1980 | 19.3 | 32.3 | (13.0) |
| 1981 | 31.4 | (5.0) | 36.4 |
| 1982 | 40.0 | 21.4 | 18.6 |
| 1983 | 32.3 | 22.4 | 9.9 |
| 1984 | 13.6 | 6.1 | 7.5 |
| 1985 | 48.2 | 31.6 | 16.6 |
| 1986 | 26.1 | 18.6 | 7.5 |
| 1987 | 19.5 | 5.1 | 14.4 |
| 1988 | 20.1 | 16.6 | 3.5 |

| Year | | S&P 500 | Difference |
|---|---|---|---|
| 1989 | 44.4 | 31.7 | 12.7 |
| 1990 | 7.4 | (3.1) | 10.5 |
| 1991 | 39.6 | 30.5 | 9.1 |
| 1992 | 20.3 | 7.6 | 12.7 |
| 1993 | 14.3 | 10.1 | 4.2 |
| 1994 | 13.9 | 1.3 | 12.6 |
| 1995 | 43.1 | 37.6 | 5.5 |
| 1996 | 31.8 | 23.0 | 8.8 |
| 1997 | 34.1 | 33.4 | 0.7 |
| 1998 | 48.3 | 28.6 | 19.7 |
| 1999 | 0.5 | 21.0 | (20.5) |
| 2000 | 6.5 | (9.1) | 15.6 |
| 2001 | (6.2) | (11.9) | 5.7 |
| 2002 | 10.0 | (22.1) | 32.1 |
| 2003 | 21.0 | 28.7 | (7.7) |
| 2004 | 10.5 | 10.9 | (0.4) |
| 2005 | 6.4 | 4.9 | 1.5 |
| 2006 | 18.4 | 15.8 | 2.6 |
| 2007 | 11.0 | 5.5 | 5.5 |
| 2008 | (9.6) | (37.0) | 27.4 |
| 2009 | 19.8 | 26.5 | (6.7) |
| 2010 | 13.0 | 15.1 | (2.1) |
| 2011 | 4.6 | 2.1 | 2.5 |
| 2012 | 14.4 | 16.0 | (1.6) |
| Compounded Annual Gain – 1965-2012 | 19.7% | 9.4% | 10.3 |
| Overall Gain – 1964-2012 | 586,817% | 7,433% | |

**Notes:** Data are for calendar years with these exceptions: 1965 and 1966, year ended 9/30; 1967, 15 months ended 12/31. Starting in 1979, accounting rules required insurance companies to value the equity securities they hold at market rather than at the lower of cost or market, which was previously the requirement. In this table, Berkshire's results through 1978 have been restated to conform to the changed rules. In all other respects, the results are calculated using the numbers originally reported. The S&P 500 numbers are **pre-tax** whereas the Berkshire numbers are **after-tax**. If a corporation such as Berkshire were simply to have owned the S&P 500 and accrued the appropriate taxes, its results would have lagged the S&P 500 in years when that index showed a positive return, but would have exceeded the S&P 500 in years when the index showed a negative return. Over the years, the tax costs would have caused the aggregate lag to be substantial.

This material is copyrighted and used with permission of the author.

**Website- www.frankjdonohue.com**

## Employment History Timeline

1. Lawn Service: Owner     1974–1975
   Seaford, NY
2. Newspaper Deliverer: Sub-contractor     1976–1978
   Long Island Press: Seaford, NY
3. Locker-room Man Assistant     Jun. 1976–Aug. 1979
   Meadow Brook Gulf Club: Jericho, NY
4. Waiter, Doorman, Parking Valet, Bus Boy     Jan. 1977–Aug. 1979
   Cook's Helper, Dishwasher, Handyman
   The Back Barn: Bethpage, NY 11714
5. Warehouse Stockman     Oct. 1977–Dec. 1978
   Unity Buying Service Co, Inc.: Hicksville, NY
6. Salesman – Barbecue Grills     May 1979–Aug. 1979
   Island Recreation: Massapequa, NY
7. Professional Painter     Sep. 1979–Nov. 1979
   J.S. Trogdon Company, Inc.: Dallas, TX
8. General Accounting Specialist     Dec. 1979–Dec. 1983
   United States Air Force: Lackland AFB, TX: Sheppard AFB, TX
   RAF Lakenheath, UK: RAF Mildenhall, UK: McClellan AFB, CA
9. College Student     Jan. 1984–Aug. 1985
   Embry-Riddle Aeronautical University: Daytona Beach, FL
10. Handy Man     Mar. 1984–Sep. 1985
    Fair Realty: Holly Hill, FL
11. Travel Accountant     Apr. 1984–Dec. 1985
    United Air Force Reserves: Patrick AFB, FL: Robbins AFB, FL

## Career Progression Timeline

1. Flight Instructor     Sep. 1985–May 1986
   Embry-Riddle Aeronautical University: Daytona Beach, FL
2. Banner Tow Pilot     Feb. 1986–Apr. 1986
   Syrmna Towing Advertising Co.: New Syrmna Airport, FL
3. Flight Instructor     May 1986 Oct. 1986
   Transamerican Airways: Atlanta, GA
4. Captain     Oct. 1986–Mar. 1987
   Midnite Express: Atlanta, GA

5. First Officer                                  Mar. 1987–Jul. 1987
   Atlantic Southeast Airlines: College Park, GA
6. Second Officer                             July 1987–Aug. 1989
   Flying Tigers: Los Angeles, CA
7. First Officer, Captain                      Aug. 1989–Present
   FedEx: Memphis, TN

## Planes I Have Flown

- Cessna C-150, C-152, C-172 P & H, C-172 RG, CT-210, CT-310, C-320, C-140, C-402 B & C
- Aztec 7E-CA
- Piper PA-28-161, PA-44-180, PA-28-180, PA-180 D, PA-23-250
- Beechcraft BE 99
- Embrea EMB-110
- Douglass DC8-63F
- Boeing B747-100, B747-200, B727-100, B727-200
- Air Bus A 310, A 300

## Countries and Airports I Have Visited

Brussels, Belgium (BRU); Berlin, Germany (TXL); Frankfurt, Germany (FRA); Cologne-Bonn, Germany (CGN); Munich, Germany (MUC); Stuttgart, Germany (STR); London, England (LHR); Prestwick, Scotland (PIK); Amsterdam, Netherlands (AMS); Paris, France (CDG); Basil, Switzerland (BSL); Zurich, Switzerland (ZRH); Milan, Italy (MXP); Guadalajara, Mexico (GDL); Mexico City, Mexico (MEX); Toluca, Mexico (TLC); Panama City, Panama (PTY); Dubai, United Arab Emirates (DXB); Anchorage, Alaska (ANC); Guam, Mariana (UAM); Taipei, Taiwan (TPE); Tokyo, Japan (NRT); Seoul, South Korea (ICN); Okinawa, Japan (DNA); Manaus, Brazil (MAO); Rio De Janerio, Brazil (GIG); San Juan, Puerto Rico (SJU); Sidney, Australia (SYD); Singapore (SIN); and Hong Kong (HKG).

## Places I Have Lived

| | | |
|---|---|---|
| 1961–1962 | Franklin Square, NY | Apartment |
| 1962–1979 | Seaford, NY | Home |
| 1979 | Dallas, TX | House |
| 1979 | Los Angeles, CA | House |
| 1980 | San Antonio, TX | Dormitory |
| 1980 | Wichita Falls, TX | Dormitory |
| 1980 | RAF Lakenheath, UK | Dormitory |
| 1981 | Bury St. Edmund, UK | Flat |
| 1982 | RAF Mildenhal, UK | Flat |
| 1983 | Sacramento, CA | Apartment |
| 1984–1985 | Daytona Beach, FL | Three houses |
| 1986 | Atlanta, GA | Apartment, house |
| 1986 | Mobile, AL | Apartment |
| 1987 | Jacksonville, FL | House |
| 1987 | Dallas, TX | Apartment |
| 1988–1989 | Long Island, NY | Home |
| 1989–1990 | Key Largo, FL | Home |
| 1990–1991 | Memphis, TN | Apartment |
| 1991 | Virginia Beach, VA | Home |

## Almost Died Stories

Age 2.   Falling out of a car on the Long Island Expressway
Age 13. Trick or Treat with a real gun?
Age 17. Auto skid during a snow storm on New York Highway 17
Age 19. Gang mugging at the New Orleans Mardi Gras
Age 21. Auto accident en route from Madrid to Benador, Spain
Age 21. Auto skid on black ice in the Midland Mountains en route to Glasglow, Scotland
Age 22. Highway break-down during the worst brush fire in Nevada
Age 26. Warrior gang attack on a New York Subway
Age 27. Near-drowning in Bondi Beach-Sydney, Australia
Age 28. Passed out and choking in Frankfurt, Germany

## Bikes, Boats and Cars

1974  Schwinn Ten-speed bicycle
1975  Sears sixteen-foot boat, ten HP
1972  Chevelle Malibu auto
1980  Suzuki 250 TS motorcycle
1968  Austin Mini auto
1970  Audi 500 GL auto
1960  Austin Cambridge auto
1972  Chevy Luv pickup truck with camper shell
1966  Chrysler Newport auto
1978  Cutlass Oldsmobile auto
1990  Checkmate sixteen-foot boat, forty HP
1990  Chris-Craft nineteen-foot boat, eighty-five HP
1986  Toyota Tercel auto
1991  Ford Taurus auto
1977  Grady White twenty-foot boat, 175 HP
1996  Chrysler Minivan auto
2001  Acura 3.2 TL auto
2002  Grady White twenty-two foot boat, 200 HP
2006  Toyota RAV4 auto
1996  Volvo 240 auto
1998  Volvo S70 auto

# Bibliography

1. Belanger, Jeff. "The History of Halloween," *Kids Ghost Village*, 2008. http://kids.ghostvillage.com/ghostsintheclassroom/historyofhalloween.shtml.

2. "Aircraft Data and History," *Airliners*. Last modified March 5, 2008 http://.airliners.net/aircraft-data/stats.html. Dec 15, 2011.

3. Marsh, Harry. *Borough of St. Edmundsbury: Official Guide.* Norwich: St. Edmundsbury Borough Council, 1976.

4. See note 2 above.

5. "Space Shuttle Missions," NASA. http://.nasa.gov/mission-pages/shuttle/launch.html (accessed Jan. 3, 2012)

6. See note 2 above.

7. "Glaze and Black Ice," *Weather Online.* http:/www.weatheronline.co.uk/reports/wxfacts/
Glaze-and-Black-Ice.html (accessed March 29, 2012)

8. "Coefficient Formulas," Roy Mech. http://www.roymech.co.uk/Useful_Tables/ Tribology/co_of_frict.html (accessed March 1, 2013)

9. "History of Bear," *Wikipedia.* http://enwikipedia.org/wiki/History_of_beer.html (accessed March 10, 2012)

10. "Hieronymus, Stan," *Craft Beer.* http://craftbeer.com/beerology/history-of-beer/early-times.html (accessed March 10, 2012)

11. "The Embry-Riddle Story," *Embry-Riddle Aeronautical University.* http://erau.edu/about/ story.html (accessed March 21, 2013)

12. Dunn, Marcia "Challenger: 25 Years Later, a Still Painful Wound," *The Associated Press.* 2011. http://community.statesmanjournal.com/blogs/science/2011/01/28/challenger-25-years-later-a-still-painful-wound/.html

13. Ibid.

14. "NTSB Identification: MIA85LKG01" *National Transportation Safety Board.* NTSB microfiche number 29830. http://ntsb.gov/aviationquery/brief.aspx?ev_id= 20001214X36273&key= 1.html (accessed March 20, 2013)

15. See note 2 above.

16. Wood, Charles. "The Instrument Landing System," *Navflight*, 2008. http://navfltsm.addr.com./ils.htm.

17. See note 2 above.

18. "Top Gun," U.S. Navy Fighter Weapons School. http://flitetime.net/tg.html (accessed March 21, 2013)

19. "Tom Cruise," *Wikipedia.* http://en.wikipedia.org/wiki/Tom_Cruise.html (accessed January 3, 2012)

20. "Top Gun Script-Dialogue," *Drew's Transcripts Script-O-Rama.* http://script-o-Rama. com/movie_scripts/t/top-gun-script-transcript-cruise.html (accessed March 21, 2013)
Top Gun excerpts used with permission of Paramount Pictures.

21. *Flying Tigers 1945–1989*, Lost Angeles: Ashbrook and Wacker, 1989.

22. "History of Flying Tiger Aircraft," *Flying Tiger Line Pilots Association.* http://.flyingtigerline.org/history.html (accessed March 21, 2012)

23. "A History of Pride: 80 Years of Pilots Putting Safety and Security First," *Air Line Pilots Association, International*, 2011, 7, http://cf.alpa.org/internet/accomplishments/safety/1930.html

24. Hopkins, George. *Flying the Line.* Washington D.C.: The Air Line Pilots Association, International, 1982.

25. "Code of Ethics," *Air Line Pilots Association, International.* http://alpa.org/Home/ WhoWeAre/CodeofEthics/tabid/2262/Default.aspx.html (accessed March 9, 2013)
This material is copyrighted and used with the permission of the author.

26. See note 2 above.

27. "NSTB Investigation: AAR-89-04, NTIS: PB89-910406," *National Transportation Safety Board*. http:// ntsb.gov/investigations/reports_aviation.html

# Bibliography

28. "Archive Fact Sheet: Arthur Guinness (1725-1803)," *Guinness Storehouse.* http://guinness-storehouse.com/en/docs/arthur_guinness.pdf.html (accessed March 21, 2013)

29. "Kilkenny Castle," *Absolute Astronomy.* http:l.absoluteastronomy.com/topics/Kilkenny_Castle.html (accessed August 25, 2012)

30. "Frederick W. Smith," *Academy of Achievement.* Last modified January 9, 2008. http://achievement.org/autodoc/page/smi0bio-1.html.

31. Greene, Meg "Fred Smith 1944-Biograhy," *Reference for Business.* http://referenceforbusiness.com/biography/S-Z/Smith-Fred-1944.html (accessed April 4, 2012)

32. See note 2 above.

33. "The Labor Movement in America," *Social Studies Help Center.* Last modified March 22, 2013 .http://socialstudieshelp.com/Eco_Unionization.htm

34. Ibid.

35. "FedEx Pilot History," *ALPA FedEx MEC.* http://crewroom.alpa.org/fdx/DesktopModules/ViewDocument.aspx?DocumentID=19085.html (accessed July 1, 2012)
This material is used with the permission of ALPA Fedex MEC secretary-treasurer.

36. Ibid.

37. U.S. Department of Federal Aviation Administration. *Electronic Code of the Federal Aviation Regulations.* Washington DC: US Government Printing Office, 2012. http://eecfr.gov/cgr-bin/text.html.

38. Ibid.

39. Ibid.

40. See note 2 above.

41. Dobson, James. *Dare to Discipline*, Wheaton. IL: Tyndale House Publishers, 1992

42. Ibid.

[43.] Ibid.

[44.] Dobson, James. *The Strong Willed Child, Birth Through Indolence*, Wheaton, IL: Tyndale House Publishers, 1978.

[45.] Phelan, Thomas. *1-2-3 Magic: Effective Discipline for Children 2-12* Glen Ellyn, IL: Child Management, Inc., 1995. 19-26

[46.] See note 41 above.

[47.] See note 44 above. 103

[48.] "20 Timeless Money Rules" *CNN Money Magazine*, August 23, 2007.

[49.] Graham, Benjamin. *The Intelligent Investor*. New York: Harper Collins, 1949.

[50.] Graham, Benjamin and Zweig, Jason. *The Intelligent Investor*. New York: Harper Business Essentials, 2003. 6, 45

[51.] Ibid. 542

[52.] Ibid. 477

[53.] Ibid. 401

[54.] Buffet, Mary and Clarke, David, *The TAO of Warren Buffet*. New York: Simon and Schuster, 2006.

[55.] "Letter to Shareholder," *Berkshirehathaway*. http://berkshirehathaway.com/letters/ 2004ltr.f.html.

[56.] Clason, George. *The Richest Man in Babylon*. New York: Hawthorn/ Dutton, 1955

[57.] Lynch, Peter and Rothchild, John. *Beating the Street*. New York: Simon and Schuster, 1993. 303

[58.] Ibid. 305
[59.] Ibid. 208,212

[60.] Ibid. 36

[61.] Ibid. 304

# Bibliography

[62.] Bogle, John. *Bogle on Mutual Funds: New Perspectives for the Intelligent Investor.* Boston: McGraw-Hill, 1993.

[63.] O'Neil, William. *24 Essential Lessons for Investment Success.* New York: McGraw-Hill, 2000. 153

[64.] "20 Timeless Money Rules" *CNN Money Magazine,* August 23, 2007.

[65.] Ibid.

[66.] Ibid.

[67.] Claman, Liz. *The Best Investment Advice I Ever Received.* New York: Warner Business Books, 2006. Jim Rogers, International Investor, and "Adventure Capitalist"

[68.] "Major Religions of the World Ranked by Numbers of Adherents," *Adherents.* Last modified August 9, 2007. http://www.adherents.com/Religions_By_Adherents.html

[69.] Clemmons, Nancy. *Exploring the Religions of Our World.* Notre Dame: Ave Maria Press, Inc., 2008. 292

[70.] Ibid. 334

[71.] Peters, F.E. "Abraham's Miraculous Journey," *U.S. News and World Report,* March 13, 2007. 18

[72.] "Jewish Virtual Library," *The American-Israel Cooperative Enterprise.* 2012. http://jewishvirtuallibrary.org/jsources/glossT.html (accessed April 5, 2012)

[73.] Ibid.

[74.] *Holy Bible, the New American Bible.* Nashville: Thomas Nelson, Inc. 1998.

[75.] "Crash Course Series on Introductory Judaism," *Hanefesh.* 2011. http://hanefesh.com/Crash_Course.html

[76.] "Web Bible," *Christian Answers.* 1998-2013. Http://christiananswers.net/bible/home.html (accessed April 4, 2012)

[77-80.] Francis, James Allan. *The Real Jesus and Other Sermons.* Philadelphia: Judson Press, 1926. 121

81. "The Profession of Faith, Catechism of the Catholic Faith," *Vatican.* 2005 http://vactican.va/archive/ccc_css/archive/catechism/credo.html (accessed March 14, 2013)

82. "The Our Father, Catechism of the Catholic Faith," Ibid.

83. Peterson, Eugene. *The Message//Remix.* Colorado Springs: Navpress Publishing Group, 2003. 1775

84. *Catholic Prayer for Catholic Families.* Chicago: Loyola Press, 2006.

85. Clemmons, Nancy. *Exploring the Religions of Our World.* Notre Dame: Ave Maria Press, Inc., 2008. 320

86. Rothemich, Stephen. "Tobacco Use," *Health Promotion and Disease Prevention in a Clinical Practice.* Philadelphia: Lippincott Williams and Wilkins, 2008. 235

87. "Commonly Abused Drug Chart," http://drugabuse.gov/ drugs-abuse/commonly-abused-drugs/commonly-abused-drugs-chart.html (accessed March 23, 2013)

88. Kim, Ben "Blood Sugar and Insulin: The Essentials," *Dr. Ben Kim, Experience Your Best Health.* http://drbenkim.com/articles-bloodsugar.html (accessed March 24, 2013)

89. Shewmake, Roger. "Nutrition," *Health Promotion and Disease Prevention in a Clinical Practice.* Philadelphia: Lippincott Williams and Wilkins, 2008. 169

90. Hensrud MD, Donald. "Nutrition and Healthy Eating," Mayo Clinic. May 6, 2010. http://mayoclinic.com/health/coffee-and-health/AN01354.html

91. Haas, Elson and Levin, Buck. *Staying Healthy with Nutrition: the Complete Guide to Diet and Nutrition Medicine.* Berkeley: Celestial Arts, 2006

92. Jonas, Steven, "Regular Exercise," Ibid. 149

93. U.S. Department of Health and Human Services, Healthy People 2010. *Physical Activity and Fitness,* chapter 22. Washington, DC: U.S. Department of Health and Human Services, 2000:22-21 Conference editions in two volumes. 157

94. See note 89. 185-187

95. "Act of Contrition, Catechism of the Catholic Faith," See note 82 above.

# Acknowledgments

I thank my administrative assistant, Jessica Hauser, for her excellent work, dedication, and time. I thank Carolyn Madison for her detailed, in-depth and top-quality line editorial work. I'd also like to thank Mark Graham and Mark Stevens for their help in develop editing and shaping the finished product. I thank Nick Zelinger for his expertise in book design and book formatting. I thank my mother and father for having and raising me, and to my loving wife and God for giving me the precious opportunity to be a father. To my sons, who have inspired me to write this book, I wish the best of all good things to come to you in this earthly life and the life after. God bless.

# About the Author

Frank Donohue earned his Bachelor degree and several pilot licenses at Embry-Riddle Aeronautical University after serving one tour of duty in the United States Air Force. Frank and his wife live in Virginia Beach but continue to travel. They have two grown children.

---

### Author's Note

"School and Schooled" was written, designed, produced and published by its author to the same high standards as the mainstream publishing industry. I invite you to post an honest and objective review of this book in the online bookstore of your choice. Your comments will help improve the quality of what good writers write and what good readers read. Thank you for your time and service.

www.frankjdonohue.com

www.ingramcontent.com/pod-product-compliance
Lightning Source LLC
Chambersburg PA
CBHW070059020526
44112CB00034B/1674